I DON'T CARE IF I NEVER COME BACK

A BASEBALL FAN AND HIS GAME

Art Hill

SIMON AND SCHUSTER
NEW YORK

Acknowledgments

I thank my wife, Mary Ellen, for her encouragement and her suggestions, and for putting up with countless problems to enable me to write this book. And for innumerable other things, too.

My sons, Terry, Tony and Chato, all made important contributions to the creation of this book. I asked, and they said, "Sure." I thank them for that, and for everything else.

Bob Creamer read my first baseball book, liked it and, more important, bothered to tell people about it. If he hadn't, this book would never have been written. I thank him, and always will.

I thank Jon Segal, my editor, who tirelessly promoted my cause and provided unlimited editorial and moral support.

I thank, also, Tom Avery (a publisher), Ken LaMotte (a good neighbor), Donald Honig (a writer), Ron Modra (a photographer), John F. Redding (librarian of the Baseball Hall of Fame), and Tony Spina (ace photographer of the *Detroit Free Press*). The last four I have never met, but they all helped.

Four men named Neft, Johnson, Cohen and Deutsch compiled *The Sports Encyclopedia: Baseball*, a stupendous collection of facts which has been my principal source of reference. I have also referred to *The Baseball Encyclopedia*, but the first book was the one I used constantly (reducing it to tatters) because it was the one I had.

This book was begun in Birmingham, Michigan, finished in Stoughton, Wisconsin, and revised on the Spanish island of Menorca. I thank my friends in all those places for their thoughtfulness and consideration.

To
Steve Chandler—
who cared about writing,
cared about me
and one day said:
"You should write a book
about baseball."

In the absence of vision, we gather around the lives of men and women who have lived to some purpose.
—Louis Simpson

No man is a hypocrite in his pleasures.
—Samuel Johnson

I think it to be, not merely my right, but my duty . . . to regard nothing as sacred and to hold nothing in religious respect.
—Leonard Woolf

(Except maybe baseball.
—Art Hill)

The tiger springs in the new year.
—T. S. Eliot

Something About the Game

"Baseball is the favorite American sport because it's so slow. Any idiot can follow it. And just about any idiot can play it." The speaker is Gene Vidal, as smugly quoted by his son Gore in *Matters of Fact and of Fiction.*

I yield to no man (except, I believe, Vidal himself) in my admiration for Gore Vidal as a writer. He has been called our finest living essayist. If not strictly true (E. B. White is still alive), it's close enough. But in this case he, like his father, is dissembling, which is to say replete with something you hate to find on your shoes. I don't know why, precisely, but I can make a good guess. Gore Vidal doesn't like baseball because there is almost nothing he does like. If he liked more things he would be a less interesting writer but, on occasion, a more reliable source. As for his father, I suspect that Gene Vidal, like many great athletes (e.g., Jim Thorpe), couldn't hit a curveball. You may have noticed how often people who can do certain things well find that the things they can't do are, after all, not worth doing.

Of all the games played by large numbers of people, baseball is the hardest to master. Hitting a baseball is the single most difficult skill in sport, as evidenced by the fact that even the best hitters do it successfully less than 20 percent of the time. And hitting is only half the story. You could take a boy out of the country, a big strong boy who had never seen a football or baseball game, and tell him to go out and play defensive tackle, and he could do it. Badly, of course, but he *could* do it. But tell him to go out and play shortstop ("When the ball is hit to you, scoop it up with your glove and throw it to first base before the batter gets there; you have four seconds from the time the ball leaves the bat") and he could *not* do it. Nor could he play any other position. If he tried, he would probably get hurt. Fielding is largely an acquired skill, but it is not acquired without some pain.

Still, as Bill Veeck, owner of the Chicago White Sox, has said, baseball is now the only team sport in this country that can be played professionally by regular people. Success in the others is dependent on accidents of birth. To excel at football, you have to be born huge. Basketball requires that you be born tall. And for hockey it is essential that you not be born in Panama.

As for the familiar charge that baseball is slow, it's specious. Speed is as important in baseball as in any other sport. If the critics mean that there is a lot of time between plays, well, we like it that way. I won't repeat all the well-worn testimony about the duel of wits between pitcher and batter, the science of positioning, the use of the hit-and-run and much more, except to say that they are a vital part of what makes baseball such a fascinating game to millions of people (and they are made possible by the interval between pitches). If other millions find it dull, that's their problem. I'm glad it's not one of mine.

Ordinarily, I do not question Gore Vidal's view of American history. He writes so expertly about it that I am not inclined to quibble over facts. Besides, I had always assumed he had his facts in order. And yet the same essay in which he describes his father's athletic prowess contains factual errors, one of which is startling.

The essay is called "West Point," and in it he refers to

Abner Doubleday, West Point 1842, as the inventor of baseball. This myth, possibly the greatest hoax since Piltdown
Man, has been so thoroughly discredited that I won't dwell
on it here. (Nobody "invented" baseball, but a man named
Alexander Cartwright established the rules and dimensions
of the game in 1845. He is the true father of American baseball as it is played today, and he is in the Baseball Hall of
Fame. Significantly, Doubleday is not, although the Hall is
in his hometown. Jane Austen did not invent baseball either,
but she has a better claim to it than Doubleday, since she
mentions the game by name in *Northanger Abbey*, a novel
written twenty-three years before Abner was born.) The
fable persists, however, and perhaps Vidal was just catering
to popular taste, like an atheist blurting, "God damn it!"

It is impossible, though, to take so casually another statement in the West Point piece. Vidal refers to "the slaughter
by the American army of three million Filipinos at the
beginning of the century." This is preposterous. The most
exaggerated estimate of Filipino dead in that shabby chapter
of our history would be less than a tenth of Vidal's figure.
I have no wish to exonerate the famous Americans who involved us in the shameful Philippine adventure, even less
to make light of two hundred thousand Filipino deaths (the
more accurate figure, which is shocking enough). But truth
is the historian's principal tool, and when our leading "history
critic" wanders so far from easily verifiable fact, it makes us
wonder where he gets the information on which he bases his
strong opinions. Obviously, his assessment of baseball is not
founded on extensive study of the game.

Having said that, I wish I could explain *my* lifelong ob-
session with baseball. But it is like trying to explain sex to
a precocious six-year-old. Not that I have ever done this,
but I assume the child would say something like "Okay, I
understand the procedure. But *why*?" There is no answer
for that. You have to be there.

With baseball, too, you have to be there. But once you have been there, and bought it, you are likely to remain hooked for the rest of your life.

There are many ways to get there. Most Americans who are addicted to baseball played the game when they were young. But this is not a rquirement. P. G. Wodehouse, the English humorist, who was writing wildly funny stories about golf before you and I were born (unless you are awfully old), discovered baseball in his seventies. He became a rabid fan of the New York Mets and remained one until his death at ninety-four. Saul Steinberg, the brilliant artist-cartoonist, did not come to the United States until he was twenty-eight, but now at sixty-five he lies in bed at night and dreams of pitching a perfect game. According to *Time*, he sees baseball as "an allegorical play about America." I don't know about that, but I know about the dreaming, although I do not entertain such grand fantasies. I dream merely of getting a hit in a big-league game. One lousy time at bat, one fat medium-speed pitch right down the middle, one sharp crack of the bat, and I'm in the book forever. That's all I ask. Is that so much?

If baseball's appeal is hard to explain, there is no shortage of people who are willing to try. A writer named Gilbert Sorrentino had a go at it in *The New York Times*. Baseball, he said, is played in a framework of space rather than time. He said that in McLuhan's terms it is a "hot" game, that it is "filled with high-definition performances," that "anything can happen," literally, because the game's length is not controlled by a clock. He did not say, because a careful writer will go to any length to avoid using a cliché, that the game is never over until the last man is out. But I think maybe that's what he meant.

And here is an article someone has sent me from a scholarly magazine called *Critical Inquiry*. The author, Dennis Porter (professor of French and comparative literature at the University of Massachusetts, Amherst), feels strongly that baseball shares a hidden structure with the Russian fairy tale, and that the game is "best understood as a nonverbal folk form." He could be right, although I almost never think of it that way.

I don't claim to know what lights the spark. I know only that every winter, when baseball is dormant, I feel as if it's gone forever. And every spring, the first time I see a shortstop charge a slow bounding ball, short-hop it on the edge of the grass and in the same motion throw to first, beating the runner by a half-step, I rediscover its magical beauty and I marvel at my good fortune.

I became a Detroit Tiger fan for life the day I saw my first major-league game at the age of nine. This, too, is significant. There are no objective baseball fans. Or none that I've ever met. You are committed to a *team*. Somewhere in Nebraska, there is an aging fan who checks the progress of the Oakland A's every day because, as a boy, he lived in Philadelphia and was bewitched by Jimmy Foxx and Lefty Grove and that bunch. Or, if he's older still, Eddie Collins and Chief Bender and *that* bunch. His family moved to Cleveland, say, when he was fifteen. When he grew up, he moved around and finally settled in North Platte, from where he has followed the A's through all their moves— Philadelphia to Kansas City to Oakland, last to first to last again. He is hypothetical, this old guy, but his counterparts exist in cities large and small throughout America—still rooting for the first team that cast its spell over them.

And not only in America. In Bratislava (or Athens or Bombay), there is a man who, whenever he gets his hands on a U.S. newspaper, peeks inside to see how the Cubs or Red Sox or Pirates are doing before getting down to the hard news.

The simple fact of baseball's appeal to millions of people is beyond argument. The deeper meaning of baseball, like that of life, is obscure. It may be that baseball is, under close analysis, pointless. What seems apparent to me is that close analysis is pointless. The game is there. It is the best game there is. That's all I need to know.

With those who don't give a damn about baseball, I can only sympathize. I do not resent them. I am even willing to concede that many of them are physically clean, good to their mothers and in favor of world peace. But while the game is on, I can't think of anything to say to them.

                                    ❀   ❀   ❀

Last year, I wrote a book called *Don't Let Baseball Die.* The title was facetious, as you will see, although it obviously expresses a sentiment I endorse. The book was produced by a small Michigan publisher with no national distribution system. So only a few people, many of whom were friends of mine, read it. But it came to the attention of a New York publisher, who suggested that I do another book on baseball, "incorporating the best parts of the first one." This idea appealed to me because I like people to read what I write, and the publisher promised that more of them would be given that opportunity. There was thus the prospect that I might also make some money out of it, although this consideration is naturally secondary to a dedicated artist.

I explain all this so you will understand that, while this book uses an actual baseball season (or part of it) as a narrative framework, it is not only, or even primarily, about that season. It is about baseball today and last year and all the years before that.

I write from the viewpoint of the average fan, although, like any average fan, I think I know more about the game than the average fan. I should, if only because I've been watching it longer than most fans. But I get my news the same way any fan does. I see a lot of games in person and on TV, I listen to them on the radio, I read the papers and an occasional magazine piece. But I don't dig for inside (or "in depth") information. For one thing, I find it wise to keep my heroes at a distance.

One more thing. I write a lot about the Detroit Tigers. I can't help it. I'm a Tiger fan and have been living in Tiger territory for the last thirty years. For this book, my publisher advised me to "get out and see some ball games in other towns." I did, and it was fun. But there is still more about the Tigers in this book than their position in the standings is likely to warrant. They are my team. That's baseball.

A Cold Thursday
in February

NO NEWS IS STILL NEWS

This is the day the baseball season begins. The pitchers and catchers of the major-league teams are gathering at their various training camps in the sunny sections of the land. In my case, the team is the Detroit Tigers and the place is Lakeland, Florida. I am in Michigan, where the actual start of the season is signaled by the first eggless-omelet story of the year. Jim Hawkins, the *Detroit Free Press* baseball writer, made it official with a "news" story that did not take my breath away. The Tigers, it seems, have a big problem: too many pitchers!

Like most baseball stories from Florida, this one contains a grain of truth. The Tigers do have a lot of pitchers in camp. But no team ever has too many *good* pitchers, and this truism is duly acknowledged by the obligatory quote from the manager to the effect that while it is a problem, it is the kind of problem he likes. The phrase "happy trouble" is almost automatic in this sort of story, but Hawkins avoids it. He may be ready for a good season.

What makes this a typical spring baseball story, however, is that it is manufactured out of very porous cloth. Hawkins did not have to go to Florida to write it. He could have written it back in Detroit two months ago, while glancing through the Tigers' roster. Tradition demands, though, that

every big-league baseball team be thoroughly covered by
reporters from the major papers in the town it represents. And
indeed, we who love the Tigers read every word of what they
write, even though most of it is of negligible importance.
It is an unwritten law (or maybe it's written) that there must
be a story from camp in the paper every day. Or several
stories, if it's a slow news day. Which is why the true baseball fan loves a slow news day in the spring.

Every story must have an angle, however obtuse. Making
up angles is the principal function of the spring baseball
reporter. The ability to make a static fact look like news
is a big part of what makes a baseball reporter (or, for that
matter, any sports reporter) a pro. I suspect that a master chef
can probably whip up something that at least looks like an
omelet even when he finds himself temporarily eggless.
Similarly, a baseball writer had damn well better be able
to concoct something that looks like a news story when there
isn't any news, especially in the spring. Otherwise he will
soon find himself out in the cold. Which means either un-
employed or covering high-school football, whichever seems
colder.

The snow is two feet deep outside my window, and the
basketball and hockey seasons are just heating up in preparation for their endless play-offs. The opening baseball game is
still six weeks away. But in the meridional latitudes of this
great nation, thanks to the newspapers, the season is on. By
this we know that the earth is on schedule in its endless
voyage through space. Thanks, Lord. Or Whoever.

Sunday
February 25th

CALIFORNIA DREAMIN'

If baseball reporters must earn their keep in the spring
by making up believable news stories without any news, they
sometimes get an assist from baseball nuts who *make* news
that is barely believable. I searched this morning's paper in
vain for such a story, because this is the first anniversary of
one of the all-time winners in that category. On this date in
1978, it was announced that a junior high school in Lindsay,
California, had been renamed after Steve Garvey, the Los
Angeles Dodgers' clean-living first baseman. If that isn't
insane (or inane) enough for you, the school's library was
named for Tom Lasorda, the Dodgers' manager, possibly in
the belief that Tom has read a book.

In addition to living clean, Garvey is a high-average long-
ball hitter, which may have been a factor in his selection for
this honor. He is also an Anglo-Saxon. How long has it been
since you heard of a junior high school named for a clean-
living spray hitter from the Dominican Republic?

The school, by the way, was formerly named for Abraham
Lincoln. You can see the reasoning. In hip Southern Cali-
fornia, who wants a school named after some dead guy?
Garvey had led the Dodgers to a pennant the previous year;
Lincoln hadn't done anything worth talking about for ages.
(He did save the Union, though. If he hadn't, Garvey, who
comes from Florida, might have been a jai alai player.)

❖   ❖   ❖

As happens far too often, one ridiculous story begets
another. Lincoln and baseball inevitably, in my case, evoke
memories of the late Bill Stern. In the old radio days, Bill
Stern (the Colgate Shave Cream man) had a weekly sports
show on which he related little-known true stories of inci-

dents in the lives of famous people. Every story had to have
a sports angle, and it had to be "inspirational." Since there
are only about five such stories (all of them duller than
Buffalo), he soon ran out of material—and that's when the
anecdotes began to get interesting. Once we realized he was
making them up out of thin air (apparently assisted by someone with a really bizarre imagination), we could hardly wait
for them. One week, he had Lincoln taking his turn at bat
in a pickup ball game on the White House lawn when they
brought him the news of the South's surrender.

Since no history book had recorded this remarkable event,
it was obviously a major scoop. But Stern had no difficulty
in topping it. A few weeks later, in a hushed and reverent
voice (Stern was the only man who ever mastered staccato
reverence), he told us how Lincoln, on his deathbed, painfully whispered to General Abner Doubleday, "Don't let
baseball die."

If Lincoln had spoken at all after being shot, it seems more
likely that he would have said, "Don't let *me* die." But
perhaps the most intriguing aspect of this fable is that if it
had happened, the General's response would doubtless have
been "Why me?" (Or conceivably, "What's baseball?")
Abner Doubleday died in 1893 without ever learning that
he was the inventor of baseball, since that fiction—fully as
fantastic as most of Stern's—wasn't fabricated until many
years later.

Thursday
March 1st

OF GATES BROWN, HIS COLOR
AND AVOIDING THE ISSUE

Gates Brown, who is back with Detroit as a coach this
year, was one of the most popular players ever to perform for

Gates Brown. An awesome pinch hitter in 1968.

the Tigers. A frightful outfielder, who occasionally played
left field at great personal risk, he was just plain frightening
to opposing pitchers when he had a bat in his powerful
hands. When Gates went up to pinch-hit with the score
tied in the bottom of the ninth, especially if a right-handed
pitcher was working, you figured it would soon be over. And
you were usually right. That was in 1968, of course, when
everything worked and the Tigers won it by twelve. In that
wonderful year, Gates Brown batted .370, going to the plate
just 92 times and getting 34 hits, 6 of them home runs and
almost half of them for extra bases. He was one of the finest
pinch hitters baseball has ever seen. And for that one year,
he was simply awesome.

Last year, after the Tigers hired Gates Brown as a batting
coach, we soon began hearing Detroit hitters mentioning his
name in connection with their improved performance. Notable among these was Aurelio Rodríguez, who started the
season like a batting champion and finished it at .265, a
modest enough figure but still 46 points better than his
previous year's average.

How did Brown do it? Frankly, I have never understood
quite what a batting coach does, since most players presumably know how to bat before they get to the bigs. But
Aurelio had a simple explanation. He said Gates told him not
to swing at bad pitches, explaining, "If you don't swing at
bad pitches, they have to throw you a good one." I already
knew that. I also knew Rodríguez was swinging at bad
pitches, notably the low curve off the plate. But it had
never occurred to me that you could correct this just by
telling him to stop.

Obviously, Gates Brown was doing something more than
stating self-evident truths, especially to hitters of the caliber
of Rusty Staub and Ron LeFlore, who also acknowledged his
assistance. Whatever it was, it was working—and with batters
of all hues. I bring this up because last year the Tigers had a
player in camp named Charlie Spikes. Spikes had been a few

years earlier, a rookie hitter of tremendous promise. The promise had never been kept, but the Tigers hoped it was still redeemable. In a routine new-player story from Florida, a *Detroit Free Press* reporter made the curious statement that Gates Brown had been hired "specifically to work with players like Spikes." I wondered what that meant. Former Cleveland players? Players from Bogalusa, Louisiana? Right-handed power hitters? What it undoubtedly *did* mean was that Charlie Spikes, who is black, still had great potential as a hitter but had lost his confidence, and that he might hope to regain it under the guidance of Gates Brown, who is also black. (Spikes never did make it, although I thought the Tigers gave up on him too soon.) That a black player should feel more comfortable with a black coach than with a white one seemed perfectly reasonable to me. But for some reason they can't (or don't) say that in the papers.

The matter of race in baseball is handled in a strangely reticent way by the newspapers. Which is to say that it is not handled at all, most of the time. I can appreciate that it is a subject which must sometimes be dealt with delicately. Apparently, sportswriters, distrustful of their ability to tread softly on rocky ground, prefer not to walk in that area at all. One odd result of this is that unless a player's picture appears in the paper (and given the quality of some newspaper photographs, often not even then), we do not know whether he is black or white. When Catfish Hunter came up with the Kansas City (later Oakland) A's, I assumed he was black because I first heard of him at about the same time I first heard of his teammate Blue Moon Odom. I knew Odom was black so, with elegant illogic, I posited that his fellow rookie with the equally colorful nickname was also.

How did I know Odom was black? I can't remember. Perhaps I saw a picture of him. Perhaps I just relied on the rule that any player named after a song is black. (This is the Night Train Lane Rule, formulated in honor of the Detroit Lions' superb defensive back of a few years ago.)

Am I being flippant about a serious subject? Well, no, I am trying to be deadly serious about what should be a subject of no importance at all: the color of a man's skin. When it is somehow taboo to mention casually that a player is black or white, the subject arises only when there is overt racial conflict. Racial harmony never makes the papers.

We who follow baseball from the outside, who never see what happens or hear what is said off the field, have very little idea of how well integrated baseball really works. I like to think that all the players look at one another simply as ballplayers and fellow human beings, that they judge one another on merit alone and are scarcely aware of differences in skin color. This is the way the world ought to be, and it's comforting to believe that the condition has actually been achieved in the small world of sport. But I have been around a bit in the world of men and women, mostly white, and I have listened in openmouthed disbelief to the outrageous qualities that supposedly intelligent people attribute to those of a different race (or religion). So I know that the Brotherhood of Man is still a few years off. Still, if we're any closer to it than we were twenty years ago (and we obviously are, no matter how far we still have to go), a good share of the credit must go to the playing fields of America.

There are doubtless many reasons for this. One is that a professional athlete, whether his neck is red or black, usually can't help admiring professional skill in another, whatever his tint. Also, in the heat of athletic battle (much as in a real war), courage is often useful, and it turns out that no race has an exclusive on it. But the biggest reason is that in team sports, a professional's livelihood depends in part (sometimes in large part) on the performance of his teammates. Ask a white shortstop from south Georgia whom he'd rather have playing second base with him in the deciding game of the play-off series—a good old boy from down home who can't make the double play . . . or a black man who can. In such situations racial animosities seem to evanesce. And sometimes respect for the player can be translated into respect for the person.

So how could sportswriters improve their coverage of this touchy subject? Certainly not by constantly mentioning a player's color. That would be as foolish as giving his weight or his age each time his name comes up. But when a decision, an incident or a remark has obvious racial overtones, that should be reported. It is conventional wisdom that you can't make a problem go away by pretending it doesn't exist. When the unpleasant facts are recorded, there will be no reason not to tell us about the hopeful things that happen as well. There *are* some of those, and I don't want to be denied the good feeling I get when I hear about them. I am a romantic, and every time I hear a story about a white man unselfishly helping a black man or vice versa, I think, By God, things are going to be okay after all, forgetting (sometimes for as long as five minutes) all the evidence to the contrary.

Saturday
March 3rd

THE HARDEST POSITION

Alan Trammell and Lou Whitaker are the two halves of the best young second-base combination to come to the majors as a unit in many years. They played together in the minors, came up to the Tigers together last year and will be together in the Detroit infield for many years to come if God's in His heaven. Long before we ever saw them, we were told that they roomed together on the road, that they eat together and, best of all, talk baseball together endlessly. Not only is this a triumph for brotherhood (Trammell is white, Whitaker black), but it takes me back to another day. In my youth, all ballplayers, according to report, spent their evenings sitting around the lobbies of second-best hotels talking baseball. The principal reason they did this, it's true, is that most of them couldn't afford to do anything else. (Now that I think of it, we never heard much about Babe Ruth sitting around hotel lobbies, but then he was always off somewhere visiting sick boys in hospitals.) Still, it's nice to read about two kids who represent an almost obsolete phenomenon: the baseball player whose primary interest is baseball.

Whitaker, the second baseman, looks like the better hitter of the pair. He has been called, by some dreamy Tiger executive, the next Rod Carew. That would be nice, but we'll settle for a steady .300 or better, which appears to be well within his capabilities.

Trammell, who hit .268 last year and should improve on that, is a fine fielder with a good arm (as is Whitaker) who makes a lot of noise out there. He is apparently a natural leader, rather in the style of Dick Bartell, a shrill little man who goaded the Tigers to a pennant in 1940 although he hit for a skimpy .233 average. Alan has a special appeal for me because, for most of my life, or so it seems, the Tigers have been looking for a shortstop. I suppose, realistically, that fans of all teams feel that way because shortstop is the hardest position to play and there have been so few really good ones. To define my terms, a "really good" shortstop is one who does the job in the field, day after day, year after year, and hits well enough so you don't mind seeing him come to the plate in a tough situation. If you have one of those, you have taken a major step toward participation in what we like to call the October Classic.

In 1945, on my way home from defending generations yet unborn from the Yellow Peril, I saw a young shortstop playing for the Marine Corps Training Center team in Pearl Harbor who looked like a future major leaguer. (Do I have to be honest? Okay, I actually saw him play only once, but I took the word of his coach, who was a friend of mine, that

The author (right) and his father at the third game of the 1945 World Series (Detroit, October 5, 1945).

he couldn't miss.) I spoke to the shortstop that evening, possibly while slightly taken in strong drink, and he said that he would love to play for the Tigers. I didn't exactly say I was with the Detroit club, but I think I rather implied that I had strong connections there. Well, come to think of it, I did. The next day I wrote my father and told him to tell his good friend Wish Egan, the Tigers' chief scout, about this bright prospect. When I got home, my father informed me that Egan had said he "knew the kid" but wasn't interested. That was my one and only attempt to scout a ballplayer, and I would have to say I scored 100 percent (although the Tigers got a zero), because the "kid" was Al Dark. And he wasn't a kid—he was twenty-three years old and ready to play. I thought about it often in the following years, especially in 1948, when Dark led the Boston Braves to a pennant with a .322 batting average; and in 1951, when the Giants won the pennant with Dark playing great shortstop and hitting .303; and in 1954, when the Giants won the Series in four straight from Cleveland with Dark hitting .417.

(There is a sentence there that I ought to clarify. Seems clear enough, but still, considering Dark's legendary probity, I had better repeat that it was I, not he, who had been drinking the night I spoke to him at Pearl Harbor. Abstinence is a practice I now share with him, but it took me another twenty years to get around to it. He and I still don't see eye to eye on the question of tithing.)

I never saw Dark again (except on the field) after that one meeting, but he might remember it. If he does, and wonders why he never heard from the Tigers, this will let him know it wasn't my fault. But I doubt that he's been brooding over it. I'm sure I felt a lot worse about it than he did.

During the '50s, the Tigers' shortstop problems were alleviated somewhat by the presence of Harvey Kuenn, one of the great natural hitters. His lifetime batting average of .303, enviable though it is, is scarcely representative of his value as a hitter during his years with the Tigers. In 1959, he led the league in batting with .353, but by then he had already deserted his shortstop post for a less taxing job in the outfield. He was then only twenty-eight, but I think he had a weight problem. I know he has one now. You can check it out for yourself the next time the Milwaukee Brewers, for whom he is a coach, come to your town.

The Tigers never won anything while Kuenn was with them, and in fact they have a peculiar history of winning championships with shortstops who could barely carry a bat to the plate. I've mentioned Bartell's .233 in 1940. In 1945, they won the pennant and the World Series with Skeeter Webb playing short and hitting .199. There were those who whispered that Webb's position as first-string shortstop was not weakened by his position as Manager Steve O'Neill's son-in-law, but that may have been unfair. They won it all.

After the war, the Tigers didn't win another pennant until 1968, the year of the Ray Oyler phenomenon. Here was a man holding down a regular position on a team that won a world's championship who had only twenty-nine hits all season. He batted .135! It was the year of the pitcher; none of the Tigers threatened .300 except Gates Brown, the miraculous pinch hitter, with .370. The Tigers' team batting average was .235, and the whole league had an average of .230. Carl Yastrzemski led the league in batting with a .301 mark. All in all, just about the worst year in history for hitters. None the less, .135 for a championship shortstop is a figure that defies comparison.

Doubtless Oyler was embarrassed by that average at the time. But as the years go by, it has become a mark of distinction, attesting, among other things, to what a fine fielder Ray was. "The best shortstop I ever played with," says Dick McAuliffe, the second baseman on that team.

But good as he was in the field, Oyler's hitting finally deteriorated to the point where something had to be done. Manager Mayo Smith decided to bring Mickey Stanley in from center field and play him at shortstop in the World Series. That won the world's championship for Detroit. It is a rule of sports journalism that you are not allowed to mention this move without calling it "daring." But I think "ingenious" is more apt. Mayo was smart to think of it, but once he had thought of it, it would have been more daring not to do it.

Oyler recalls how Mayo broke the news to him a couple of weeks before the Series: "He said, 'Now, look, Ray, I'm going to have to do it because we need hitting to beat St. Louis.' Stanley's bat was much better; I have to admit my bat wasn't that good."

True, but beside the point. Stanley was going to play in any case. What the move did was make room for Al Kaline in the outfield. (Al had broken his arm earlier in the year, and had finished the season on the bench.) And that simply meant the difference between winning the World Series and losing it. Kaline had 11 hits—at least 10 more than Oyler would have had—including 2 home runs and the biggest single of his career, the one that turned the tide in the seventh inning of the fifth game, just when the Tigers looked as if they were ready to hang it up and go fishing. From that moment on, it was Detroit's Series, and they won it going away.

So it is possible for a team to be successful with a puny-hitting shortstop. (Note: .250 is weak; .200 is puny.) A shortstop who can make the "impossible" play repeatedly (assuming he doesn't mess up the easy ones) can get by with an average that most players would find conducive to unemployment. The Tigers proved this one more time in 1972, when they won their division with Eddie Brinkman playing short and hitting .203. But Eddie, besides being an incredible fielder, was also a clutch hitter who seemed to hit the ball hardest when it counted most. No doubt this is exaggerated in my memory (winning teams always get larger as the years usher them farther into the past), but it only takes two or three *key* hits in a season to make the difference in a close race. The Tigers beat out Boston by just half a game in '72, so it's safe to say that Brinkman's selective hitting played a vital role in their victory.

In addition to all this, Brinkman was a team leader. A brash, outspoken, good-natured, sometimes obscene man (his joyously uncensored outburst on live TV the night the Tigers wrapped it up is still fondly remembered by many), he contributed even more to the team's success than his glove and his bat.

If winning with a weak-hitting shortstop is feasible, it's more fun to win with one who can hit a little. The Tigers have done that, too, but you have to go back to 1934 and '35 for an instance. That was when hard-nosed Billy Rogell played short alongside the flawless second baseman Charlie Gehringer. Rogell's batting averages for the pennant years, .296 and .275, were among the lowest on those hard-hitting teams, but they are numbers that any manager today would like to see following his shortstop's name. And here's another. Rogell drove in 100 runs in '34, a surprising total for a .296 hitter with only three home runs.

Nowadays, if you fly out of Detroit's Metro Airport, you will probably approach it by car along William G. Rogell Drive. That honor didn't come to Billy because of his short-stopping. His famous manager on those Tiger teams, Mickey Cochrane, had a street named after him while he was still a baseball hero. Rogell had to get elected to the Detroit city council a dozen times or so before becoming an eponym. (Neither of these thoroughfares, it should be noted, is a tree-lined boulevard. Cochrane Street is a narrow passageway behind the ball park. Rogell Drive is a sort of airport off-ramp.) Now white-haired and rising seventy-five, Councilman Rogell can still be seen from time to time on the eleven-o'clock news, and he's usually mad about something. Through the years, he has made the traditional transition, brought on by age and a changing world, from voice of the working stiff to cantankerous conservative. But he's just as hard-nosed as ever.

I don't know how Alan Trammell feels about municipal politics. If he lives up to his promise, he'll probably be able

Billy Rogell.
Baseball to
politics.

to buy his own town before he's through. But on the field he could do worse than emulate the attributes that made Billy Rogell a champion all those years ago: good field, good hit, true grit. Trammell seems to have the tools. A couple of pennants would complete the picture.

❀   ❀   ❀

Skeeter Webb wasn't the only unusual player on the 1945 Tigers. That was wartime baseball, and there were many odd entries on the Tiger roster. One was an outfielder named Chuck Hostetler, best remembered for falling down while rounding third with what would have been the winning run in the sixth game of the World Series. No matter, they won the Series the next day, and Chuck was a member of the world's champions. Not bad for a guy who had played his first major-league game the year before at the age of forty.

Another member of that team who has always interested me was Bob Maier. I know very little about him because I was in the far Pacific that year (as I mention from time to time), but he was the Tigers' regular third baseman, playing in 132 games and hitting a respectable .263. Although he was only twenty-nine, he never played again after 1945, and he had never played a major-league game before that year. He wrapped up a highly successful career—first-string player, pennant, world's championship—in a neat one-year package. Although I got home in time to see the second and third games of the Series, I never saw Maier play, because Jimmy Outlaw had replaced him at third base at the end of the year. They might have done better to stick with Maier. Outlaw batted .179 in the Series, and Maier, who pinch-hit once, batted 1.000.

❀   ❀   ❀

Mention of Wish Egan, the man who didn't think Al Dark was good enough, recalls the time I heard him tell how the Tigers got George Kell. Egan was a huge red-faced Irishman who had had a negligible career as a pitcher many years earlier. He was in his mid-sixties and, although the record book gives his playing weight as 185, he must have been a hundred pounds heavier than that when I met him. He had a reputation among baseball men as a brilliant judge of talent. (They didn't know about Al Dark.)

As Egan told the story, he was assigned to negotiate a deal with Connie Mack for Kell in the early weeks of the 1946 season. Kell was only twent-two at the time, but he had already demonstrated that he was a third baseman of rare quality. When his name was brought up, Mack was taken aback. "Oh, my," he said, "George is a fine ballplayer. I couldn't let him go for anyone less than Barney McCosky."

"I was stunned," Egan related, "but not for the reason he thought. We were quite prepared to give him McCosky and another good player for Kell. But I had to make a show of resistance. I pointed out that McCosky was one of my boys. I had signed him for the Tigers. I couldn't think of trading him. But Mr. Mack was determined to have him, and I finally let myself be talked into an even trade. I didn't know how to feel about it. I was delighted with the deal, but at the same time I was a little ashamed of myself for taking advantage of the old man." Connie Mack was then eighty-four.

There is no doubt that this was a fine trade for Detroit. Kell was probably the best third baseman in the league for several years, and an excellent hitter, besides being several years younger than McCosky. But Barney wasn't exactly a bum. He went to Philadelphia that year and batted .354, following it with years of .328 and .326. He was also a good outfielder. A back injury hampered his career after 1948, but that sort of thing is unpredictable and can hardly be considered in evaluating a trade.

There's a footnote to the story. Connie Mack was old, but he was skinny. He outlived Wish Egan by five years.

Monday
March 5th

THE MISSING GAME

After I wrote (while discussing Eddie Brinkman, above) that the Tigers won their division by half a game in 1972, it started to bug me. According to the rules, no team *can* finish first by half a game. All teams are scheduled to play the same number of games, and all rained-out games must be made up *if they have a bearing on first place*, even if it means extending the season. So . . . back to the old record book, where I discovered that the Tigers had played only 156 games that year, and the Red Sox only 155 (whereas the schedule called for 162). Then it all came back to me: 1972 was the year of the players' strike, which lasted for ten days at the start of the year. When the season finally did begin, all the unplayed games were simply dropped from the schedule. The Red Sox had missed seven games, the Tigers only six. It seemed unimportant at the time, but it proved unfortunate for the Boston club at the finish.

When the Red Sox came to town for the final three-game series with the Tigers, they were 1½ games behind, which meant they had to sweep the series to win the divisional championship. If they had played that missing game and won it, they would have started the last series only one game behind, and could have tied the Tigers by winning just two of the three games, which in fact they did. But here's the key point. Even if the Red Sox had played the missing game and *lost* it, they would have been no worse off than they actually were. They would have been only two games behind, and still could have won the division title by taking all three games from the Tigers. So the one extra game the Tigers played could have made all the difference. I'm sure the Red Sox thought it did.

Tuesday
March 6th

NO FIGURES FOR FIELDING

Baseball lives on statistics. Without them, baseball fans wouldn't know who their favorites were. This is not quite literally true, but almost. There have always been players who, without compiling impressive figures, had a flair for doing the right thing at the crucial moment, and they have usually been popular and comparatively well paid. But the guys who come in demanding million-dollar deals, if they want to be taken seriously, had better have big numbers in the proper columns after their names. And for the most part, these are the fellows who draw the loudest cheers, too.

The proper columns, for a hitter, are batting average, runs batted in, home runs. Doubles, triples and runs scored are a good measure of a hitter's skill too, but *BA*, *RBI* and *HR* are the three columns the fans look at first, and thus the ones that sell tickets. Owners know this, and pay accordingly.

With pitchers, it's games won and earned-run average (ERA). Canny old baseball men are said to pay a lot more attention to the ERA than they pay to the won–lost mark, for the obvious reason that a pitcher with a good team is bound to win a lot more games than one with a terrible team. But whatever his team does, a pitcher who wins twenty is doing a good job and can count on being amply rewarded for it; he'll be a "twenty-game winner," which, like a .300 hitter, is something special—so much better than a nineteen-game winner or a .299 hitter.

This reverence for statistics doesn't exist in any other sport. Pro football fans may be equally rabid, but they seldom quote figures to prove their point. Except for a few superlative numbers, like O. J. Simpson's 2000-yard season, they don't carry figures around in their heads, to be used as weapons in barroom arguments. Baseball fans do, and wouldn't have it any other way.

All this being true, it is unfortunate that there are no statistics to reflect the single most exciting skill in baseball: the ability to make the astonishing fielding play time after time. The fielding averages, meticulously compiled and involving hundreds of plays per season for every regular player, don't even give a true picture of the comparative merits of the players of ordinary skill. Most record books don't bother to include them. And when it comes to the plays that take your breath away, there is nothing you can put on paper that conveys what they mean to the player, to the fan and to the game.

Aurelio Rodríguez, the Tigers' third baseman, has a life-time batting average of .239, so he hasn't spent twelve years in the major leagues on the strength of his hitting. Because he doesn't hit much, he lives constantly with the possibility that he'll be replaced by someone with a bigger bat. Last year he was platooned with Phil Mankowski, a left-handed hitter, and it worked out pretty well. Rodríguez, in fact, had his best year ever at the plate. So the strategy was justified, but for me something important is missing if Aurelio isn't out there performing his daily miracle.

Of course, I do not go to a Tiger game with the intention of seeing Rodríguez or anyone else make a great fielding play. Like most fans, I am looking forward to seeing Jason Thompson hit one of his booming home runs, or Ron LeFlore lash a line drive to right center—a cinch double for any-one else—and race around to third easily before the out-fielders can catch up with the ball. That's a reasonable hope because I know that Thompson and LeFlore will each come to bat four or five times during the game. I do not know that any line shots will be hit just inside third base, affording Rodríguez the opportunity to grab a two-base hit out of left field and with his incredible throwing arm turn it into a routine out. In some games, there are no outstanding fielding plays. But when it happens, it's what I remember longest. I may go home talking about a game-winning hit, but years later, when the actual game is forgotten, the super fielding play will still be a sharp, clear picture in my mind.

It's too bad there isn't any way to capture it in a line of type.

Wednesday
March 7th

DEATH OF A FAT MAN

Steve Bilko died a year ago today. Hardly anyone noticed the three-inch story in the paper which related that he had died of "an undisclosed illness" after a long stay in the hospital. I observe the anniversary of his death only because I wrote a few notes about him at the time. Steve didn't quite make it to his fiftieth birthday, which is too bad, but he played in 600 major-league games, which is something.

Remembering people like Steve Bilko is what separates the fans from the mere passersby in baseball. (Football fans remember Bruno Banducci.) Steve was a huge man with a funny name who could hit a baseball half a mile, but seldom did. All told, he hit only 76 big-league home runs, which is not many for a man whose entire career was based on the assumption that he could hit home runs. (He *did* hit 56 of them one year in the minors.)

I remember Bilko, of course. (Hell, I remember Lou Brower.) But my sons remember him, too, even though they were just kids during the one mediocre season he spent with the Tigers. He was one of those people whose presence outshines their ability. Phil Silvers even borrowed his name (I feel reasonably sure) for the bumptious sergeant he played in his hit TV series.

In the minors, Bilko once played for Rochester of the International League, a team that traveled by train to Canada to play the Toronto Maple Leafs and the Montreal Royals. The story goes that the first time Bilko was questioned at the border by Canadian immigration officers, he was asked, "Place of birth?" and replied, "Lower six."

I have to believe that this is merely a lighthearted fable, but it illustrates the sort of thing that big strong ballplayers who are not noted for their grace have to put up with. Awkwardness in the field is taken as an indication of mental inertia. Nowadays, Bilko would have an agent and a writer and could probably command a $100,000 contract on bulk alone. But at the time he fitted the popular stereotype of the brute ballplayer.

Zeke Bonura, a much better hitter (lifetime .307) who played for the White Sox and Washington in the '30s, had to endure the same sort of thing. He was, I believe, the worst-fielding first baseman I ever saw. He played the position so badly that he *looked* dumb. And there were countless stories about his colorful and hilarious conflicts with the rules of rational behavior. He was depicted as a hopeless rube barely bright enough to order his own dinner. In fact, Bonura was born and raised in New Orleans, hardly a rustic setting, and he was a college man, which (being one myself) I like to think indicates at least a modicum of intelligence. There were few college products in professional baseball in the '30s, so it's safe to assume that Bonura's mind was equal to those of most of his teammates. But we believed the caricature. In those pre-television days, we rarely saw the players close up, and almost never heard them speak. So we accepted the myth. And it's true, when Bonura went after a ground ball to his right, it was hard to believe he was an educated man.

I wonder what Steve Bilko thought about during the long days and nights of his last undisclosed illness. The traditional happy moments with family and friends, I suppose, plus a few bitter ones. A little fear, surely, or maybe a lot. I wonder if he recalled the night in Detroit when he hit one over the left-field stands in a pre-game long-ball hitting contest. No one had ever done that in a game. (It was, I thought, the most dramatic demonstration possible of the difference between hitting against a real pitcher and swinging against someone throwing setups down the middle.)

I feel sure, though, that what he remembered best was 1953, the only year he was really a first-string ballplayer. He

Steve Bilko. Did he remember 1953?

played the entire season at first base for the Cardinals, hit 21 home runs, drove in 84 runs. He was a regular on a pretty good big-league team, playing alongside Stan Musial and Red Schoendienst. At twenty-four, he was the youngest player on an aging club. From here on in, he must have thought, it can't get anything but better. From there on in, as it turned out, it was all downhill. And fast. Two years later, he was out of the majors. He worked his way back up, but it took several years, and he was never more than a fringe player after that one semi-glorious season.

I don't know why Bilko declined with such startling speed after a single highly promising year. It may have been simple bad luck, or it may have been something he blamed himself for later. But I'll bet, at the end, he wasn't thinking of that. My guess is that all his baseball memories centered on that year when he was almost a star, and that they could be summed up in some such simple phrase as "Damn, wasn't it great!"

Tuesday
March 13th

TAKE ME OUT TO THE KITCHEN

Rusty Staub, the Brillat-Savarin of designated hitters, apparently finds baseball a bit tedious after sixteen years of working at it. He is thinking of packing it in, and turning his talents to his true love, which he never calls "grub." He might be dissuaded from this radical change of course, but it would take a lot of money. To lure him out of the pantry, the Tigers would have to guarantee him a million dollars over the next five years. If they won't, *zut alors!* it's off to *la cuisine*, where his gentle touch with a *crème caramel* (whisk control, in the patois of the trade) is properly appreciated.

Staub has a contract with the Tigers that runs through 1980 and pays him $200,000 a year for stepping up to the plate four or five times a day and, when he can manage it, lashing a baseball into right field or, if possible, beyond it. This works out to about $277.77 each time he picks up a bat, which would satisfy me but seems insufficiently rewarding to Rusty when he contemplates the really big bucks that certain unidentified big spenders are anxious to pay him for his skill in the preparation and serving of what he never calls "eats" either.

In his current profession Rusty gets paid even if he pops up, which is the equivalent of burning the prime rib in his new field. It is only fair to mention, though, that he did hit the ball well and truly often enough last year to drive in 121 runs, a total exceeded in all of baseball only by Boston's Jim Rice, who had one of those years Babe Ruth used to dream about.

Gazing dreamily at these figures, Rusty got the idea that he was worth more money than he was getting for hitting baseballs. But he did not, he emphasizes, ask for a raise. He is happy with the two hundred thou annually. He would just like to be guaranteed that he will get it for the next *five* years, rather than two. This would assure him of $200,000 in 1982 and a like sum in 1983, even if he drives in only 12 runs in 1981.

There are those who say Rusty has a point. Jim Campbell, the Tigers' general manager, is not among them. He maintains that far from having a point, Rusty has a contract, and that a contract is a contract. This is the conditioned-reflex expression for everyone who agrees with Campbell. Ask anyone in Detroit what he thinks of the Staub controversy, and he will probably answer, according to his leaning, either "Campbell had better sit down and talk with Rusty, or the Tigers can kiss the pennant goodbye" or "Dammit, a contract is a contract."

Rusty, to give him his due, knows that a contract is a contract, and being a man with a sense of propriety, he declines to use the brazen maneuver which is usual in such cases, the straightforward holdup. Normally, a ballplayer who is tied to a long-term contract and who feels he is underpaid goes to the man with the money and says something like this: "Look, I know I have a contract, but I am not getting what I deserve. Now, either you renegotiate upward or trade me, or if you won't do either of those things, I am going to be unhappy." This last would not seem like much of an argument, but it carries a sinister implication. It suggests, none too subtly, that the player will be brooding so over his maltreatment that he won't be able to hit the ball as far or as often, or strike out as many batters, as he used to when he was happy. It comes very close to being a threat to dog it. This, if you could prove it, and if the major leagues were to buy a backbone for the commissioner (or, alternatively, appoint a commissioner who already has one), would be grounds for expulsion from the grand old game.

These people who come in demanding that their contracts be renegotiated are always armed with long lists of figures involving other ballplayers who are making a lot more money and who batted 40 points worse than the plaintiff last year, or drove in only half as many runs or (if the unhappy one is a pitcher) won only half as many games. These lists are easy to compile because the very prevalence of long-term contracts in baseball today makes it an absolute certainty that if you have a good year, there will be at least ten players in the game who had worse years than you but are getting more money. Yet this circumstance seems to justify the demand, because there is no case on record of any of these other players' going to *their* general managers and suggesting that their long-term contracts be adjusted downward to bring them into line with the guy who had the good year.

Rusty, as I have said, was above this sort of shabby logic. He did the blasé bit. His future, he says, probably stifling a yawn, is in the restaurant business, and he would just as soon get at it without delay. But if the ball club should see fit to make him an offer too good to refuse he would be willing to postpone his *restaurative* career to accommodate the Tigers and help them win a lot of games.

Now, while I am perhaps laying it on a bit thick, I am not twisting the basic facts. Staub actually said, when all this started, that he had offers from certain restaurant people that would bring him *more* money than he could make in baseball.

The problem with this, although to my knowledge no one has come right out and said it, is that nobody believes him. (What I mean, of course, is that I don't believe him. I'm only guessing about the rest of the world.) Oh, I have no doubt there's big money to be made in the restaurant business, but only if you're successful. Any new business is a gamble, and when it comes to long odds I would put the restaurant business right up there with buying all the possible combinations in the daily double.

So what Rusty meant, presumably, was that he would have a *chance* to make more money in the catering game than he does in baseball, although he didn't put it quite that way. But that's obviously the way Jim Campbell interpreted it. He seemed undaunted by the prospect of Rusty's career switch, and even went so far as to take a little dig at him. "If baseball is going to be his avocation," he said, "then he may be doing us a favor by getting out of the game." Unkind, perhaps, but it put the shuttlecock in Rusty's airspace.

On the late news tonight, Marvin Miller, the head of the major-league players' association, had something to say on the matter. Naturally, he's on Rusty's side, but his reasoning was meretricious. "Rusty is *not* trying to renegotiate," he said, "he's just asking for an extension. Owners do this all the time . . . and they don't call it renegotiating."

Mr. Miller is an expert labor negotiator, so it goes without saying that he is a master of the pinchbeck analogy, and in this one the base metal is showing through. It's true, certainly, that owners offer to extend players' contracts if it appears to be to their advantage. But if the player declines, that's the end of it. The owner cannot forbid him to play or withhold his salary. Quite unlike Rusty's demand, which carries with it the threat to withhold services, the owner's

offer has no clout behind it, and it will be accepted only if
the player considers it also to *his* advantage.

It has been pointed out that there is a false note in Campbell's "contract is a contract" hymn. This stems from the
universal conviction that contract or no, if Rusty were ten
years younger (he is thirty-five) and making the same demand, Jim would be unrolling the foolscap and inking the
quill before the words were out of his mouth. But that's
really irrelevant. A contract is an agreement between two
parties. It can be canceled as easily as it was entered into,
and in the same way—*by mutual consent.* The only point
of a contract is to protect each party against the possibility
of the other party's changing his mind. If the million-dollar
player becomes dime-a-dozen during the second year of his
five-year contract, the owner still has to pay him the million
if that's what the contract says. The owner would be met
with hoots of derision if he tried to persuade the deteriorat-
ing player to take a cut, or to reduce the term of his contract.
The player knows that and wholeheartedly approves. But
he doesn't think the same conditions should apply to him.
Or, perhaps to state it better, he thinks an exception should
be made in his case. Clearly, however, a "contract" that is
binding on only one of the parties involved is not a contract
at all.

I guess I have just revealed where I stand in this matter.
But actually, my feelings are mixed. I wish Campbell had
handled it quietly and privately. I don't know how, exactly,
but then, I am not handsomely paid to know how. If I were,
I would certainly have tried to accommodate Rusty in some
way, or convince him of the futility of his position, before
the thing became a *cause célèbre.* I don't say it would have
been easy, but then, as a man once said in another context,
if it were easy we'd get someone off the street to do it.

When all bets are down, though, in the final analysis (and
when the roll is called up yonder), I do indeed believe that
a contract is a contract. All my life I have been mystified by

the spectacle of the one-way sports "contract." This is most notable in the common case of the famous football coach who jumps to a better job, although we clearly remember that he signed a highly publicized five-year contract just two years ago. That wasn't a contract, it was a guarantee that he couldn't be fired for five years, apparently demanding no assurances from him in return. We can understand how a great university might find it embarrassing to try to force a man to remain on the job when he wants to leave it (with all the publicity that would attend the controversy), but what about the man himself? Doesn't any football coach ever feel an obligation to live up to his contract? A contract is a promise, and when you deliberately break a promise you are a liar. Football coaches are supposed to be men of character. I believe, despite the win-at-any-price stereotype, that many of them are, in most respects. But if they sign contracts they have no intention of honoring, given a better offer, they are also liars.

Last year, the New England Patriots, a football team that does not represent any university, and so didn't mind the controversy, actually tried to make their coach live up to his contract. When he jumped to a college job, they made a stink about it, at great expense and possibly even some embarrassment to his new employer, the University of Colorado. I applaud them, and I hope the case sets a precedent.

And that's how I feel about the Rusty Staub case.

Thursday
March 15th

MEMORIES OF THE GENTLE GIANT

Today, the Ides of March, is my birthday, and I have officially been declared an antique. It occurs to me that if I live to be ninety-nine, which God forbid (one prayer that

Hank Greenberg. Ten years, 1276 RBI's.

will doubtless be answered), I will see the year 2019. Dimly, to be sure, but still . . . That seems unbelievably remote, but no more so than 1979 seemed in 1939. In 1939, when World War I was known simply as "the World War," my baseball hero was Hank Greenberg. I've had a lot of favorites since, none of them quite as big as Hank. Heroes increase in stature as memories are gilded over. But Hank was a great one even without benefit of hindsight.

"You've often heard "It was a home run from the moment it left the bat." That was Greenberg's trademark. The big, brutal swing, followed (unless he had guessed wrong) by the sweet sharp crack of the bat, and it was all over. All but the shouting, which was immediate. With Hank, there was no waiting.

Greenberg's career was curtailed by the war (he was drafted a year *before* Pearl Harbor) and one serious injury. So he played not quite ten full seasons, but in that short span he batted in 1276 runs. Six times he had more than 125 RBI's, three times more than 150. In 1946, after being away four and a half years, he led both leagues in home runs with 44.

As a fielder, Greenberg was an object lesson for every kid who has ever turned his face away from a hard ground ball. Because that's exactly what Hank used to do when he first came to the Tigers. But he *made* himself a good fielder. Even as a superstar, he was always the first one at the park. I know because more than once, three hours before game time, I was the only one in the stands watching him. Endlessly, he would hurl a ball against the outfield wall and field it on the hop, like a kid in his own backyard who has no one to play catch with.

Hank was, I think, the only player ever to win Most Valuable Player awards at two different positions. He moved in mid-career from first base to the outfield, so Rudy York, who couldn't play anywhere else, could play first.

And one more thing. In his final days with Pittsburgh, Hank was one of the very few players to buck the trend and openly encourage the rookie Jackie Robinson to hang in there. As the game's greatest Jewish player, Hank was no stranger to big-league bigotry, and he knew it could be surmounted. Robinson proved him right, too.

While it's true that boyhood heroes tend to grow larger than life, Hank was large enough *in* life. The statistics I cited speak for themselves. Because of his shortened career, his totals (331 home runs, for example) aren't as impressive as those of some others. But make no mistake, among hitters Hank Greenberg ranks with the very best.

Imagine a boy of today growing old in 2019. When he looks back at the '70s, which sports hero will he remember? If there is one whose individual feats he can recall as clearly as I recall so many of Hank's, he will have something special to think about while waiting for the iceman.

Saturday
March 17th

THANK GOD I'M A COUNTRY BOY

Les Moss was born in Tulsa, Oklahoma, according to the baseball record book. The year was 1925, which means he is coming up on fifty-four. He is one of those people who seem old to me even though they are younger than I am. He wears steel-rimmed glasses and a short haircut, and looks as though he'd just dropped in for a cup of coffee after finishing the milking. I see him in bib overalls seated at an oilcloth-covered kitchen table saying, "Shucks, if we don't get rain right soon the weevils are agoin' to die of thirst," or something similar in a Southern rural-humor vein.

My total impression of the new Tiger manager is derived from a few newspaper articles, a few pictures and some brief remarks in a couple of TV interviews he did last fall right after he was appointed. I remember him as a major-league catcher who hung around for a good many years. Better say I don't remember him at all as a player. What I remember is his name and the fact that he was a catcher. He played in 824 major-league games (733 more than Ralph Houk, his predecessor), but I don't remember any of them.

I don't know if Les Moss ever lived on a farm in his life,

but he has the look and sound of pure country. I cannot honestly attest that he said "shucks" even once during his TV interviews, but he always seemed as if he were going to.

On television, Moss looked rather slight, which is surprising because the book gives his playing weight as 205 and his height as five-eleven. Those are stocky figures. If he still weighs 205 pounds, he has a number of them well hidden.

When questioned on camera about his reputation as a stern boss, Moss looked embarrassed and suggested that this was an exaggeration. "I never fined anyone more than twenty-five dollars," he said, "so I can't be too tough." Maybe not, but the fact that he fined players at all for misplays on the field (as distinct from forbidden extracurricular activities) is an indication of the way he feels about how baseball should be played.

He did confirm that he runs a hardworking training camp. When the season starts, he said, he intends to have his team in shape and ready to play in the big leagues. There may be some Tigers who need that, and some who resent it—and they may be the same people. You can't fire a baseball player; they cost too much. But contrary to some managerial opinion, you *can* make a highly paid star sit down and watch if he's not showing enough interest in the game. Moss seems like the kind of manager who will do that (unlike Houk, who seemed only to want to be loved). Maybe, when the chips are in the center of the table, he won't have the nerve. I hope he will. If not, we're in for another drab season.

Monday
March 19th

NO VISIBLE MEANS OF SUPPORT

Why is there a baseball team in Oakland, California? The obvious answer is that no one has yet made Charlie Finley

an offer he cannot refuse, free of restrictive conditions. Last
year at this time, the club was "sold" to a man who owned
a lot of oil, except that at the last minute Finley called it off.
Since everyone who lists oil among his assets seems to be
twice as rich now as he was a year ago, I think it's high
time he made another offer.

I recall the whole episode with a full measure of glee,
mainly because a Detroit sportscaster named Jim Forney
reported on the eleven-o'clock news that the Oakland A's
had been sold to Marvin Barnes, which, if true, would have
been the most improbable news event of recent years. Marvin
Barnes is a basketball player with a shaky grip on reality.
He once played with the Detroit Pistons, so Forney figured
the name was his to use in perpetuity, whenever he couldn't
remember the last name of anyone named Marvin. This was
a habit of his which provided endless amusement to the
shut-in. I waited in vain for the day when he would confuse
Angie and Emily Dickinson, or Pete and Tokyo Rose.

Actually, it seemed that the Oakland A's had been sold to
Marvin *Davis*, whose full title was Wealthy Oilman Marvin
Davis. He planned to move the team to Denver and have the
players wear real baseball uniforms. The deal was said to be
"90 percent sure," but where Finley is concerned, ninety is a
long way from a hundred, and he called it off, apparently
because there was a proviso in the contract that he drop all
litigation against major-league baseball, and he refused to
do that. Can't say I blamed him. He had (and I guess still
has) two huge lawsuits going against the commissioner, by
whom he has been ill used. Just about every time Charlie
wants to sell a player for cash (usually one whom he is about
to lose in the free-agent draft), the commissioner vetoes it
on the grounds that it is harmful to the structure of baseball
—or something. Just why it should be harmful to baseball
for Finley to sell a player for a million dollars and *not* be
harmful for the same player, a year later, to sell himself for

a similar sum is hard to understand. But that's the way
Bowie Kuhn apparently sees it.

Other owners seem to make big cash deals with impunity,
usually by including some second-line player to make it look
as if the cash is not the primary consideration. Unless the
chicanery is too shameless to ignore, there is normally no
objection from what is loosely called the top.

I suspect the commissioner takes out all his wrath on
Charlie Finley (who, Lord knows, deserves it) because he
knows he won't get any flak from the baseball establish-
ment, since all the other owners hate Finley too.

All this financial and legal maneuvering is extremely com-
plex, and I don't claim to understand it fully, so it could be
that I am maligning the commissioner unfairly, although
that would seem to be extremely difficult.

Anyway, the result of it all is that the American League is
stuck with a virtually worthless franchise in Oakland. Finley
is deliberately letting it go to wrack and ruin, in an effort to
force the other owners to let him sell the club on his terms.
Last year he hired two college kids to broadcast the games
and put them on a ten-watt station that could, I gather,
barely be heard beyond medium-deep center field. He does
not promote the games or attempt, in any way, to get people
to come see them. I presume the only people happy about it
all are the few devoted fans who do show up, because they
have unlimited choice of seats and a clear view of the field.
And it's still baseball.

What, if anything, has become of Wealthy Oilman Marvin
Davis? Is he still lurking in the wings waiting for a chance
to buy the club? If so, I think baseball had better make peace
with Finley, or do whatever it takes to let this deal go
through. If W. O. Marvin Davis has lost interest, another
buyer, possibly Marvin Barnes, will have to be found somewhere. But whoever finally buys the club, I hope he doesn't
change the name. The first big-league game I ever saw was

between the Tigers and the A's, the latter then working out of Philadelphia. Since then they have been the home team in Kansas City and Oakland, and they will be headed elsewhere sooner or later. No one ever calls them the Athletics anymore, but the truncated version of the old name still provides a small link with the past, and I hope they keep it.

Tuesday
March 20th

DANGER, HISTORIANS AT WORK

The Las Vegas telephone directory, which I chanced upon yesterday, contains a one-page history of the city. From its pious beginnings as a fort established by soldiers under orders from Brigham Young, to serve as a base for Mormon missionaries spreading their faith, the story traces the community's rapid recent growth to its current position as one of the most famous cities in the world. The anonymous author of this brief chronicle attributes the city's present renown to its "worldwide reputation as a holiday and vacation mecca." There is no mention of gambling.

(The foregoing has nothing to do with baseball. It is published here as a public service for those who have not yet learned how many ways there are to tell a lie.)

Friday
March 23rd

TO THE LAST MAN

There is a twenty-fifth man on every major-league roster. He is not so designated, but everybody knows who he is. On a very good team or a very poor one, there may be some argument as to his identity, but it's generally fairly obvious.

The twenty-fifth man is there because the player limit is

twenty-five. He is the man who wouldn't be there if the
limit were twenty-four. Or, rather, he is the one who would
go if the team had to get rid of one player outright—as distinguished from sending him to the minors for more season-
ing. He is usually a plumber, a man who can plug a hole in
an emergency, and often makes the team because he can
play several positions adequately.

Before last year the Tigers fielded several terrible teams
in a row, and for the last two or three of those seasons their
No. 25 man was Wayne Allison (Chuck) Scrivener. Scrivener,
who could play any position in the infield but couldn't hit a
lick, was almost a prototype of the genus. Mister Twenty-
five. He began playing professional ball in 1968, knocked
around the minors for seven or eight years, and the best he
ever hit at *any* level was .253 at Toledo in 1972. His major-
league average in a little over two seasons with Detroit was
under .200, and in his final season with the Tigers it sank to
a level too shocking to be quoted here.

He did the job, though. He got into quite a few games,
usually as a late-inning replacement for an infielder who had
been removed for a pinch hitter. But always, fulfilling the
criterion, he was the expendable man if it had been necessary
to expend anyone. He was, as I have indicated, of no per-
ceptible value offensively. Always a weak hitter, he became
almost a non-hitter. But that was okay. The Tigers weren't
going anywhere, and he was useful in the late innings.

Last spring, things were different. The Tigers were looking at themselves as a team that had a shot at the pennant.
Whether this was realistic or not, it was obvious from the
first day of spring training that there would be no place
on the club for Chuck Scrivener, and I'm sure he knew it.

Like all baseball fans, I admire and envy the big stars.
But I identify with the Scriveners, the guys who have devoted a large part of their life to this game, only to have
their highest aspirations end in frustration and failure. Except
that to me, it wouldn't have been failure. He played on a

big-league team. For two whole seasons, he wore that uniform, traveled first class, ate in the good restaurants, engaged in the colorful semi-articulate, generally obscene
banter of the best baseball players in the world. He was at
home in a big-league locker room and on a big-league field.
Marginal or not, he was a major-league ballplayer.

I speculate on what might have happened if I had spent
my entire childhood and youth learning to play baseball. It's
pure fantasy, but on the popular (if highly dubious) postu-
late that you can get anything if you want it badly enough,
I theorize that I, too, might have become a major leaguer.
The friends of my youth who recall my athletic short-
comings (featuring a breathtaking lack of speed) are doubtless giggling at this, but let's assume I would have made it
somehow. At best, I would have been a borderline player,
sitting on the bench almost all the time, filling in during the
late innings of lost games while the spectators are edging
toward the exits, unknown but to a few fanatics who collect
minutiae about *all* the players. A year or two of this, and
then back to the minors and out.

What I want to know, Chuck, is was it worth it? Considering that Scrivener is thirty-one years old and still trying, I
suspect I know the answer.

✿   ✿   ✿

My own baseball career can be summed up very briefly,
and I think it has one unique distinction. When I was in the
ninth grade at Manila Central High School in the Philippines,
several co-conspirators and I organized (and thus became)
the school's varsity baseball team. All the best athletes at
Central ignored us, preferring to devote their time to
basketball and track, sports at which the school excelled.
We invited them all, but we didn't urge them too hard
because, obviously, if they had come out they would have
taken our positions away from us.

We joined the local high-school league and played a full

schedule consisting of five games, none of which we were
ever in danger of winning. Our pitcher, whose name was Bill
Carpenter, I think (it's been forty-four years), was a handsome *mestizo* boy who could have thrown a baseball through
a brick wall if he could have hit a brick wall. He had batters
diving for safety even before he released the ball, which
often reflected excellent judgment on their part. And no
matter where he threw, he always threw as hard as he could.
Once he tried to pick a runner off first and hit him in the
back when he was still five feet from the base. I was the
first baseman. I picked up the ball while the runner was
writhing on the ground, and then attempted to help him to
his feet. In doing so I touched him with the ball, and the
umpire apologetically called him out. He protested bitterly,
but he was still out. It was the high point of our season. Or
low point, if you prefer. But I remember it with hilarious
satisfaction as the only thing we ever tried that worked.

(Oddly, although I have told this story many times, complete with funny dialogue, it never struck me as strange
before that the runner protested in English, although I
assume both he and the umpire would have been more at
home in Tagalog. One speaks the native language of the
game, I guess.)

The Central High baseball team did not survive that
season, but I did get one more chance to play on a school
team, three years later at Mason (Michigan) High School.
The star of the team was a boy named Joe DeRose, a good
hitter who, unfortunately for me, played first base, the only
position for which my physical equipment fitted me. But
Joe also pitched, and when he did I was allowed to play
first. I got into quite a few games that way, including three
that we won. I remember those three games with utmost
clarity, even including the names of the teams we beat (St.
Johns, East Lansing, Charlotte), and I remember every hit
I got. All my hits were singles through the infield, most of
them rather scratchy, but I remember them. I do not re-

member a thing about the games we lost, or the times I failed to hit, which were in the majority. Like an old soldier, an aging baseball player, meager though his talents, has a highly selective memory.

I estimate the distance between Manila, P.I., and Mason, Michigan, as roughly ten thousand miles. Therein lies my only claim to fame as a ballplayer. I doubt that anyone else ever played baseball for two such widely separated high schools. I am reasonably certain, however, that no documentary evidence remains of my exploits in either location, so you'll have to take them on faith. And the *Guinness Book of World Records* will have to carry on without me.

*   *   *

I come from a baseball family. Anyone who has known me for any length of time knows that. Let me briefly trace the history of baseball in my family. My father was a ballplayer. That's it—the beginning and end of our hall of fame. A baseball dynasty built on the performance of one man, whose own achievements have probably been somewhat magnified over the years. The ensuing generations, although fully committed to baseball as a way of life, have done more talking than playing. My brothers weren't any better at the game than I was, and I have two sons who gave it their best shot and were forever being elected "team sparkplug" or "most popular player"—the baseball equivalent of Miss Congeniality. I knew just how they felt, and I bled for them, especially since I was sure I was to blame. They obviously inherited their batting ability from me. Like me, they paid their dues and became pretty good fielders. Just as I had taken countless ground balls on the face, arms and shoulders in the uneven backyards of all the houses we lived in when I was a kid, so did they. Like my father, I was a stern teacher: "We can't stop for tears now. Get back out there and keep your eye on the ball." And crack! Another hot smash right at the feet of the novice shortstop. Like me, they worked hard at it, had a lot of fun and weren't quite good enough.

I have a third son (actually the middle one) who never had much interest in baseball, but we all like him anyway. He took up a *useful* avocation and became a marvelous carpenter (he can fix *any*thing), the first Hill in several generations who could pound a nail straight. The rest of us marvel at his skill, and wonder where it came from.

Despite his lack of interest in the game, Tony used to go through the motions when he was small. Growing up in our family, he probably thought it was something you had to do, like washing your hands before dinner. Not long ago, he said to me, "You ought to put something in the book about Grandfather Hill, and how he used to cut the pocket out of his glove." This is a family joke. My father, like a father, took a dim view of the comforts enjoyed by succeeding generations that had been denied him. He would hold a first baseman's mitt owned by one of my sons in his hand disdainfully, as if torn between amusement and disgust. "Where did you get this bushel basket?" he would scoff. Their (and my) fielder's gloves inspired a similar reaction. "You can't even get hold of the ball with one of these things," he would say. "Why, when I was playing, we used to cut the center out of our gloves, right in the pocket, so you could really get the *feel* of the ball. That was baseball." It was indeed, and even with today's bushel baskets, it still is—the game that brings generations together. Because one of the most remarkable things about baseball is that it has changed so little over the years. The players of fifty or sixty years ago look funny to us now, with their baggy pants and heavy shirts, but the game they played was remarkably similar to the one that's played today. Football and basketball have evolved over the years into something quite different from what they were. Baseball is still essentially the same game.

My father never actually produced one of those gloves

with the pocket cut out. He did show us once a fielder's glove that appeared to have been cut out of two pieces of thin leather, which were then sewn together. This two-dimensional curiosity, he claimed, had been his brother's. I don't question that, but I wonder at what age his brother used it, and whether he ever caught anything with it that couldn't as easily have been caught with the bare hand.

We made fun of my father's antiquated notions, as children and grandchildren have always done, but we secretly respected him because, of us all, he was the only one who had the credentials. He played three years at the University of Michigan, and was captain in his senior year, 1911. He was always a first baseman, except for one year when he was beaten out of that job by a player named George Sisler, one of the greatest hitters of all time. (Sisler's lifetime batting average in the majors was .340, his highest single-season average .420.) During Sisler's year at Michigan my father became a catcher, and he continued to catch occasionally in amateur baseball after college. He had the gnarled fingers to prove it.

My father's coach at Michigan was Branch Rickey, and they remained friends until Rickey's death. When Rickey left Ann Arbor to become manager of the St. Louis Browns, he invited my father to come along with him, but he declined. Baseball, he told me, was not considered a respectable job for an educated man in those days. As a small boy, I used to decry the insensitivity of this man who had so casually denied me the chance to be the son of a big-league ballplayer.

In discussing his college career, my father, like all ballplayers, used to talk about the home runs he hit, and I guess there were a few of those. But recently, while examining some ancient box scores, I discovered to my surprise that he had been a leadoff hitter in his last year at Michigan. This implies a certain amount of speed afoot, which, if he really had it, is just one more attribute he failed to pass on to me.

Monday
March 26th

PLAIN LANGUAGE FROM TRUTHFUL NICKIE

Not one to mince words, Nickie McWhirter thinks Jim Campbell is a jerk. Rusty Staub, she says, may be a jerk too, but she considers that irrelevant.

Nickie McWhirter is a *Detroit Free Press* columnist. She writes about anything that appeals to her, is very good at it and almost always says exactly what she thinks. I include the qualifying adverb only because I know that nobody *always* says exactly what he thinks, but she tries as hard as anyone.

In today's column, Ms. McWhirter more or less echoes what I said back on March 13th, that Campbell didn't try hard enough to settle the matter before it got out of hand. But I guess it's not a true echo because, of course, she hadn't read what I wrote and, more to the point, an echo is seldom louder than the original noise. I said it rather as an after-thought; she puts it bluntly and plainly.

What she says, in brief, is that Campbell has loused up the ball club just to show Rusty who's boss, that a general manager's job in any field is to keep the business running smoothly and the employees working at top efficiency. This, she says, is precisely what Campbell has not done; the players are all worried about how Rusty's absence (or presence) is going to affect their status; the new manager, Les Moss, cannot plan strategy because he doesn't know whether one of his key employees will be present or absent. "All Campbell has shown," she says, "is his own ability to handicap an entire organization by being stubborn and unskilled."

Another precinct heard from. I don't know that I agree with her entirely, but I listen when she speaks.

COLOR HIM BLACK

Luke Easter, who was shot to death yesterday, was a symbol of our times. A powerful black man who could hit a baseball great distances, he didn't get to the major leagues until an age when most players are over the hill. When he joined the Cleveland Indians in 1949, he gave his age as twenty-eight, but he was a lot older than that. The story of his death in today's paper says he was born August 4th, 1915. The baseball record book agrees on the date, but gives the year as 1914. Assuming the book is correct, he was almost thirty-five when he joined the Cleveland Indians as a rookie in 1949. He spent six years with the Cleveland club, his best being 1952, when he hit thirty-one home runs and drove in ninety-seven runs. During that season, he turned thirty-eight.

He was, as I said at the beginning, black. That fact is what kept him out of the major leagues until long past his prime. Considering that he hit some of the longest home runs ever seen in the Cleveland park at an age when he should rightfully have been retired, it's not hard to imagine what kind of record he would have compiled if he'd come to the big leagues at twenty-two or so.

He died when two hoods shot him for the money he was carrying from the bank as part of his job. So he got a raw deal in life—and in death. About the first he never complained. About the second, he never had a chance to complain. Taken together, these two facts made him, as I also said at the beginning, a symbol of our times. Which, besides being a cliché, is damned small consolation once you're dead.

Wednesday
April 4th

ONE FOR THE MONEY

'Tis the season to pick winners. The money games start tomorrow, so all and sundry are making their choices in the newspapers. Why they do this has always been something of a mystery to me. Obviously, it is the sort of thing readers like, or newspapers wouldn't devote so much space to it. But why? Every fan, of even modest intelligence, must know they are only guessing—and that the fan's guess is as good as the baseball writer's. Still, they do it, and we read it.

As for me, I like the Tigers. And do not dismiss that too lightly. I picked them in '68, when they won it all, and in '72 when they won the division and were barely beaten in the play-offs by Oakland, the eventual Series winner. This fact would doubtless be more impressive if I withheld the news that I also picked them in '75, the second of Ralph Houk's five rebuilding years. That year they lost 102 games and were fortunate enough to have 3 rained out.

I believe there was one year I didn't pick the Tigers to win the flag. That was 1952, when the club lost 104 games (in a shorter schedule) and featured three pretty good pitchers, Ted Gray, Art Houtteman and Virgil Trucks, who lost a total of 56 games. Trucks, who won 5 games and lost 19, pitched two no-hit games that year, but was lucky to win them since the Tigers got him the minimum number of runs with which it is possible to win two games—i.e., two.

That was a bad team. I showed good judgment in not pegging it for the elusive gonfalon. (It's been years since I've heard anyone refer to the pennant as the gonfalon. A sad loss to the sporting lexicon.) I may, however, have suggested that those '52 Tigers were "capable of making a run for it if they get a few breaks."

This blind, chauvinistic belief in one's own team, often against all reason, is foolish and marvelous. It is the muscle and magic of the game's attraction, and you cannot crush it. Every time a sixth-place team wins four or five games in a row, hope is rekindled and the pennant, so recently despaired of, seems attainable after all "if they get a few breaks."

What's more, the knowledgeable fan can justify his faith, especially at the start of the season. I could, if it wouldn't bore you catatonic, run down the Tiger lineup, position by position, and prove that the team can hardly miss being a winner this year. (And if The Bird comes back, well, I hardly need tell you . . .) As a matter of fact, I just did that very thing—on a separate sheet, which you will *not* find enclosed—and I'm getting more excited than ever about the team's prospects.

The secret of such partisan analyses is that you never look on the dark side. You point out that Lance Parrish has been compared to the young Johnny Bench, that he has a great arm and hits with power. You ignore the fact that he has a lot to learn about catching, and hit .219 last year.

Unconsciously, I do this every spring with the Tigers. I don't have any doubt that somebody did it with the '38 Phillies and when the season ended (Phils last, 24½ games behind the Dodgers, who finished seventh) was looking for little signs of better things to come in '39.

It is, surely, significant that baseball begins in the spring. The bosses have damaged the symbolism somewhat by moving the opener back to early April, the cruelest part of the cruelest month, thus reducing to near nil the chances of starting the season on the first warm day of the year. But the first game, mixing memory and desire, is still a herald of sunny, maybe even better days ahead.

No one has ever accused me of looking at the world through rose-tinted glasses. At least, not lately. I was a slow learner, but I finally figured out that nobody lives happily ever after and *la vie en rose* is only a song. I suppose the

simpleminded optimism with which I, as well as millions
of others, greet every new baseball season is a response to
the realization, conscious or not, that life is not quite the
glorious adventure we had rather counted on. If a man must
yet believe in something, what better than a baseball team
that is annually reborn; a team that, no matter how low it
may sink in the darkening days of late September, starts
out again tied for first the following spring?

So I do not apologize for my exaggerated zeal for these
Tigers, these young men I have never met who play a game
I never mastered. They are, in my eyes, *l'équipe en rose.*

Start the season.

Friday
April 6th

RUSTY'S RICH SOUFFLÉ IS SAGGING

The deal that Rusty Staub had cooking seems to have
fallen flat. Although Rusty insists he is still in line to make a
pile of money in the restaurant business, he now pleads with
the Tigers to trade him, rather than "let him rot," because
he really wants to play baseball.

This is a radical switch from his earlier position when
Staub said he was ready and eager to plunge into his culinary
pursuits full time. He strongly implied that baseball was no
longer necessary to him, although he was willing to go on
with it if the money was good enough. (Incidentally, it seems
I was wrong about his salary demands. It develops that he
wanted his contract extended for three years at a substantial
increase in pay, rather than at the same salary.) Now, coming
full circle, he says he has postponed his restaurant plans on
the slim chance that the Tigers will trade him. (Actually, he
said he has "retarded" his plans, and Jim Hawkins of the
Free Press was unkind enough to quote him verbatim.)

Rusty Staub. His two favorite fields of endeavor.

It has become a sad story. It's depressing to think of this good hitter withering into putrefaction at thirty-five, an age that I think of as the very apogee of youth. Rusty Staub is a proud man. Opinionated and stubborn, but also proud—and with a distinguished career behind him to justify his pride. But he guessed wrong this time. He overvalued his hand and bet more than he could afford. It's embarrassing to see him now, backtracking and temporizing, all the while insisting he hasn't retreated an inch from his original stand.

It's becoming more and more apparent that he will eventually capitulate. He'll make surrender sound like vindication, but it won't be. Campbell will gloat a little—he's proved his point—but he won't have much reason to. What he will have won is a Pyrrhic victory. You will recall the words of Pyrrhus, who said (loosely translated from the Greek): "Another victory like this one and we've had it!"

Who's to blame? From the standpoint of the Tigers and their fans, it's immaterial. Rusty won't be the player he was before, and the team has been irreparably damaged. Kiss the pennant goodbye? Well, it was only a dream, anyway, but most things are dreams until they come true. This one's chances of coming true have been substantially reduced.

Saturday
April 7th

LOSING THE OPENER

Today was opening day. The game had been postponed twice by hideous weather, and it was finally played today in almost equally hideous weather. The Tigers rose to the occasion by playing hideous baseball, and lost to Texas, 6 to 2. Not being a devotee of ice fishing or any of the other arctic sports popular in these parts, I stayed indoors and watched the game on television. It might have been more palatable on radio.

Last year, however, it was different. The scheduled opening game was canceled, naturally—that's routine in Detroit and points north; but the following day everything fell into place. The weather, the Toronto Blue Jays and the gods who are in charge of The Bird's arm all cooperated. So let me describe for you a typical Detroit opening day, when everything goes well—or as well as can be expected on opening day. A year ago today, I wrote:

NOT LOSING THE OPENER

Opening day II. Perfect weather, A well-pitched game by Fidrych, home runs by May, Mankowski and Jason Thompson. Tigers win the opener, thus negating the perennial Detroit joke, which has held up for several years and goes like this: "They can't serve beer at Tiger Stadium this season." "Why not?" "They lost the opener."

I am in a position to report that they can and do serve beer at Tiger Stadium—and that in fact, most of the people sitting around me seemed to be there for no other reason.

Opening day is usually carried out without me. The only thing I like about it is the baseball game. There are several things I don't like about it: the vast numbers of people who don't care much about the game, the difficulty of getting tickets and finding a place to park, the governor, the mayor. Not that I have anything against the governor and the mayor as politicians. Although they are of sharply divergent political persuasions, they both strike me as being rather good at their jobs. I feel about them the way Whitey Herzog, the Kansas City manager, felt about John Mayberry when he shipped him off to Toronto the other day. I like each of them "as a person" but I don't care for them on a baseball field. It always annoys me to see a public servant stand on the mound and lob a ball awkwardly in the general direction of the plate, where another public servant completes the ceremony by dropping it. I keep wondering: this man must have played ball when he was a kid, so why can't he throw properly? But he never can. Apparently holding elective office causes the throwing muscles to atrophy. (I am secretly thinking, naturally, that if *I* were out there they'd see a first pitch correctly thrown. But maybe not. Maybe it's the sight of fifty thousand people in the stands, rather than the rigors of politics, that makes a governor release a baseball like a man throwing darts in a London pub.)

But I am nitpicking. The real curse of opening day is the crowd. If you get a capacity crowd at a game later in the season, it is presumably made up of people who are excited about baseball. Opening day attracts hordes of "fans" who are there principally because it's a semi-official holiday in Detroit, and Tiger Stadium is the place to be. The game is incidental; the revelry is paramount.

With me it's just the opposite. I find the opening of the baseball season so exciting, so fraught with promise of wonders to come, that I don't *have* to be there. I can catch the game on radio, if it's not televised, and enjoy every minute of it (if the Tigers are winning or at least close). And then next week I can go to a game without being elbowed to death by tourists. To me, the sixth game or the tenth is just as exciting as the first.

At the last moment, though, my youngest son, Chato, called and said he had an extra ticket, so off I went. It was a fine game, but I had difficulty seeing some of it because of the endless stream of people going in and out, mostly to buy beer. Alleged baseball fans would leave their seats with men on base and one out, and be gone for two or three innings because the beer counters were so crowded. One man, who sat (when he sat) in the row in front of ours, seemed to prefer our row for his exits and entrances. About the fourth time he crawled over me, I said, "For X sake, why don't you go out through your own row?"

He seemed dismayed that I had addressed him so rudely. Self-righteously he replied, "I bought seats in *both* these rows." This was probably true, since he obviously knew the people sitting behind him. But it struck me as shoddy reasoning. *His* seat was in the other row. If he had bought seats for his friends (or his customers) in twenty different rows, would that give him crawling privileges in all of them?

After the game, pursuant to two-year-old tradition, we stood around until Mark Fidrych came out to take his bow. Since we were standing in the left-field upper deck, they could have sent out Ella Fitzgerald in a Tiger jacket and we wouldn't have known the difference. But The Bird is a consummate showman, and if it makes him happy it's okay with me. The truth is, though, that the ceremony has lost its spontaneity, and with it much of its charm. When Mark first captured the imagination of this town (and most of the civilized world), the post-game chorus of "We want The Bird!" was unrehearsed and delightful. Now it has become a ritual act of devotion, like the Stations of the Cross, and it all seems rather staged.

Still, you can't knock The Bird. He puts on a show, but he is also an amazing pitcher. I have never seen one quite like him in the way he seems to get stronger and throw harder in the late innings, especially when he is protecting a slim lead. When he does that, the excitement in the stands is real enough. I hope he pitches for our side forever. Or until I die. Whichever comes first.

❖   ❖   ❖

Only a year ago, but it seems like a story out of the dim past. It's hard to believe that just one year ago Mark Fidrych was throwing that low fastball over the corner, apparently as well as ever. It's hard to believe it was only *three* years ago that he came out of nowhere to become the most exciting new ballplayer the game had seen in many a season. It seems as if he has always been here, and that for most of that time we have been waiting for his arm to heal.

Mark did not pitch the opening game this year. And it's an open question when he will pitch again. Perhaps in a month or two. Perhaps next year. Perhaps never.

I'll keep you posted.

Thursday
April 12th

WHITHER THOU GOEST, I WILL GO

When I was a kid, we used to play an impromptu game with a stick and a tennis ball on a rock-hard grassless field. When a fly ball hit the ground, it would bounce fifteen or twenty feet in the air, and the fielder would have to wait until it came down before he could throw it back to the infield. It was fun, but we never thought it was baseball—which is interesting because it strongly resembled the game the Tigers and Blue Jays are playing in Toronto these days.

Okay, I admit that my distaste for baseball played on what appears to be a giant game board is intensified by the fact that it helped the Tigers kick away a game against Toronto, although it must be admitted that the way they were playing, they didn't need much help.

There is no excuse for the artificial baseball field, but like executive cupidity (its *raison d'être*), it is obviously here to stay, and I will adjust. I don't think there is anything the lords of baseball can do to make me dislike the game, although they keep trying. I just wish they'd remember that the corollary to "thy people shall be my people" is "where thou diest, I will die."

Several errors in the current series have been directly

attributable to the pool-table surface in Exhibition Park, but it was in today's game, which the Tigers won, that absurdity peaked. In the sixth inning, Roy Howell of Toronto looped a short fly into left field for a double. Steve Kemp had no chance to catch it, but he made a valiant try and arrived in the vicinity of the ball just as it hit the ground (or whatever)—and then had to stand around waiting for it to come down from a giant bounce. It is doubtful that Kemp could have thrown Howell out at second, even on a real baseball field. But it sure looked silly. It looked like a game played with a stick and a tennis ball. I tell you, it took me back.

None of this is to be interpreted as a knock on Toronto, a city for which I have the highest esteem. (Toronto, after all, did not invent the cement playing field.) You may, however, consider it a hymn of thanksgiving to Bill Veeck. When he took over the Chicago White Sox a couple of years ago, he ripped up the existing carpet and replaced it with creeping red fescue. That must have cost him a buck or two, and Veeck dearly loves a buck. But he differs from some other big-league owners in that he also loves baseball. Luck to him!

❋   ❋   ❋

The Toronto TV games, which are occasionally visible in Detroit on Channel 9, Windsor, Ontario, are sponsored by Labatt's beer, which is not surprising since the brewery owns the ball club. One of its brands is Labatt's Blue, and the team was reportedly named the Blue Jays in the hope that the headline writers would shorten it to Blues. Naturally, everyone calls them the Jays. A bit more foresight might have produced Bluestockings or—a really good name for a Canadian team—the Blue Northers.

I am partial to the Labatt's commercials because they are usually delivered in correct English, a clever device which U.S. advertisers would do well to imitate if they can find some copywriters who have learned English. Like every other brewery, Labatt's has recognized the recent mania for watery beer by creating a "light" one. In their advertising, they describe it as having "one third fewer calories," whereas all American light beers are said to have "one third *less* calories," a locution that makes my skin crawl— although it's not as bad as the weathercasters' perennial "the most amount of rain." The idea that "less" can be properly used with a plural noun in such a construction has become one of the dominant principles of American advertising, not to mention American journalism and American speech. The French are always bitching about English expressions' creeping into their language. I knew they were going somewhere.

Speaking of TV advertising, I look forward to seeing, in some better time, a yogurt commercial that begins: "In Soviet Georgia, there are two remarkable things about the people. They eat a lot of yogurt, and they lie about their age." I suppose I should be more tolerant of those old guys who claim to be a hundred thirty-two. What else is there to do in Soviet Georgia?

I am also intensely irritated by that Alpo commercial in which Lorne Greene fondles a dog and says, "This husky fellow is fifteen years old. That's a hundred and five for you and me." Analogies of human and animal ages seem to fascinate people, which would be okay if they weren't so obviously false. Every other dog lover you meet tells you he has, or had, a fifteen-year-old dog. But how many hundred-and-five-year-old people do you run into? We had two cats who lived to be eighteen. That must be at least a hundred on the mythical cat–man scale. But you almost never run across anyone who has raised two *people* to the age of a hundred.

And another thing. How come, when you do see a picture in the paper of some old codger celebrating (in a loose sense) his hundred-and-fifth birthday, it is never pointed out that this is equal to fifteen years for a dog?

Digression is good for the soul.

Wednesday
April 18th

REPORT FROM THE STICKS

On a quick trip through the hinterlands of Illinois, I chanced to buy a copy of the *Rockford Register Star*, a journal of the Gannett chain, once classified by its own ace Washington correspondent as a "bunch of shitkicker papers." The man who used this colorful term is known in the trade as one of the best reporters around, so I cannot but accept his word. Possibly not coincidentally, he now works elsewhere. (When you are that good a reporter, you have to be careful not to report too close to home.) But I assume his assessment still stands. The word he used is a big-city dysphemism for "farmer," and I suppose he simply meant that the papers of this chain (including the one in Guam) are narrow, self-centered and parochial. A fairly accurate description of most small-town papers, as well as a good many metropolitan ones. If he had used some other, less aromatic phrase, it might well have slipped by almost unnoticed.

In any case, I was curious to see how a paper so characterized would handle its baseball news. It came as no surprise to me that its coverage did not differ, in any noticeable degree, from that in the Detroit papers or those of any other large city. Rockford, close to Chicago, looks to the Cubs and White Sox for its rooting interest. The lead story in today's *Register Star* recounts Kenny Holtzman's 5–3 victory over the Cardinals. Holtzman, who spent two years in limbo with the Yankees, is now back with the Cubs, where he pitched two no-hit games before going on to Oakland and World Series glory. (Remember when Oakland was the best team in baseball? Good Lord, it was only five years ago!) Gary Stein, who wrote the game story, also has a pretty good feature on Scot Thompson, the Cubs' hot-hitting rookie, implying that he will replace Bobby Murcer in the outfield before the season is over.

Over on page three, there's an interesting column by Chuck Keefer on Bill Veeck and how attention to detail pays off when you're running a ball club on short money. Veeck and the White Sox vice-president, Chuck Hemond, it seems, spent hours poring over hundreds of pages of league documents before uncovering a pitcher, one Mike Proly, who was eligible for the re-entry draft but hadn't been so designated by the commissioner's office. Actually, Veeck had the idea and Hemond did the poring, as is traditional in such relationships. (I am reminded of a Marine Corps colonel I once knew whose grammar was uncertain but whose sense of position was impeccable. He said of his executive officer: "Ah calls him Charlie 'cause he's a lieutenant colonel; he calls me Colonel 'cause ah'm a full colonel.") Between them, though, they dug up a pretty good young pitcher and relieved the Minnesota Twins of his services. "If it wasn't for Veeck and Hemond, I'd probably still be in Tacoma," Proly says. He may end up back there anyway, or someplace equally obscure. But for the moment, he's happy to be in the majors, Veeck and Hemond are happy to have picked up a promising young pitcher for peanuts and Chuck Keefer is presumably happy at having written a good story with an unusual angle.

In summation, however, I must report that I *did* find the Rockford paper's coverage narrow and parochial. In the whole damn paper, there's only one paragraph about the Tigers' victory over Kansas City. How country can you get?

What I would like to convey here is the odd sense of wonder I always experience when I read baseball coverage in a paper oriented to some other team than mine. Having a fairly good set of values, I am invariably surprised by the intense interest in, and loyalty to, their teams which such papers' sports columns reflect. It is, I feel, a bit childish to get so worked up over what is after all only a game. If it were the Tigers, I could understand it, but the Cubs and the White Sox!

In more reasonable moments, of course, I understand it perfectly, although I still can't explain it. Consider that Bill Buckner is a hero to Cub fans, as Jason Thompson is to Tiger fans. But if they were traded for each other tomorrow, after a certain period of grousing on both sides, and assuming they both continued to play well, they would probably become *local* heroes all over again. It's always the *team*, almost an abstract concept, that commands the fans' loyalty. This is mysterious, and it is also why baseball won't die in our time unless they think up some way to ruin it far more effectively than those which have been tried thus far.

*   *   *

While writing the preceding segment, I encountered (and deftly sidestepped) the interesting question: What is the singular of Sox? In the days when ballplayers were often fairly happy where they were, there were frequent stories about this fact, usually with headlines like "It's great to be a Yankee!" Could Mike Proly, then, write an article entitled "It's great to be a White Sock"?

*   *   *

Note to Tiger Management: The hypothetical trade I mentioned was not meant as a suggestion. Buckner is a fine ballplayer, but he's no Thompson (and he's five years older). Just so there won't be any misunderstanding.

Thursday
April 19th

A IS FOR APPLE, B IS FOR BUNT

Ron LeFlore doesn't bunt. I intend to discuss this singular fact at length before this journal runs its course. But for the moment, I state it merely as simple truth.

In a recent game on the road, the Tigers had gone into the ninth inning leading by one run. Alan Trammell was on first with no one out. Baseball strategy, in such a case, demands that you move that "insurance" run to second base, from where the runner can score on a clean single. But LeFlore, the next batter, swung away and hit a line drive to the third baseman, who doubled Trammell off first.

We have here a man with outstanding batting skill and tremendous speed who apparently doesn't know how to bunt, and it leads to some ludicrous situations. This was one of them. The Tigers, as it happened, won the game, but LeFlore's failure to bunt in a situation where it was virtually forbidden to do anything else was bad baseball.

Incidentally, when Trammell was doubled off first, he violated one of Paul Richards' baseball maxims. Richards, who managed in the major leagues for many years, was a student and a *teacher* of the game, an almost unknown phenomenon in baseball today. He believed that it was a manager's job to instill in his players certain truths which he holds to be self-evident, and to make them live by them. In Donald Honig's book *The Man in the Dugout*, Richards expounds: "Sometimes, you see a man doubled off on a line drive, and later on somebody will say, 'He couldn't help it.' Well, that's wrong. He could help it." Richards maintains it should *never* happen with the bases full and nobody out—and on teams he managed it almost never did. You shouldn't really have to teach a major-league player fundamentals, says

Richards, but it doesn't hurt to remind him—fifty times, if twenty isn't enough.

I do not quite agree with Richards' contention that a runner is always at fault when doubled off. I have seen situations where I thought the runner couldn't help it (a line drive to the first baseman, right on the bag, for instance). But there's a more important point to this story: Richards understood that a ballplayer should continue to learn throughout his career. It is ironic that while this is far more true today than it was even a dozen years ago, the teaching manager has almost ceased to exist.

In the old days (how abruptly that phrase gives a man's age away), when a ballplayer reached the major leagues, it was taken for granted that he had mastered the basics of the game. Today a lot of raw young players are carried on major-league rosters who didn't spend enough time in the minors to learn their trade. In most instances, their talent is unquestioned. Otherwise, they wouldn't have been signed to lucrative contracts while still in college (or high school). But they don't really know how to play baseball.

This being true, it should be apparent that a different kind of manager is needed in the majors, one who will insist that his players be taught the ABC's of baseball. If he doesn't want to do it himself, or doesn't have time, he should make his coaches do it. Teaching ability should be the prime criterion in selecting coaches, instead of whatever the prime criterion is now, which is something of a mystery.

Last year, when Ralph Houk was still managing the Tigers he said of LeFlore, 'I think it's remarkable the way Ronnie steals bases when he hasn't even learned to take a lead yet." What I thought remarkable was that LeFlore had been playing under Houk's leadership (if that's the word) for four years and no one had taught him to take a lead. Stranger still was the fact that Houk apparently felt no embarrassment in admitting it.

I don't know how good a teacher Les Moss is, but I have the impression that he's willing to try. That's a start.

Friday
April 20th

HASTEN, JASON

Jason Thompson is a strong young man who plays first base for the Tigers rather well and hits with great power. Last year he hit 26 home runs, which led the team in that department but was still disappointing. He had 17 home runs by the end of June, and figured to hit at least 35 over the season. But he hit only 9 the rest of the way, which was a letdown. He was reportedly "playing hurt," though, so we look for him to break loose this year. He certainly has the tools, he has improved his batting average substantially in every year since he joined the club and he won't be twenty-five for another couple of months.

What makes everyone so sure Thompson *will* break loose is not so much the number of his home runs, but the tremendous distance of some of them. He hit one in last year's opening game that bounced off the roof of the right-field stands. He has, in fact, done this several times, and very few other players have done it even once.

As a consequence of his blast in last year's opener, his teammates began calling him "Rooftop," but the nickname was not spontaneous. It was coined in response to a publicity-gimmick campaign by one of the Detroit papers to select an "official" nickname for Jason. It is perhaps significant that the players themselves came up with the best one, but even so it is rarely used. The great nicknames are not made up by committees. The ones that actually replace the names the players were born with are usually the product of a jest, a flash of insight, an impulsive remark.

Jason Thompson hits the roof.

Three that come quickly to mind are Schoolboy Rowe, Goose Goslin and Babe Ruth. Lynwood, Leon and George. Ask any old baseball fan what Babe Ruth's nickname was, and chances are he'll say "the Sultan of Swat" or "the Bambino." "Babe" had long ago ceased to be a nickname and become his *name*.

Schoolboy Rowe, the great Tiger pitcher of the '30s, is an interesting case. The name, whatever its origin, was definitive; that is, it had effectively replaced his Christian name. But "Schoolboy" is an awkward word for everyday purposes, so his teammates seldom used it. But they didn't call him Lyn (some of them probably didn't even know his baptismal handle); they called him Schoolie.

A famous instance of a nickname *for* a nickname involves the pitcher who won more games than any other in history. He was born March 29, 1867, and christened Denton True Young. According to legend, someone who saw him pitch as a young man promptly dubbed him "Cyclone." The name stuck but was almost immediately shortened to Cy. During a career that lasted twenty-two years, Cy Young not only won 511 games and lost 313 (also a record), he also lost forever the name his parents had given him. Denton True Young died in 1955, but the name of Cy Young will live as long as baseball is played.

Who are the modern-day—let's say the post-war—counterparts of Schoolboy, Goose and the Babe, players whose nicknames have replaced their real names in the public consciousness? Offhand, I can think of a few. Can you come up with the last names that go with these beginnings: James Augustus, Johnny Lee, Leroy Robert, Lawrence Peter? Actually, you don't even need the surnames when you know that their baseball names are Catfish, Blue Moon, Satchel and Yogi.

❁   ❁   ❁

Maybe today's ballplayers take themselves too seriously. With so much money involved, maybe they have to. But for whatever reason, there are no pitchers around these days with nicknames derived from their inability to win games. In other days, there were a lot of them, and they bore the names with good humor, sometimes even considering them a kind of backhanded compliment. Walter (Boom-Boom) Beck of the Phillies used to march in from the bullpen with his head erect as the crowd chanted, "Boom *boom*, boom *boom*, boom *boom*," in a sort of ragged unison. (The crowd noises at Phillies games in those days were no better coordinated than the players.)

Another favorite of mine was Lynn (Line Drive) Nelson, who pitched for the Athletics and, briefly, the Tigers. He was a good hitter, and he always affected to believe his nickname derived from that fact. It didn't.

One of the most derogatory nicknames ever pinned on a ballplayer was that attached to Hugh Mulcahy, who pitched for the terrible Phillies of the late Depression years. And it was, in fact, a badge of honor. Hughie Mulcahy was not a great pitcher, but he was a pretty good one. In three seasons (1938–40) he started 101 games for the Phils, completed 49 and actually managed to win 32. Not bad pitching for a team that finished last by an average of 20 games over that period. (Twenty games behind the *next-to-last* team, that is.) The best pitcher on a horrible team always piles up an impressive number of losses, and Mulcahy was no exception. His name appeared in box scores as the losing pitcher so often that he became known far and wide as Hugh (Losing Pitcher) Mulcahy.

In 1941, Hugh Mulcahy went into the Army. I assume he volunteered, probably hoping to find a service team that could score some runs for him. (The 1940 Phils averaged 3.2 runs per game.) He returned to baseball after the war, but he'd grown old during his absence, and he didn't pitch

Hugh (Losing Pitcher) Mulcahy.

much. In 1947, his last year in the game, he finally escaped from Philadelphia; he was traded to Pittsburgh. The Pirates finished last—tied with the Phillies.

Saturday
April 21st

THE EARLY DAYS

"We'd like to take you back to the early days of baseball" came the announcement on a Madison, Wisconsin, TV station. They were promoting a show coming up later that week. I pictured grainy, flickering films of Sam Crawford and Three Finger Brown, crowd shots of audiences unanimously male and derby-hatted. But the announcer went on. "The time," he said, "was twenty-five years ago. The place: Milwaukee, Wisconsin. The team: the world-famous Milwaukee Braves." The *early* days of baseball! When the Braves moved to Milwaukee, I was approaching Rusty Staub's present age. My oldest son remembers it. They had television!

It's been a few days since I heard that announcement. I've thought about it a little, and decided that one man's early days are another man's yesterday, and what does it matter? The game's the thing. I think of the early days of baseball as the turn of the century, long before I was born. I think of the '30s, so remote to most people, as the days beyond compare. Is anyone today in the same class with Lefty Grove, Jimmy Foxx, Lou Gehrig, Joe DiMaggio, Hank Greenberg, Charlie Gehringer? Probably, but not in my eyes, which are the eyes of a boy.

My bias is plainly American League, but the National League had its nonpareils, too. Mel Ott, Joe Medwick, Carl Hubbell and Bill Terry come immediately to mind. And Hack Wilson, although he was a product more of the '20s

than of the '30s. When the Depression replaced the Jazz
Age, Hack seemed to fade away, as was perhaps appropriate
considering his roistering nature.

Hack Wilson has finally been admitted to the Hall of
Fame, almost fifty years after his magnificent season. Baseball has a strong moralistic streak, seldom apparent among
its practitioners, which seems to surface when old-timers
consider the past. Perhaps that's what kept Hack Wilson
waiting outside the shrine for so long. But he's made it now,
as well he should. The Hall of Fame is properly restricted
to players who have proved their greatness over a full career
(as Wilson did), but if ever a man deserved a bid on the
basis of a single season it was Hack. In 1930, playing for the
Cubs, Hack Wilson hit .356, hit 56 home runs (still the
league record), and batted in 190 runs! Many players have
hit for a higher average, a few have hit more home runs;
none has ever had more RBI's. And no one has ever come
close to putting them all together in one incredible season
as he did.

Hack Wilson died in 1948 after a short life and, for a
while, a merry one. He did not require a very long casket.
He was only 5 feet 6 inches tall, perhaps the most surprising statistic of all.

Monday
April 23rd

DREAMS OF GLORY

Dave Rozema is back, and the Tigers are ready to make
their move. It seems to me I've heard that song before.
Rozema, who had an outstanding rookie year in 1977, was
ineffective most of last season and hasn't looked much better
this spring. His career has, in fact, borne a disturbing re-
semblance to that of Mark Fidrych. The ups and downs

haven't been quite so dramatic, but they have been almost as regular. Great start, followed by intermittent sore-arm problems and periodic sojourns on the injured list. If the Tigers are ever to be contenders with their present personnel, Rozema must regain his rookie form and maintain it through a full season. And if The Bird came back at the same time, of course, we'd be off and running. But how many times can we dream that dream?

Anyway, taking it a little at a time, Rozema pitched an excellent game yesterday, holding the Blue Jays to three hits, working on a no-hitter for the first six or seven innings. Lance Parrish hit a tremendous home run, and the Tigers climbed over .500 for the first time this year. All good signs for the future.

Last year, after a flying start, the Tigers fell out of the pennant picture almost overnight. They climbed back to a respectable ten games above .500 at the finish, but still finished fifth. This year, I figure, they'll have to do it with consistent play, winning a few more than they lose, month after month, right on through the season. *Et voilà!* Come journey's end, there they'll be, playing California or Texas or Kansas City for the A.L. flag. Then, bring on the Dodgers, Pirates, Cubs, Expos, Reds, or Giants!

Piece of cake.

Thursday
April 26th

RAIN

The Tigers have had six or seven games rained out already this spring. I'm not sure of the number, partly because the opening game was rained out twice. In any case, it has played havoc with their pitching rotation. And the double-headers are starting to pile up for July and August. This means trouble, especially for a team with a thin pitching staff.

Rain has also had a debilitating effect on Mark Wagner's batting statistics. Wagner has been playing shortstop in place of Alan Trammell and doing a surprisingly good job at the plate. His numbers would look even better if he hadn't had some deplorable treatment from the elements in the last couple of days. Twice the Tigers started games in Milwaukee, and both of them were halted by rain before the requisite five innings could be played to make them official. Wagner came to bat three times in these non-games, and had a home run, a double and a single. As far as baseball history is concerned, these hits did not happen. They are as non-existent as if Mark had never left the hotel.

I maintain that all the at-bats, hits and other figures compiled in a game cut short before the fifth inning should count in the final totals, just as they would in a game that went the distance. These game fragments are not exhibition games; everyone's doing his best; nobody *knows* it isn't going to be an official game while it's happening. So why shouldn't everything count?

Consider the case of a player who goes to bat three times in the first five innings and strikes out each time. At the end of five innings, with the score tied, it starts to rain. And it never stops. The game is called. Nothing has been decided. Since it was a tie, the game will have to be replayed. But because it went five innings it's "official," and our man is charged with three strikeouts.

The next day, he hits two home runs in his first two times at bat, but this time the rains arrive at the end of the fourth inning. Same result. The game is called, and must be replayed at a later date. But our man loses his two home runs.

I seem to recall that Lou Gehrig once had three triples in the first four innings of a game that didn't go the "official" route. I can't prove it, and there's no way to check it (save hunting through hundreds of old newspapers), because this is one baseball statistic you *can't* look up. All we know for sure is that as far as baseball is concerned, it never happened (even if it did).

Everything should count—everything that takes place under game conditions on a major-league field with official umpires working and all eligibility rules in effect. I find this view so utterly logical that I can't understand why most people to whom I suggest it seem to find it illogical. But there is hope for my position. I feel sure that Bowie Kuhn would find the idea ludicrous, which would be a powerful argument in its favor.

I think Al Kaline might side with me. In his illustrious career, Al had 399 home runs. The mystique of round numbers being what it is, he would very much like to have had 400, and he has been heard to bemoan the "five or six" home runs he lost because of early rain. I don't blame him. If you ask me, he was robbed.

Wednesday
May 2nd

THE DESIGNATED PRODIGAL RETURNS

Rusty Staub came back to the Tigers yesterday. He joined them in Chicago, where they were playing a series with the White Sox. He says he returned because Campbell has agreed to talk seriously about his demands. Campbell says he hasn't promised a thing he hadn't promised from the beginning. But nobody cares. Everyone's hoping Rusty will be as good as ever, which would obviously make the Tigers a much better team.

Jim Hawkins, the *Detroit Free Press* baseball writer, relates that Rusty went directly to the ball park to take batting practice. Eddie Brinkman, the old Tiger shortstop, now a coach, was doing the pitching. "On his first swing," says

Hawkins, "Staub bounced the ball back up the middle, and Brinkman let out a whelp."

I trust we will hear more about this.

Saturday
May 5th

THE INSCRUTABLE RON

I am not a television snob. I have been known to watch stuff with no redeeming merit, social or otherwise, except that it killed an hour I had no other use for. Once, when physically exhausted, I watched an entire episode of *Charlie's Angels*, filled with the most mindless dialogue since the glory days of *Mr. Keene, Tracer of Lost Persons*. Looking at those girls can hardly do you any harm, I figured, especially Kate Jackson, although to me she will always be Jill Danko, the nurse on *The Rookies* who personally cared for every person in the city of Los Angeles who was shot or smashed up in a high-speed car chase or otherwise damaged in a police-related accident.

What I am trying to say here (and I think I have already said it) is that I am not above watching crap on television, although I may tell my friends that I spent the evening trying to work out a new perspective on the early Pound cantos.

Since I am a sports fan, and since I have no scruples about watching junk, why, then, have I never seen even one minute of those shows in which superstars of sport vie with each other for large monetary prizes in contests alien to their natural bent? Basketball players play tennis against jockeys. Bowlers high-jump against golfers. I am a little vague about exactly what they do because I have never watched them do it. I don't look down on it. No one who has seen a whole episode of *Charlie's Angels* can afford to look down on anything the TV people think up. But it simply never interested me. Who wants to watch a professional boxer rowing a boat, when any expert boat rower could do it better, although he might not be able to punch his way out of a roomful of elderly midgets?

Once, on a Saturday afternoon between seasons, I chanced upon the national arm-wrestling championship, live from Petaluma, California, Great hairy-armed people (of both sexes) made faces at each other and uttered sudden strange, involuntary noises, until finally one of them slapped his opponent's arm down onto the surface of a sort of raised platform especially built for the occasion. (Roone Arledge, or whoever, would not want his stars performing on top of a bar, the way it's usually done by amateurs competing for beers.) Dozens cheered. Against my better judgment, I watched these people for more than half an hour, and I learned a few things. I learned, for example, that in arm wrestling the battle *is* always to the strong. The wiry guys ("don't be fooled by his build; there's hidden power there") always lost to the guys with bigger, and usually hairier, arms. And I found out why the national arm-wrestling championships are held in a shed in Petaluma, California, rather than in Yankee Stadium. They are, after the initial flash of interest at the discovery that they exist at all, dull. And yet you can make a case for them. Those are presumably the best arm wrestlers in the land up there arm wrestling, and thus more deserving of an audience than a middle linebacker swimming the fifty-meter butterfly.

Still, my attitude toward trash sports was liberal, recalling Voltaire's toward those whom he considered unenlightened or offensive. I disapproved of what they did, but I would defend their right to do it. Voltaire actually said "defend to the death," but I think that might be a bit beyond the depth of my commitment in this case. Or, probably, of Voltaire's. He never watched a weight lifter playing Ping-Pong.

Or a baseball player lifting weights, and it is here that the

promoters of Eclectic Misfits, or whatever it's called, have
finally over-extended their credit with me. They did this by
spoiling Ron LeFlore's arm, which, besides making it nearly
impossible for him to throw a runner out at third base, has
proved prejudicial to the maintenance of good order and
discipline on the baseball team for which he plays. This is a
story based on rumors and secondhand reports, but they all
ring fairly true, and since I have no source of ultimate truth,
I think they deserve comment. Only one thing is certain.
There *is* something wrong with Ron LeFlore's arm. He cannot throw very well, and the Tigers' opponents have been
taking advantage of it. The prevailing rumor is that Ronnie
hurt his arm during the winter while lifting weights in a
superstars' contest on TV. The adjective most often applied
to LeFlore's arm injury is "mysterious," since no one admits
for the record to knowing what caused it. Ron's arm muscles
may be damaged, but his figurative muscle has poked the
first hole in Les Moss's unexpectedly thin armor.

LeFlore himself says nothing, which is very wise and
reflects the rather surprising good judgment that he often
displays in his relations with the press. Ron is not, as most
of the world knows, the product of a college education, or
indeed of much formal education at all. But he shows exceptional good sense in deciding when to sound off and when to
clam. It seems apparent that the arm was not injured in a
baseball game. If it had been, everyone would know about it
and there would be no comment necessary except "That's
too bad." But if he hurt it in a stupid weight-lifting contest,
or in any of a hundred other ways in which people hurt
themselves, most of which seem stupid in retrospect, he cannot do himself any good by admitting it. Or by making up
some thin story that no one will believe. So he says nothing,
and since no one knows the cause of his injury, there is no
basis for serious criticism. Silence is, in this case, the only
sensible course. But a lot of athletes who did go to college
would not have been smart enough to realize it.

Unfortunately, though, the whole business has had repercussions beyond the immediate problem. One of them surfaced with the return of Rusty Staub. With Staub filling the designated-hitter spot full time, Les Moss figured he would be able to settle on a regular outfield. LeFlore, who had been doing some DH'ing, would go back to the outfield, but to left field instead of his old position in center field, at least until his arm was better. Steve Kemp would move to right, Jerry Morales to center. This was routinely reported in the papers, and the ink was hardly dry before LeFlore was publicly demanding a conference with the manager. Center field is the place of honor in the outfield, and Ron has always played there because of his speed. He obviously considered the planned move humiliating. After a short meeting with Ron, Moss announced that LeFlore would stay in center field. The unspoken message was as clear as the spoken one: the manager of the baseball team is not in complete control. This is bad news. When a big-league manager, even today when the iron hand is no longer fashionable, can be so easily over-ruled by one of his players on a matter of strategy, he is in trouble. The point is not that LeFlore got him to change his mind—any manager ought to be willing to consider his players' suggestions and complaints—but that he did it so openly and defiantly. The stern, no-nonsense image of Les Moss has been severely debased.

LeFlore's statement on the matter was less diplomatic than his silence on the question of how the arm got hurt. "If I can't throw well from center field, then I wouldn't be able to throw well from left field, would I?" A clear instance of stating a self-evident truth which is, at the same time, nonsense. The move was not intended to strengthen his arm, but to transfer it to the area where it would do the least damage. Ron knew that, of course.

From the standpoint of pure strategy, LeFlore may have been on firm ground. Although he is not a great outfielder, his speed often enables him to catch fly balls that others would not get near. But his little victory was a defeat for team morale. Planting the notion that the players, at least the name players, need take orders from the manager only when they find them congenial is step one on the road to anarchy. Anarchy, on defense and on the bases, was last year's Tiger thing. It didn't work, and those of us who take an interest in these matters were hoping for a new policy this year: outfielders backing up infielders, infielders backing up infielders, outfielders backing up outfielders. Last year, one got the impression that each man was playing an independent game, oblivious to the needs of his teammates, which has the effect of nullifying the concept implicit in the word "team."

Nowhere was this more conspicuous than in running the bases. You do not criticize a man too much when he gets thrown out trying to take an extra base, as long as he makes it close. But over-running a base and then getting tagged out trying to get back to it is a capital crime, and the Tigers had a crowded rap sheet on this offense alone last year.

The architect of the new policy (which might be summed up as "playing the game on a professional level" or simply "paying attention to what's going on") was to have been Les Moss, but an architect whose plans are subject to capricious revision by the builders is not likely to create an arch of triumph. Moss's capacity to run the team has been somewhat reduced by this incident. Maybe more than somewhat, although I hope not.

❀   ❀   ❀

When, at the beginning of this segment, I characterized Ron LeFlore as "inscrutable," I did not mean to imply that he was a silent, withdrawn introvert. Nor when I said that he knew when it was to his advantage to keep quiet did I mean to suggest that he did it all the time.

What I meant was that Ron is mysterious or, to put it in less melodramatic terms, hard to figure. Notwithstanding his evident wisdom in keeping quiet about the origin of his arm problem, Ron is normally rather outspoken on any matter that appears to affect his welfare. But he doesn't talk much about bunting.

Ron does not bunt. Why? I don't know, for sure. It is patently absurd for a hitter with Ron's speed and power not to lay one down occasionally. He could bunt for base hits, and when the infield shortened up to defend against the bunt, he would become much more effective when he swung away. But he won't do it. True, he doesn't know how to do it very well, but that leaves unanswered the question of why he hasn't bothered to learn. (There's no trick to it, except practice. You just stand up there and do it a hundred times a day until you become pretty good at it. Some players become expert at it, but pretty good will do.) I think, believe it or not, that he doesn't do it because he thinks it's effeminate, that it is somehow an admission of weakness.

LeFlore comes out of a background and culture that is obsessed with manhood. Black players in general, living in a society that for centuries pretended to look upon people of their race as children, are wont to state that they want to be treated like men. A white player having a public dispute with his manager might say that he wants to be treated like an "adult" or a "human being," but a black player will almost always use the word "man." It is, for one thing, the antithesis of the hated "boy." It's also an answer to the sociologists who have characterized black America in a thousand learned essays as a matriarchal society.

It's no secret (he wrote a book about it) that Ron LeFlore joined the Tiger organization direct from a period of enforced residence in Jackson (Michigan) State Prison. Befriended by a prisoner with baseball coaching experience, Ron learned to play the game behind those walls. Under such impossible conditions, he became good enough to convince a major-league team that he deserved a shot at the big time. After just a year in the minors, he made it to the big

Ron LeFlore. One in a million.

club, and has perched precariously on the edge of greatness
almost since the day he got here.

I cannot exaggerate the dimensions of this achievement.
That a kid (young man, that is) with virtually no experience
in anything beyond street stickball could make the jump
from prison to the big leagues in such a short time is little

short of miraculous. It is, as the title of the movie about him suggested, a one-in-a-million story.

LeFlore has so much natural ability that even when he has a disappointing year, he is a great asset to the team. This is fortunate because, in one way or another, most of his seasons with the Tigers have been disappointing. In 1977 he hit .325 and looked ready to take his place at the very top, where he seems to belong. But '78 was again a disappointment. He finished the year with pretty good numbers, but far short of what the previous season had seemed to portend. He started miserably, picked up a little, and then went into a hideous slump. Three months into the season, he was hitting .259 and looked almost helpless against right-handed pitching, which had never troubled him much in the past. People said they couldn't figure out what was wrong with him. But I went ahead and tried anyway.

To start with the specific, Ron had been bailing out against right-handed pitchers like a high-school kid. The reason a player does that, I think, is dumbness. And I don't mean that LeFlore was dumb in the usual sense. He reportedly has an IQ of 130. But baseball smartness has very little relationship to native intelligence. Yogi Berra, for example, never struck me as being very bright. Even his famous malapropisms and non sequiturs were mostly made up by sportswriters. But he was referred to as a "smart ballplayer." And in a game, he was.

Smartness, on the baseball field, consists largely of two elements: experience and concentration. You learn by doing; that's experience. Once you have learned, you *always* remember; that's concentration. In the field, a "smart" player always knows how many are out and precisely what he is going to do on the next pitch, no matter what happens. That's all there is to it.

At bat, concentration is equally important. If a man who has always hit right-handed pitching well goes 3-for-30 against right-handers, as LeFlore had recently done, he is obviously doing something wrong. LeFlore had been bailing out. You could see it clearly on the center-field-camera shot on TV.

The term "bailing out" simply means backing away from an inside pitch. If you are batting right-handed, when a right-handed pitcher releases the ball it looks as if it is aimed right at you (unless he throws full overhand, which few pitchers do). It does not look like it will get into the strike zone until it reaches the plate. Inexperienced batters tend to pull back, not only from a curveball but even from a fastball that nicks the inside corner. (Most of us who played ball in our youth have had the embarrassing experience of leaping back, or hitting the dirt, on a pitch that was called a strike. It usually happens the first time you face a pitcher who actually knows how to pitch, which most schoolboy pitchers don't.) A good batter does not back off. He stands in there and hits the ball. That's how, occasionally, you get hit by a pitch. Obviously, no batter would ever be hit by a pitch if he were concentrating solely on not getting hit.

There are players, of course, who can hit an inside pitch while giving ground, but they lose power, and they cannot hit the *outside* pitch, which will surely follow the close one, once the batter has established a pattern of bailing.

What it takes to stand in there against a pitch that looks as if it's coming out of left field, follow it all the way to the plate and then, if it's over, have a good cut at it is *concentration.* (What it would take for you or me to do it is exceptional courage, but a hitter is supposed to have conquered that problem by the time he gets to the bigs.) LeFlore, who is a natural athlete with both speed and strength—what a halfback he would make!—has always been prone to lapses of concentration, both in the field and at bat. I don't know why. Last year there had been a lot of extraneous activity surrounding him, mainly in connection with a TV movie being made about his life. That may have affected him, but I don't think it was the whole story, because he has always tended to suffer through periods of apparent inattention. I suspect it is because he *is* so physically gifted that he occasionally lapses into a deadly complacency.

I am convinced that Ron LeFlore could be a superstar if his dedication were constantly on a par with his unquestioned ability.

This year he has gotten off to an uncharacteristically excellent start. Last time I looked, he was hitting .340. If he can avoid a prolonged slump, and play to his full potential throughout the year, he will indeed be a threat to Rod Carew or anyone else who has his eye on the batting championship.

         ✿   ✿   ✿

When I reviewed Ron LeFlore's book, *Breakout: From Prison to the Big Leagues* (ghosted for him by Jim Hawkins), I found it very disturbing. I don't mean shocking. We are no longer easily shocked, even by the sordid details of life in a penitentiary. I was disturbed by the total absence of anything that could have been interpreted as regret, disavowal, swearing off.

I didn't expect remorse, contrition. Largely because of his color, LeFlore was born into a world that no one could tolerate, and he reacted to it in what he considered a perfectly normal manner. He became, at an early age, a hustler, con man and thief. LeFlore's position is that he did what he had to do to live, and he makes no apology. I wouldn't argue with that unless I could swear that I would have acted more nobly under the circumstances—which I certainly cannot. What I found disquieting in the book, however, was the strong impression it conveyed that were he not making big money as a ballplayer, he would have had no qualms about going back to the same life he left behind when he went to prison. (I couldn't help wondering if Hawkins, the actual author, realized how strongly his words were transmitting that message.)

There was one bit of unconscious humor in the book that

delighted me. After describing the homosexual activities of some of his fellow prisoners in rather more lucid detail than seemed absolutely necessary, Ron relates how he reacted to a homosexual advance. He knocked the man down with a baseball bat, hit him a couple of times, then began kicking him, all the while shouting, "I'm a man! I ain't no homosexual!" I place that near the top of my list of unlikely shouts. Obviously, there is one pressure group in this country that Hawkins doesn't want to mess with.

About three months after I had recorded my impressions of LeFlore's book, I saw the TV movie, *One in a Million*, based on the same life. The credits, in fact, said: "Based on the book *Breakout* by Ron LeFlore and Jim Hawkins." But, as with *The Godfather* and *Gone With the Wind*, the movie was better than the book. I thought it was excellent, in fact, although it did not half succeed in capturing the true misery of ghetto and prison life, just as *Roots* did not reveal the real degradation of slavery, and *The Holocaust* failed even to suggest the incredible agony of the Jews under Hitler. This seems to be endemic to television drama, which tries above all not to drive anyone away. The truth may be that there simply *is* no way to get the message through, but I sometimes think they could try a little harder.

Television and most movies try to substitute incident for atmosphere. In *Roots*, half a man's foot is cut off; in *One in a Million*, Ron's brother is shot to death in an apparent argument over dope. These are both shocking incidents, but they occupy a relatively short time in the drama. A tragic *event* can be outlived and finally almost forgotten. But slavery, concentration camps and urban poverty are *conditions of life* which go on day after day, year after year. The belief that there is no escape (and in truth, there usually is none) grinds people down until they become less than complete human beings. Some of this is suggested by the gradual deterioration of Ron's brother, Gerald (skillfully played by Larry B. Scott), throughout the film. But I guess it takes a director like Scorsese to make you *feel* it. And TV is not yet his medium.

Still, within the limits imposed by the small screen, *One in a Million* was an admirable effort, and LeVar Burton (who, during the filming, was described by several ball-players as "too small" or "not the athletic type") did a superb job as LeFlore. He is a gifted, intelligent actor, who understood Ron better than his biographer did. He also did a far better job of pretending to be a ballplayer than certain more renowned actors have managed in the past.

To me, the biggest revelation in the movie related to my earlier comments about the implication that LeFlore would have returned to crime if he hadn't been offered the Tiger contract. Watching the film, I got the same impression and I realized I had probably been naive. That *was* the message, and the moral seems to be that a criminal *can* be rehabilitated *if* he learns a useful trade in prison and has a good job waiting for him when he gets out. Considering how few convicts can be offered jobs with the opportunity for advancement that LeFlore had, though, it is hard to see how Ron's experience can help much in solving the problem of rampant recidivism.

      ✿   ✿   ✿

I have dealt with the story of Ron LeFlore here at far greater length than I intended to when I started this segment. But perhaps I was justified. It is, I'd venture to say, the most dramatic individual story now going on in baseball. And the nice thing about it is that it has a happy ending. Thus far, anyway. I hope, for Ron's sake, that it always will. Just *how* happy, of course, depends on how expertly he makes use of his amazing (*truly* amazing) skills. I hope—for my sake, too—that he gets it all together just once. If he does, he can lead the league in batting, hits, runs, stolen bases, doubles and probably triples. (Home runs are not his forte, although I wouldn't even bet that he couldn't make a run at that title, too, if he wanted to sacrifice the others.) He can be the best player in baseball—for one year, at least. Maybe he ought to save it for next year, when the Tigers make their real move. No later than that, please. Since 1980 is the last year of his Tiger contract, we don't know where he'll be in '81. I wonder if Jim Campbell does.

If, in conclusion, I might address one piece of advice directly to Ron LeFlore, it would be this: Learn to bunt, Ron. It's not sissy.

Monday
May 7th

ON TACTICAL SILENCE AND PARTIAL SCORES

Thinking over Ron LeFlore's judicious silence on the matter of his shoulder injury, I remembered a friend of mine who once used the same tactic. We were close friends in college. He now lives a great distance from me, so I seldom see him, but I like to think we still are friends. When Pearl Harbor exploded, right in the middle of our fourth year at Ann Arbor, we both went off to war, but in different branches of the service.

Sam (not his name) joined the Navy, went overseas, saw some action and came back with two fingers missing. After I had spent enough time with him to be sure he wasn't neurotic about it, I asked him how it had happened. He wouldn't tell me. He never did tell me. Or anyone else, as far as I know. He always passed it off with a joke. "The sign *said* don't feed the animals, but . . ." He is a funny man, and he seemed to have an endless supply of comic answers to the inevitable question.

I still don't know how Sam lost those fingers. It is quite possible that he gave them up in some brave action which he is reluctant to talk about, either because of modesty or because the memory is painful. It is equally possible that he dropped a torpedo on them, or suffered some even more bizarre (and thus embarrassing) accident. Anyway, after all this time, almost any answer would be a letdown, and I no longer want to know. I haven't thought about it in years, but while I did I pictured him alternately as a heroic figure and as a buffoon. Which is, come to think of it, the way I think of myself and most of the people I like. So his tactical silence worked. He became Everyman. Or at least Everysoldier.

But this is a baseball book, so I ought to tie up this story with a baseball anecdote. Luckily, there is one. While he was overseas, Sam's parents tried to keep him liberally supplied with baseball news. They had both been born in the Old Country (do we still say that?) and didn't know baseball from hopscotch, but they knew Sam was an avid fan, and nothing was too good for their boy in the service.

In those days, all metropolitan newspapers published five or six editions every day. The first editions of the afternoon papers would come out in mid-morning, and would be followed by succeeding editions every hour or so, right up to the Five Star Final at about five thirty. The banner headlines on these intermediate editions often dealt with the progress of the local baseball team that day. Sox Lead. Yanks Get 5 in First. That sort of thing. (During the '30s, both Detroit afternoon papers kept a huge headline reading Hank Homers set permanently in type.) At the bottom of the front page would appear running scores of all games in progress, updated by an inning or two in each edition.

Over in Espíritu Santo, or wherever he was, my friend Sam waited in vain for some genuine baseball news. He never got any from his parents, although they tried. Every week a thick envelope would arrive filled with clippings, not from the sports pages but from the front pages, reading:

AMERICAN LEAGUE

Boston	000 01
New York	000 1
Detroit	020 000
Chicago	101 01
St. Louis	0
Cleveland	

Tuesday
May 8th

THE GOING RATE

This will be short. I hope so, anyway, because I don't even want to talk about the umpires' strike. It is, to me, inconceivable that it hasn't been settled before this. The issue is so simple it defies every attempt to make it complicated. The umpires are not getting a decent wage. Their salaries sound pretty good, but the expense money they are given is so niggardly that they cannot get by on it—especially since the league insists they travel in a style befitting the dignity of the game. "Don't carry your own bags," they are told, and obviously it would be even less dignified to stiff the bellboy. They are asked to make a first-class impression on second-class money.

There is no need to quote long figures. All that's necessary is to point out that professional basketball and hockey officials at every level of seniority get more money for half as many games. On a straight per-game basis, the baseball umpires are paid a little more than a third of what officials in these other sports get.

The umpires say they are not on strike because they don't

have contracts. The league executives say the umps *do* have an agreement, however, which still has a couple of years to run. An "agreement," if it's signed and sealed, *is* a contract, obviously. And as we all know, a contract is a contract, so perhaps I am being inconsistent with my position in the Staub case. So be it. A foolish consistency is the hobgoblin of small minds. Everybody knows that.

The point here is that for an outlay of $20,000 per team, the umpires could be satisfied, and baseball could regain some of the dignity it is sacrificing every day the substitute umpires continue working. These stopgap officials are doing the best they can, and some of them are good, but they lack the experience, the confidence and the authority of the real thing. In some cases, their indecision and timidity have led to farcical situations. And in every city pitchers and batters alike complain of the constant fluctuations in the ostensible size of the strike zone. When pitchers cannot work the corners and batters are unsure of their rights, the game loses its precision, becomes a makeshift—negating the very skills which distinguish a professional of the top class from a talented amateur.

The whole thing could be solved in five minutes if our intrepid commissioner would step into the picture and come right out in favor of justice. Do not look for this to happen. In any situation requiring firm action, the commissioner can be relied on to issue a strong statement to the effect that it is "a league matter" in which he cannot become involved. (What, in baseball, is *not* a league matter?) His only apparent functions are to invalidate all sales of ballplayers by Charlie Finley and show up in the winners' dressing room after the final game of the World Series.

I've gone on about this too long already. By the time you read it, the regulars will be back at work (I'll be properly aghast at some of their decisions, too), and you will hardly remember the umpires' strike. But it's one more example of how the nabobs of the game can build a minor problem into a major crisis, with complete disregard for the interest of the fans, who merely continue pouring ever-increasing millions into their pockets every year.

*   *   *

You may get the idea that I have no sympathy for Baseball Commissioner Bowie Kuhn. Wrong. I have great sympathy for the position in which he finds himself. He has an easy job with great prestige and a good salary, and he doesn't want to lose it. I have no trouble identifying with that. In my time, I have lost some uneasy jobs with no prestige and punk salaries, and I was always distressed. When I realize how my distress would have been multiplied if the jobs had actually been desirable ones, I can quite understand the commissioner's reluctance to risk his sinecure by actually doing something.

The man is in an anomalous position. He was hired to preside over the very people who hired him, who don't really want to be presided over. Clearly, then, his safest course is to do as little as possible. To pretend to preside, instead of actually presiding. Fine, if that's what he wants. But those of us who care about the game, and who have an idealistic notion of what a commissioner ought to be (firm, fair, fearless and infinitely wise), do not feel obligated to respect him if that's the course he chooses. Once in a while, we feel, he ought to take a stand on a mildly controversial matter of importance to baseball. If he did, he'd have the prestige and our esteem, too. Of course, he might not have the job and the salary for long. But that's the chance you take when you start thinking in terms of right-and-wrong, instead of what's-in-it-for-me.

Mind you, I'm not saying I would do any better. Give me the commissioner's job, with the salary and the expense account (and free tickets—don't forget those), and I might become as timorous as Bowie. But then I wouldn't deserve your respect any more than he does.

Sunday
May 13th

HI HO, STEVERINO

Steve Kemp is off to an absolutely sensational start this year. In his last time at bat in the final exhibition game of the spring, he was hit on the head with a pitched ball. There was concern, as there always is, that this would affect his hitting. But seldom, if ever, has a batter come back from a beaning with such style. He is hitting close to .400 and, what's more surprising, playing his position with authority. This is quite possibly the best news since the invention of peanut butter, because Kemp has been a favorite of mine almost from the moment he arrived on the Detroit scene, slashing at thrown balls as if he wanted to render them useless for further play. That was a mere two years ago. He came in wearing a large red tag labeled GOOD HIT, NO FIELD. But his rookie season belied at least the second half of this appraisal. He hit only .257, but he had 18 home runs and 88 runs batted in—impressive figures for a rookie. And his fielding turned out to be very adequate (or, certainly, adequate enough).

Last year, Kemp and Jason Thompson reported in a day late to spring training, a gesture of dissatisfaction with the salaries they had been offered by the Tigers. Kemp's was said to be $55,000, which struck me as rather handsome compensation for a kid with one year's experience. It was, as it turned out, very reasonable for the year he had. He raised his average to .277, but his power fell off, and his fielding deteriorated badly. Even worse, he didn't seem to care. He was a puzzling ballplayer. There was never any question about his all-out effort in games, but he seemed unwilling to do anything *between* games to improve himself. I made some snide comments about him. I said, Sure, he always gives you 110 percent in a game, but he's only

Steve Kemp. Keeping his promise.

half the ballplayer he ought to be, and 50 percent of 110 percent is only 55 percent—or, in layman's terms, not enough. Rather mean stuff, but I was deeply disappointed in Kemp. He had seemed to me the kind of old-fashioned, college-try ballplayer who wins pennants, and (though he didn't know I existed) he had let me down.

I have no idea what has brought about the change, but this year Kemp reminds me of Dick McAuliffe. The comparison is, in a sense, farfetched, because McAuliffe (second baseman on the 1968 Tiger team that won the World Series) had a funny batting stance and wasn't half the hitter Kemp is, but he was the most *determined* hitter I can recall. I always thought that a batter who had McAuliffe's fierce resolve plus all the other attributes of a good hitter (eye, strength, coordination) would be a cinch for the Hall of Fame. It's a bit early yet to enter Kemp's nomination, but this year he has the look. What's more, he looks like a legitimate big-league outfielder on defense. So all is forgiven. And if he can maintain his present pace or, more realistically, something like it, he won't have to worry about the size of his paycheck for years to come. He is going to get rich. I only hope, given the state of baseball today, that he gets rich playing for the Tigers.

❁   ❁   ❁

When I commented rather acidly on Kemp's salary demands last year, I suppose there were those spiteful enough to suggest that my remarks were motivated by envy. If so, they were right. I envied him his youth, naturally, but I'm not sure I would change places with him just for that. (Would I like rock music? If so, how would I explain it?) Mainly, I envied him his chance to play in the big leagues. I would have sold at least a portion of my soul for that chance. And like many a red-blooded American boy, I continued to harbor the dream that I would somehow find myself in a major-league game until I was almost too old to play in a neighborhood softball game. We didn't think about being stars or making big money. Just to put on the uniform and run out on the field would have been a kind of bliss akin to . . . what? For a few of us, there was no other dream quite like it. Not riches, nor pliant movie beauties, nor world renown, nor anything else you can think of, moved us like the thought of being big-league ballplayers. We wanted all those other things, too, of course, but the baseball fantasy was, somehow, different. I like to think Steve Kemp felt that way once. And that he still gets a special thrill every time he puts on the suit, even if he thinks he ought to be paid more for doing it.

To be honest, I also envied him the $55,000 a year.

✿   ✿   ✿

One of the nice things, to me, about the new salary picture in baseball is not that some players can get rich, but that the ones whose numbers will never be retired (or even re-membered) can make a living wage. It wasn't always thus. Fringe players used to be paid starvation wages, and the term is almost literally exact. In the minor leagues, it *was* exact. I don't suppose any minor-league player actually died of starvation. But you can be terribly hungry without dying.

I remember a conversation I had with Walt Peckinpaugh in Ann Arbor around 1940. Walt had been baseball captain at Michigan and then had gone off to play minor-league ball, hoping to follow in the somewhat illustrious footsteps of his father, Roger Peckinpaugh, onetime boy manager of the Yankees (at twenty-three in 1914) and much later adult manager of the Indians. Walt told me how it was in the minor leagues in those days. He played for Opelousas in the Evangeline League (this was when the minor leagues were really minor), a Class D circuit in Louisiana. The salary, as I recall, was $15 a week. They played all their games at night under lights more suitable for an intimate dinner than for an athletic contest. The gnats, he said, were a major hazard, especially if they swarmed around you at the same time a ball was a hit in your direction.

Since all the teams in the Evangeline League were within sixty miles of Opelousas, the club cut its hotel bills to zero by having the players dress at home, drive to the games in two or three cars (gasoline was 15 cents a gallon) and drive back home afterward. This meant the players never got any traveling meal money, which was a large part of what most minor-league players lived on. You had to love baseball to play in the Evangeline League. The wonder is that there were thousands of players around the country living under conditions not much better than that. Today, I suppose, a player who is just good enough to play in the Evangeline League doesn't play professional baseball at all. Nowadays, there are several colleges which regularly produce out-standing major-league candidates. But in 1940 a team like Opelousas, with a total payroll of less than $1000 a month, could undoubtedly have whipped any college team in the country.

In the majors the pay was better, but sometimes not by much. I met a fellow during the war (the one called II) who had been in the Philadelphia Athletics' system, and he told me about Connie Mack's pay scale. I mentioned the name of Tony Freitas, a little guy who pitched briefly for the A's in the '30s. He said that Freitas had been paid $50 a week, and I imagine the figure was fairly accurate. Now, let's face it, Tony Freitas was no superstar, but he did win 12 and lose only 5 one year. A pitcher today coming off a 12–5 year—and free to bargain—would sneer at anything less than $5000 a week. That works out to about $125,000 for a season, enough so he wouldn't have to hustle a lunch pail during the winter. Tony Freitas, on the other hand, was faced with the problem of finding other employment the day the season ended.

Major-league players today, whatever their level of skill, get a minimum salary in the neighborhood of $20,000 a year, which at least enables them to buy a round occasionally. It must have been tough holding up your end of the camaraderie when salaries varied from $80,000 a year (Babe Ruth) to $50 a week (Connie Mack's pitching staff).

BIRD WATCHING

As a student of the contemporary press, I am always intrigued by the impulse that prompts an editor to devote his entire front page to coverage of a single event. Obviously, for this to happen the event must be of such transcending importance that it literally drives all other news—even that which might get a good play on an ordinary day—into the inside pages.

Thus, when a war ends, or a president resigns, we may expect to see a front page dominated by a lead story announcing the fact (WAR ENDS, DICK QUITS, whatever) and filled out with sidebars on peripheral aspects of the big news: JULIE INDIGNANT; PAT STOICAL, GRIM; PRESIDENT ATE OATMEAL FOR BREAKFAST; NEW PREZ VOWS TO BIND UP WOUNDS and the like. Nothing else makes page one, so anyone seeking eternal fame is well advised to avoid doing anything important—even dying—on such a day.

In the smaller world of athletics, a comparable event is one that monopolizes the front page of the sports section. If you want to make a big splash in the Detroit papers, do not run your three-minute mile on the day the Tigers win the World Series. In 1932, Lou Gehrig became the first American League player ever to hit four home runs in one game, but it took some time for the news to get around, especially in New York, because he did it the same day John McGraw resigned after thirty years as manager of the Giants.

All this is prologue to disclosure of the singular fact that *The Detroit News*, a couple of weeks ago, devoted its entire first sports page to a report of an exhibition game between the Tigers and the Cincinnati Reds. Detroit won the game handily, but no one really cared about that. What they did care about was Mark Fidrych. The Bird started for Detroit and went six innings, the most he had pitched against major-league opposition in more than a year. He looked great, too. The Reds got to him for three hits and two runs in the fourth, but in the other five innings he was almost perfect. In all, he gave up four hits and two runs, and to all appearances was ready to take his place in the starting rotation. But appearances, as has been remarked, are deceiving. And never more so than when The Bird is concerned. The numbers were good, but the actual performance was lacking in . . . something. Those best qualified to comment (his manager, his catchers, Al Kaline) all said he had done just fine, which was in harmony with the consensus among ordinary mortals. But they said it with something less than complete conviction.

The general feeling among these professional observers seemed to be that The Bird's fastball didn't "move" the way it had in the magic year of '76. In the language of an earlier baseball era, it didn't have any "hop" on it. What this means, really, is that it reacted normally to the pull of gravity. The best pitchers, the ones you always think are going to beat you, seem to defy Newton's law.

The instant a thrown ball leaves a pitcher's hand, it is subject to the force of gravity. This is equally true of a bullet when it leaves the muzzle of a gun. If fired in a direction parallel to the ground, it begins to drop *immediately* upon release from its source of energy.

When a baseball is thrown at a speed approaching—sometimes exceeding—90 miles an hour over a distance of just 60 feet, the effect of gravity upon it is not easily apparent to anyone not personally involved with it. It appears to travel in a straight line. (Similarly, a bullet, although it cannot be seen, is assumed by the casual onlooker to follow a perfectly straight course to its target, say 200 yards away. But gravity is always at work, which is why the gun's muzzle must be raised ever so slightly when the shooter switches to a target 300 yards distant.) The batter, however, knows that the ball is dropping, so he adjusts his swing to compensate for it. In effect, he swings the bat a fraction of an inch below the line which the ball seems to be traveling.

I do not, I must hastily point out, mean to imply that the batter *consciously* makes this adjustment. Most batters, we can safely assume, do not even know they do it. It is so automatic as to be almost instinctive. But it is learned— learned over a lifetime of swinging at pitched balls, starting at age five and on up through every level of competition, all the way to the major leagues.

What the batter is doing, in short, is looking at the ball when it reaches a point 15 or 20 feet from him, gauging its speed, guessing the height at which it will cross the plate and then swinging at it. All in a fraction of a second, and all without realizing he is doing it.

Now, it follows as the night the day that if the batter underestimates the speed of the ball, he will swing a bit too low and produce a foul ball or a pop fly, or perhaps miss it altogether.

But how, you ask, *can* the batter miscalculate when the level of his swing is determined automatically, instinctively, *without* conscious calculation? With this clever question, you have brought us to the origin of one of baseball's most persistent fables: the myth of the fastball that hops. It doesn't, but when thrown by a pitcher to whom the gift has been given, it seems to. This is an optical illusion, brought about by the simple fact that the ball is traveling so fast that its downward trajectory is minimized. It still drops (bound by the laws of physics, it has no choice), but so slightly that it appears to rise. This is the coveted hop.

All of the great pitchers whose fame was based on the speed with which they threw a baseball were renowned for the hop on their fastball. Walter Johnson, Lefty Grove, Bob Feller. When they turned the ball loose, it *moved*. It crackled. It hopped. Everyone said so. Not surprising, be- cause these are all legendary fireball pitchers. What *is* sur- prising is that you often hear it said of a pitcher that "he's not terribly fast but his fastball really moves." So, obviously, it isn't sheer speed that's involved here. The key factor is deceptive speed—the ability to throw a ball that travels slightly faster than it appears to, sometimes known as the "sneaky" fastball. I don't know the secret. I doubt if those who exploit it know. But it is what makes the difference between speed and smoke, between a pitcher who is described hopefully as "a big strong kid" and a twenty-game winner.

The hop, the crackle, the fastball that moves is what Mark Fidrych had when he was twenty-one years old, lost when he was twenty-two and has been trying to get back ever since. He won 19 games in that first incredible season. Three years later, he has made little progress toward winning his second 19. But Detroit, and the whole baseball world, follow every move of this, his third comeback attempt in three years, with the intensity of spectators watching a tightrope walker tiptoeing across Niagara Falls.

That explains why the *News* chose to devote all of its first sports page to reports of an essentially meaningless game. But, of course, it doesn't entirely explain it. Other pitchers with bad arms have made comebacks, some from farther away than The Bird. Tommy John, for example, was told flatly that he would never pitch again. After a pair of operations, in which a tendon in John's right arm was removed and converted into a ligament in his left elbow, Tommy came back to become one of the best pitchers in the game. But even this miracle cure was not attended by the constant morbid publicity that has relentlessly tracked Fidrych for two and a half years—beginning with a knee injury in Florida in the spring of '77.

The plain fact is that in the whole history of baseball, Fidrych is unique. There have been better pitchers. There have probably been better *rookie* pitchers. But there has never been another ballplayer—nay, another athlete—who has captured the fancy of America as rapidly as Markie. (The

Mark The Bird Fidrych.

whole world calls him The Bird, but his mother calls him Markie, which is okay with me.)

So completely did Mark Fidrych dominate the baseball news in 1976 that it would be almost indecent to write a book about baseball in the '70s without including him. But it is hard to say anything about him that hasn't already been said. He is indeed "irrepressible." His golden hair is, as advertised, "unruly." And what a pitcher he was—and may be again. If he could regain his '76 form, twenty wins a season for the next ten years would be a piece of cake for the irrepressible Bird. With the unruly locks.

Consider that Mark Fidrych made his first appearance in a big-league game on May 15, 1976, and that less than two months later he was the starting pitcher for the American League in the All-Star Game. His became one of the handful of names in American sport that get instant recognition. Muhammad Ali, Joe Namath, O. J. Simpson . . . and Mark The Bird. Housewives in Pocatello and Cedar Rapids who had never seen a ball game knew The Bird. And it all happened over the space of half a baseball season.

Without a doubt, the single most famous fact about Fidrych was that he "talked to the ball." He didn't, of course. Like many athletes, he talked to himself. Between pitches, he maintained his concentration (which was exceptional) by giving himself a pep talk. But you could see his lips moving, and when he leaned forward to see the catcher's signs and held the ball in front of his face, he *looked* as if he were talking to it. Once he had proved he could also win ball games (a losing eccentric is just a clown), the sportswriters jumped on this apparently singular habit, and bingo —household word.

Mark The Bird Fidrych. The intervening sobriquet no longer required the customary parentheses; it had become part of the name. It seemed a shame that he would never pitch against Harry The Cat Brecheen, the Cardinals' ace of some years back, who enjoyed a similar distinction. "BIRD TOYS WITH CAT IN SERIES OPENER!" Only a dream.

The sad truth is that three years later, there is considerable doubt that Mark Fidrych will ever pitch in a World Series, or that he has any real future in baseball at all. He has fallen victim to the Shoulder Monster, that cruel and mysterious beast who habitually strikes when the pitcher is hot. Fidrych's prospects are, at this writing, still in grave doubt.

After The Bird's good (but not really good enough) showing against the Reds, the Tigers had to decide what to do with him—whether to send him down to Evansville or put him on the major-league active list. In the bushes, he could pitch every four or five days and perhaps regain something like his old form. The vital consideration, though, was that if he stayed with the big club he would *still* have to pitch every four or five days—against the frightening hitters of the Milwaukee Brewers and the New York Yankees. There would be no point in keeping him in Detroit and letting him sit on the bench. Wherever he was, he had to pitch.

My feeling was that they might as well keep him in Detroit. I might not have felt that way if the Tigers had been winning. But they had been losing, and the reason was bad pitching. *Terrible* pitching. The Tigers' staff, so promising in Florida, was having trouble getting anybody out for money. So what could they lose by letting Markie pitch? He could hardly be worse than what they were getting.

Apparently the Tigers, although they did not deign to consult me, agreed. They kept The Bird and they let him pitch. At this writing, he has started two games, won none and lost one. But it hasn't all been disaster. In his last start, he held Milwaukee to one run in five innings. At that point, although no one mentioned it, he had turned in the best performance of any Tiger pitcher in more than a week.

Unfortunately, he stayed in and got bombarded before

he could get the second out in the sixth. He was, of course, bitterly disappointed, but there is a bright side to the story. Not exactly glowing, but worth thinking about. The best thing that seems to be true of Fidrych right now is that his arm doesn't hurt. He hasn't been dominating enemy batters, so this significant fact has been largely overlooked. But if we had been told two months ago that The Bird would be throwing hard without pain by the middle of May, we would have been dancing in the streets.

My cautious opinion is that *if nothing more goes wrong*, Mark Fidrych can be a successful pitcher again in the major leagues. Maybe he can be as good as he was at twenty-one, but no one really expects that. Not now, anyway. What we hope is that he'll work his way past the tentative stage and become a regular member of the staff, pitching every fifth day not because he needs the work but because the Tigers need him.

Les Moss, the Tigers manager, is demonstrating an almost abnormal sensitivity to Fidrych's situation, and to the team's position in relation to this unusual young man. If he's ready by June, says Moss, that will be great, but if it takes till September that will be okay, too. It is easy enough to say that Moss has little choice in the matter since the Tigers aren't going anywhere anyway. But the fact is that it is almost unprecedented for a pitcher who is trying to work his way back into condition after an injury to be given a regular spot in the starting rotation. Every fifth day, weather permitting, Fidrych starts a big-league game (thus far, each time against a very rough team), although his chances of winning are roughly those of an untried rookie. This treatment gives some idea of the almost reverent regard in which his former skills are held. A man who has lost a priceless diamond ring in five acres of thick brush will search for it endlessly against all odds of ever finding it. To the Tigers, Mark Fidrych is that ring, and since they have seen an ephemeral gemlike glint at a great distance (the arm doesn't hurt), they will keep at it until either they find it or all hope is gone.

If Moss's attitude is surprising, The Bird's is remarkably mature for one who so recently was considered an incurable flake. His behavior on the field hasn't changed: he still kneels down and landscapes the mound before an inning; he still waves his arms and shouts encouragement to his teammates after a putout; he still asks for a new ball every time the other team gets a hit—all the things, in fact, that made him so endearing in the first place. But off the field, he has become a thoughtful, even a serious, adult. It must be remembered that Fidrych is a celebrity. He cannot, like some pitchers, slink off into the darkness after a defeat, or just shake it off with "you win some, you lose some." After every game, he must submit to a televised interview, answering the same questions over and over again. No, the arm didn't hurt. Yes, he felt good out there, but he was coming in too high; he has to keep the ball low to be effective. No, he doesn't know when he'll pitch again; that's up to the manager; when you work for a company you do what you're told to do. Since he hasn't had a really good outing yet, these interviews cannot be much fun, but in the main he handles them with dignity and quiet composure, both qualities foreign to The Bird we used to know. If it's all over, he says, "that's a part of life I'll have to accept."

What must also be remembered is that Mark Fidrych did not prepare for this year's comeback attempt by rest and light exercise. He *worked*. His physical therapists have reported on how hard he worked, day after day, dragging himself out of bed on cold winter mornings to go to the gym and put himself through hours of boring and exhausting physical toil. So he might be forgiven for thinking life has dealt him a bum hand if it turns out that all his labor has gone for naught. But "I look at what I had before and what I have now, and now is a lot better," says Mark.

The Shoulder Monster is a merciless and unpredictable enemy. If it is destined to end Mark's playing career at the age of twenty-five, he'll be all right. The physical pain he has endured during the last three years may, indeed, conquer him. But the mental anguish, which must have been worse, has made a survivor of him. If it ends this year (or whenever it ends), Mark will be ready for it. "When it's gone," he says, "all you can say is: it's gone, and this is what I got out of it."

Baseball can hardly afford to lose so skillful and colorful a player. But it now seems that he can face the future without baseball, or at least without fame. He has learned, the hard way, what some veterans don't find out until they are thirty-five or forty (or never): after baseball, there is still a life to live. Mark says he's gotten religion. I am not one to knock the Almighty (I know when I'm overmatched), but I think there's a better way of putting it. He has grown up.

❊   ❊   ❊

The reader is warned. Do not, under pain of legal action, quote me as saying that a curveball doesn't curve. That old canard has been discredited a hundred times since it first turned up, which was, I suppose, two days after the first curveball was thrown. Many years ago, *Life* magazine dug up a physicist and a former big-league pitcher, who collaborated in a series of experiments which purported to prove that the curve was an optical illusion somehow induced by the spin of the ball.

The piece was thoroughly unconvincing and easily refuted. I recall the comment of a ballplayer who was a contemporary of the pitcher involved. "I always knew *his* curveball didn't curve," he said. (I have forgotten the names of both pitcher and critic. Sorry.)

Assuredly, however, a real curveball does curve. A good curveball pitcher can hit you in the knee while you're standing behind a tree. The curve may break in toward the batter or out away from him, depending on the pitcher's level of skill and whether he is right- or left-handed. It invariably breaks downward at the same time. It may drop sharply ("like it rolled off a table" is the prescribed description for the sinker of great merit) or ever so slightly. But it always happens.

So I didn't say a curveball doesn't really curve. What I *did* say is that a fastball doesn't really hop. It is physically impossible to throw a ball overhand and make it curve up. It's an optical illusion. But it works.

Friday
May 18th

THE WINDS OF DESPAIR

When the wind is favorable in the Windy City, rare things happen—as they happened yesterday in Wrigley Field. The Phillies and Cubs went right down to the wire in a sort of pitchers' duel (the pitchers vied with each other to see which could remain alive longest)—past the wire actually, because it took an extra furlong to decide the winner. Mike Schmidt's home run in the tenth pulled it out for the Phils, 23 to 22.

There were 11 home runs altogether. Schmidt had 2; Dave Kingman of the Cubs had 3. Bill Buckner of the Cubs drove in 7 runs, Kingman 6. Bob Boone led the Phils in RBI's with a rather modest 5.

In any game as wild as this, I look for the odd little circumstance that nobody else saw fit to comment on, but which plainly affected the outcome of the game. It's almost always there, but sometimes you have to see the game to spot it. In this case it's crystal clear; it jumps right out of the box score at you. It involves Randy Louis Lerch, the Phillies'

starting pitcher and a man I have always admired on the
strength of his name alone. Randy Louis didn't pitch very
well; he retired only one man and he gave up five hits and
five runs before they could get him off the field. But he
made his contribution. Fortunately for him, his team batted
first, and because they were on a hitting spree they ran clear
through the lineup. So Lerch got a chance to bat before he
was ever required to pitch. He hit a home run. Because of
his bat, the first inning ended with the Phils leading, 7–6,
instead of tied at 6-all. Was it important? Well, when you
win by one run, it's fair to say that *every* run is the winning
run.

The papers report that the Phils were jubilant in the dressing room after the game. That's natural enough, I guess, but
in the larger view I don't think either club had much to
cheer about. These are two teams picked to contend for the
divisional title. (That is, the consensus picked the Phils,
and I sort of liked the Cubs.) What this game says about
the Cubs' pitching does not sound like championship to me.
And a team whose pitching staff gives up 22 runs has
scarcely more reason for optimism than one whose staff
gives up 23.

*   *   *

Home runs are no novelty for Randy Lerch. He hit two
of them last September 30th in a title-clinching victory over
Pittsburgh on the next-to-last day of the season. This is
something we have lost in the American League—the thrill
of the unexpected hit by the pitcher. What Tiger fan can
forget Mickey Lolich's single in the seventh inning of the
fifth game of the '68 World Series? It started the rally that
won the game and kept the Tigers alive just when everyone
was pronouncing them dead.

The key fact here, though, was that it took nerve for
Mayo Smith, the Tiger manager, to let Lolich bat at all. Trailing, 3 to 2, with only three innings to play, he could not have

been criticized for sending Gates Brown (the best pinch hitter in baseball) up to hit for the pitcher. But Mayo still wanted Lolich's arm in the game.

The designated-hitter rule in the American League has perhaps added some excitement to the sport. After all, most pitchers *are* lousy hitters. But it has eliminated the single most important question in managerial strategy—when to hit for a pitcher who is one run behind but pitching well— and to that extent the game in our league has become less interesting.

❊   ❊   ❊

Musing on Mickey Lolich's three World Series wins in 1968, that wonderful year, I got to wondering if any pitcher had ever won three games for a team that *lost* the Series. So it was off to the record book for a little of the nitpicking research for which I am justly famed. (Actually, it's only nitpicking if you are, say, a tax examiner; in a baseball fan it's classified as harmless dementia.) I found my man, and an interesting story. In the World Series of 1903, Deacon Phillippe pitched *five complete games* for Pittsburgh. He won three of them, and pitched well enough to have won one of the others if his team had gotten him some runs.

The 1903 Series, the first ever played, was scheduled for nine games and actually went eight before Boston won it. The Red Sox also had a three-game winner in that Series, Bill Dinneen, who shut out the Pirates in the final game for his third victory (Phillippe's second loss). Besides the Deacon—Charles Louis Phillippe of Rural Retreat Virginia —Pittsburgh used four other pitchers in the Series. Boston used only three in all, and could have done better with two. Between them, Dinneen and Cy Young pitched sixty-nine of the seventy-one innings in which the Pirates batted.

The generations overlap. Twenty-six years after his Series heroics, Bill Dinneen was an umpire in the first major-league game I ever saw.

Wednesday
May 23rd

AN OLD SUMMER BOY

Gee Walker is paralyzed. The last news I heard was that he had been lying in a Mississippi state hospital for more than a year, the victim of an accident. He would like to hear from old friends in Detroit, they say. Well, I imagine he has a few friends here, and I'm reasonably certain they're old. Few pieces of information are better calculated to mark the relentless passage of time for me than the simple realization that Gee Walker is seventy-one years old.

Gerald Holmes (Gee) Walker, who played in the outfield for the Tigers in the '30s, was one of my heroes, one of the "boys of summer" of my springtime years, in Roger Kahn's felicitous phrase. (No one ever borrowed a title from a poet to happier purpose.)

Gee Walker was one of those players whose legend was larger than life, who inspired extravagant stories, many of which are probably true. One of the most famous Walker stories concerns the time he stole second base when it was already occupied. Sliding into the bag, he looked up into the face of another Tiger, who inquired, "Where do you think you're going?"

"Back to first if I can get there," said Gee. He didn't make it, but he gave it the old Walker try.

The current cliché "He came to play" might have been coined for Gee Walker. He *played* baseball as if it were a game instead of a business. And he was good at it. Tales of his reckless antics have tended to disguise the fact that he was a very good ballplayer. Look at the record: 1,784 games, a lifetime batting average of .294, 399 doubles, 124 home runs, 997 RBI's, 223 stolen bases. Not bad at all.

There was an interesting, if rather mystifying, story about the time Gee Walker was sent out to coach first base. A Tiger hitter tried to stretch a clean single into a double and was thrown out easily at second. "Why didn't you hold him up?" was the irate, but reasonable, question put to Walker when he returned to the dugout.

"I yelled, 'Gee!' real loud," Walker indignantly replied.

Even back in the '30s, that took some explaining. Walker was a Mississippi farm boy, and as everyone who had ever driven a team of horses knew, "Gee" means turn right. If he had wanted the runner to turn left—i.e., go to second base—he would have yelled, "Haw!" Unfortunately, the runner was apparently a city boy and required instructions of a more urban character.

Like many players of volatile temperament, Gee Walker occasionally got into trouble with his manager, and I still recall the play that put him in a doghouse it took him years to get out of. Batting with two out in the late innings of a game in August of 1933, he slashed a shot directly at the second baseman, who scooped it up before Gee could get out of the batter's box. In disgust, he threw down the bat and trotted out to his position in left field. The second baseman thought it was some kind of trick (in those days, you always ran out ground balls). Cautiously, he edged toward first, finally tossing the ball underhand to the first baseman. Everyone laughed but Bucky Harris, the Tiger manager. He sent Jo-Jo White out to replace Walker in the outfield, and there he stayed throughout the 1934 and '35 seasons, while the Tigers won two pennants and a World Series.

It cannot be assumed, naturally, that Gee Walker would have been a starter on those championship teams if it hadn't been for his little fit of temper. But there is no doubt that the incident gave Jo-Jo White the chance to display his skills, and he made the most of it. He was a fine fielder and in 1934 he became (for one year only) a .313 hitter.

Mickey Cochrane took over as Tiger manager in '34, and he made White his regular center fielder. Gee Walker was

Gerald Holmes (Gee) Walker. The people's choice.

hardly forgotten; he was the fourth outfielder and, in fact, played almost as much as White did in the pennant-winning years. He hit .300 in '34 and .301 in '35, so there's no question about his contribution to the victorious cause. But he was never officially a *regular*, and the knowledge that one impulsive act may have cost him that honorable designation must have been painful.

In 1936, playing full time again, Walker hit .353, an average that would have led the league a year earlier. But '36 was a hitters' year, and .353 was bettered by no fewer than five batters, led by Luke Appling with .388.

Gerald Walker was a first-class ballplayer, but he was somewhat overshadowed on a team that had Hank Greenberg, Charlie Gehringer, Goose Goslin and Mickey Cochrane. (I note that without conscious intent, I have just named four Hall of Fame players from the same lineup.) With the fans, though, he was king, one of those rare players whose crowd appeal transcends even their unquestioned ability. He was "the people's choice," and if the Tigers had been run by popular vote he would have started every game.

The true measure of Gee Walker's popularity in Detroit was indicated by the strange fate of his successor. After the 1937 season, the Tigers traded Gee to the White Sox and replaced him with Dixie Walker (no relation). Dixie Walker was a good outfielder and a .300 hitter, but the Detroit fans were outraged. With the irrational cruelty of which "sporting" crowds are often capable, they made the new man's life miserable. Dixie Walker was hated in Detroit—not because he didn't have a good year (he hit .308), but simply because he wasn't Gee. It was brutally unfair, but it was also the best possible evidence of the esteem in which Gerald Walker was held in Detroit.

Dixie Walker was driven out of town by the Tiger fans. Early in his second season with the team, he was sent to the Brooklyn Dodgers in what I guess was a straight cash deal, because I don't recall that Detroit got anything visible in return for him. (We fans were not allowed to look at the cash.) He had a long and successful career with the Dodgers, where he played on a couple of pennant winners, won a batting championship and by ironic co-incidence achieved the same kind of popularity with the Brooklyn fans that his namesake had known in Detroit. Some sportswriter referred to him as "the people's cherce," and the Brooklynese nickname caught on around the league, which must have puzzled his kinfolk down in Georgia.

Detroit fans were wrong about Dixie Walker, obviously. Fans often are. But they felt that the Walker playing left field for the Tigers was an impostor. And they wouldn't have it.

What made Gee Walker such a favorite? I suppose the crowds somehow sensed that he loved playing this little boys' game, and loved being applauded when he did it well. I hope he remembers the affection he generated in Detroit, and the joy he brought to many people in those Depression years when joy was in short supply. But how could he forget?

Saturday
May 26th

HIBERNATION

It's all over for The Bird. At least for now. He has gone inactive, and in all probability won't pitch again this season. His good effort against Milwaukee turned out to be a mirage, and the Yankees destroyed him next time out. I wasn't convinced, even then, that he should be taken off the active list. Why not let him build up his arm by using it? But I am on the outside looking in, and those who are on the inside looking puzzled don't feel that this is the answer. He can rebuild the strength in his arm better by exercise and specialized treatment than by pitching, they say. And thinking it over, I don't suppose an 0–16 record would do much for his morale, either.

So that's the way it stands now. The arm does not hurt. The arm is weak. If the arm can be made strong again (and still doesn't hurt), it's on to '80, when once more into the fray The Bird will march. The phrase that has become such an integral part of Mark's life, "doctors are hopeful," has been called into service again. If doctors are hopeful, can The Bird be less so? I am afraid that if I were he, I would be teetering on the brink of despair. He says he's not. I applaud him . . . and will continue to hope for his slow, painful recovery.

Incidentally, it turned out that the Tigers couldn't have sent him to Evansville if they had wanted to. He would have to clear waivers, and one team has refused to let him pass. Well, if it's true that pitching every five days is not the answer to his problem, that would appear to be academic.

Monday
May 28th

ON THE ROAD

TORONTO—All baseball fans are provincial. They don't want the best team to win, they want *their* team to win. That's what keeps the game going. To verify this thesis, you have only to go to Toronto.

Toronto is not only the provincial capital of Ontario, but the seat of provincial baseball loyalties which range across the continent. There is a large brotherhood of Yankee fans here. There are Dodger fans, Red Sox fans, virtually every kind of fan, including probably at least one Cleveland fan.

Toronto, you see, has been a good baseball town for almost as long as Detroit and New York. The old Maple Leafs of the International League had a long and glorious history;

some of the great major-league stars began their careers here. So Toronto people knew and followed the game, and developed loyalties to teams they had never seen. When the Blue Jays came to town two years ago, they did more than give local fans a big-league team of their own to root for; they also gave all those New York and Boston and Detroit fans a chance to see their favorite teams in the flesh once in a while. (Dodger fans will have to wait for a World Series, which may be quite a wait.) During the Blue Jays' first season, I attended a Yankees game here, and found myself surrounded by New York fans screaming for Blue Jay blood. These were Toronto people, you understand, doubtless fiercely loyal to their city, but in baseball they had been Yankee fans for years, and you can't change that overnight —or, in some cases, ever.

Baseball is fun in Toronto, one of the most attractive cities in the world. The Blue Jay fans are enthusiastic, grateful for small favors (a home run, a good catch) and reasonably good-natured about losing, although that can't go on much longer. The team improved slightly in its second season, but seems headed for the worst year of its short history in '79. If so, no doubt heads will roll. The grace period is running out.

Exhibition Park is a football stadium temporarily converted. It makes a nice enough ball park, although like most new parks it's a bit too symmetrical for my taste. (That is, it is symmetrical.) The only incongruous note is the sight of those left-field stands stretching off almost to infinity, the most distant seats seeming to be part of some other time warp. If those seats are ever sold (which I assume a benevolent management has no intention of doing), the buyers will do well to save the tickets for souvenirs, stay home and listen to the radio.

The Blue Jays have one or two proven ballplayers. Rico Carty is forty years old, more or less (more, I suspect), still hits with power and has a lifetime batting average of .303.

He can't run at all and is a grateful beneficiary of the designated-hitter rule. He is not, obviously, the sort of player around whom one builds for the future.

John Mayberry is a strange case. He is a huge, powerful black man who had three fine years in Kansas City, still delivers the odd home run (22 last year), but unaccountably seems to be growing old at twenty-nine. Too bad, because he is, according to Ken Becker, a Toronto writer, "the most intrinsically decent human being" on the club. When he sold Mayberry to Toronto last year, Whitey Herzog, the Kansas City manager, said, "I still like John as a person, but I just didn't want him playing for us anymore." Apparently everyone thinks he's a great guy, but the official accolade "wonderful human being" is reserved for the reasonably well-behaved ballplayer who also hits a ton. John probably rated that title in 1975, when he had 34 home runs and 106 RBI's. Two years later, when his batting average fell to .230, although his character remained good, the Royals didn't want him playing for them anymore. He was still a great guy, but no longer a wonderful human being.

None the less, the Jays had better hang on to him unless they can get a legitimate big-league ballplayer for him. At the moment, he's the only one they have. This is apparent from the fact that the local hero is an outfielder named Rick Bosetti, who would have a hard time making the starting lineup of a contending team. He is twenty-six years old, a sensational (if occasionally uncertain) fielder with a good arm, and has a lifetime batting average of .256, with five home runs in 655 times at bat. He is said to be a coming star, so maybe he *is* the kind of player around whom you build a winner. But the figures don't show it.

✿　　✿　　✿

My son Terry and I saw a good ball game (from a Detroit standpoint) tonight. The Tigers won it, 6 to 2, with Jack Morris holding the Jays to seven hits. Four of these, and the two runs, came in the second inning. For the rest of the game, he was almost perfect. The Tigers got thirteen hits off Dave Lemanczyk in less than seven innings. Lemanczyk is having a good year for the Jays and is considered their stopper. Pitchers get better with experience, of course, but somehow, remembering his futile efforts with Detroit, I find it hard to think of Dave as the cornerstone of a winning staff.

The hitting star for the Tigers was Champ Summers, a man I had never heard of before. First time up, he pulled a long home run over the right-field fence, winning my heart before I even knew who he was. (He is, it turns out, a former National League fringe player who had a sensational year at Indianapolis last year: .368, 124 RBI's, 34 HR's.) It seems I can't turn my back for a moment without the Tigers' making a deal. This one was with the Reds for a player (whom?) to be named later.

❋ ❋ ❋

The American League Red Book for 1979, in appraising the Blue Jays' chances, says that moving Luis Gomez to second base will "free Dave McKay for a reserve role." To "free" a player, in this sort of context, means to permit him to return to the position he plays best. I guess this lets McKay know where he stands. Or sits.

Tuesday
May 29th

CONDUCT UNBECOMING

TORONTO—"It was easy to think of baseball players I know and like, because there is no finer, friendlier, cleaner-cut group of citizens than the men who play our national pastime." Thus spake Malcolm Child in the preface to his book *How to Play Big League Baseball*, published in 1951.

Now comes Ken Becker, writing in *Toronto Life* magazine in 1979. He gave up a plush job as baseball writer for *The Toronto Sun*, he says, because he was ashamed of glorifying a bunch of guys who were, in the main, stupid, narrow-minded and insensitive—"a secret society, a narcissistic cult of perpetual children, rewarded and adored beyond any equitable scale of human accomplishment."

It wouldn't have been quite so bad, says Becker, "if they felt some sense of responsibility for the position they enjoy in our society. They don't. They abuse it." They live, he says, "in Never Never Land, a land we created for them but a land we must enter with caution unless bearing only praise and adulation."

It is sad but true that ballplayers are the very antithesis of the intellectual. By this I do not mean that they don't write learned books, or read them. I mean they do not read any books. (I am exaggerating, but not much.) I have never understood this. I am not being naive. I am well aware that college football players are not recruited for their academic prowess, and that the first-string athlete who graduates *summa cum laude* is so rare as to provoke newspaper columns redolent of awe. Yet I have known good football players who were intelligent and reasonably well read, outstanding athletes who had heard of Virginia Woolf. But there is a fine line between the merely excellent athlete and the one who becomes a professional. In some cases, the man who does not make it may have superior skills, but he lacks certain attributes required of the pro—one of which, it seems clear, is a total absence of intellectual curiosity.

I am, you were about to say, spouting generalities. This is said to be a cardinal sin for a serious writer (and I am reasonably serious), but in this case I offer no apology for the stereotype. Among baseball players especially, it is *almost* absolute.

Obviously, there are exceptions. Rhodes scholars in pro football and basketball. Whizzer White. Jim Brosnan. Jim

Bouton. Sparky Lyle. See how quickly, when discussing literate ballplayers, one descends from the sublime to the ridiculous.

I have always felt that the reason most ballplayers hated Jim Bouton was not that he wrote a book about some of their naughty little habits and practices, but simply that he wrote a book. As for Sparky Lyle, who "wrote" a best seller, *The Bronx Zoo*, he hastens to point out that it's the only book he has ever read. I detect in this a subtle artifice to fend off the question "Who read it to you?"

Unquestionably the most famous intellectual in baseball history was the late Moe Berg—lawyer; philosopher; secret agent; fluent speaker of nine, eleven or seventeen languages; graduate of the Sorbonne. Berg was an authentic super-mentality and a fascinating man. Unfortunately, he wasn't much of a ballplayer, but he spent fifteen years in the major leagues. He was in love with the game, and managers liked having a genius on the roster.

Having paid my respects to the exceptions, I return to my original contention. The baseball player who is seen reading a book—not Aldous Huxley but, say, *The Thorn Birds* or *The Day of the Jackal*—is usually regarded by his team-mates as some sort of freak. This is too bad, I guess, although it wouldn't matter much if that were the only problem. But it's not, as Becker points out in his shocking article. It shocked me a bit, and I am not particularly susceptible to shock; I assume it would stagger Malcolm Child, who saw professional ballplayers as fine, friendly and clean-cut.

I suspect, oddly enough, that both Child and Becker are accurate reporters. Writing in 1951, Child was dealing with players who were well paid but far from rich. They appreciated their preferred status and, although I doubt they were all quite as lily-white as Child implies, did not wish deliberately to do anything to endanger it. Like well-paid people in any field, they recognized their responsibility to their profession and to their own self-esteem. Today's players, grossly overpaid, cannot believe they are not entitled to behave as grossly as they wish, and a lot of them do. They are largely amoral, because morality (or, for that matter, immorality) requires a basic sense of right-and-wrong, which in turn calls for the capacity to reason. Reasoning is a function of the intellect, which most ballplayers specifically and deliberately reject. (I stress that when I say they are "grossly overpaid," I don't mean the million-dollar players. I mean the utility infielder who makes more than a corporation vice-president, the mop-up relief pitcher who seldom gets into a game but is paid more than a distinguished professor of law. When they are rewarded so amply for such meager talents, is it any wonder they lose all perspective?)

Am I exaggerating the situation? Well, listen to Becker, who traveled for a year with the Toronto Blue Jays. "There was," he says, "the barmaid in the Kansas City hotel who told of ballplayers walking in and shouting, 'Who wants to screw a ballplayer?'" And "the stewardess in San Francisco who said one of her colleagues was raped in a toilet at 35,000 feet but no one believed she wasn't merely trying to score a jock.

"There was the charter flight with the Blue Jays when one of the players exposed and fondled himself every time the stewardesses walked past him; the same player bragged that he had urinated during a game on every grass field in the American League. There was also a commercial flight when a couple of the Blue Jays . . . refused to buckle their seat belts and put out their cigarettes" and a team official had to make a special request to them "to conform to the regulations routinely followed by the rest of us."

There is a lot more, equally horrendous, but you *must* get the picture by now; it's ugly. And bear in mind that these are the Toronto Blue Jays, a bunch of Humpty Dumptys with scarcely enough talent among them to equal a single George Kell (one of the 1951 players included in the earlier book). "They betray the child's perception of them, the perception we all once shared," says Becker, and he relates a story about a little boy who politely asked Rick Bosetti for an autograph and was greeted with a friendly obscenity. He reported that incident, says Becker, and Bosetti was fined $250 for it. A couple of months later, the Jays hired Bosetti to be the team's goodwill ambassador during the off-season.

The question you must be asking (as I certainly am) is why this is allowed to go on. Why are ballplayers coddled and handled with kid gloves—especially ballplayers who ought to be incredulously grateful for their undeserved good fortune? Can't baseball teams demand the same public conduct from their employees that any other company surely would? Can't they fine and suspend players for this sort of behavior? (There is hardly a player on the Toronto team who couldn't be suspended for the rest of the season without any visible effect on the team's performance.) Are they afraid that the big-name players might refuse to conform, and that they might have to suspend one of them? Are they afraid of flak from the players' union? Would Marvin Miller leap piously to the defense of a player's right to expose and fondle himself?

Baseball had better clean up its act. Unless nobody cares. I would hate to think nobody cares. Or, worse yet, that most fans *do* think it's cute.

      ❀   ❀   ❀

In case you're wondering, I see no inconsistency between my earlier statement that I approve of fringe players' being paid a living wage and my present one that many of them are horribly overpaid. None at all. There may be some inconsistency with my expressed wish to have shared the "colorful, semi-articulate, generally obscene banter" of big-league players, in the light of what I have said here. But I don't really think so. I hadn't read Becker's article when I wrote that. And he wasn't much concerned with banter.

Finally, I guess I should point out that Becker was apparently talking about a minority of the Blue Jays, although he mentioned enough separate incidents to make it clear it was a good-sized minority. But the others, as he points out, share the guilt. They are "silent accomplices, too self-obsessed to see or hear, much less react" to their team-mates' odious conduct.

Wednesday
May 30th

DECLINE OF THE CARDS

MONTREAL—A week or two ago, I got a call from a young friend of mine who lives in Arizona, writes mournfully funny poetry and views the world through glasses ground to an unregistered prescription. He was concerned about the future of baseball. So are we all, but not surprisingly, Steve's apprehensions are prompted by considerations that wouldn't occur to most people. He is, for one thing, heart-sick over the baseball-card situation, which has apparently reached crisis proportions without my even being aware of it.

Steve is in his early thirties and I have known him since he was a little kid, hanging around with my oldest son, making slightly off-center comments about commonplace things and occasionally writing secret messages on dollar bills and sending them back into the marketplace. (That eventually brought a visit from our local FBI man. No rough stuff, though. This was in the old days, when boys were still thought to be boys.) When Steve got older, he joined the Army, where he once showed up for morning formation wearing a Confederate uniform.

"The problem, as I see it," he said earnestly from far away among the cacti, "is that the players are making so much money now they refuse to pose for the Topps photographers." (Topps is the bubble-gum company that distributes the baseball cards.) "So they are using candid shots, telephoto shots, whatever they can get. It's terrible. Some of the cards show guys clowning in the dugout, getting a drink from the water cooler, anything. When I think of the beautiful, carefully posed cards we had when I was a kid . . . remember George Crowe?"

I didn't, in fact, remember George Crowe very well. He was a fringe player for several National League teams during the '50s, a former pro basketball player who was almost thirty when he made the baseball major leagues. He was a hitter with some power, but this was almost irrelevant to the value of his card; cards were judged primarily on aesthetic appeal. I recall that a particular favorite of my son's was a far more obscure player, a relief pitcher for the Giants named Sherman (Roadblock) Jones. On the strength of a handsome baseball card and a winning nickname, Roadblock looked like a cinch for immortality. Sadly, however, his lifetime total of games won (two) proved a disqualifying factor.

Sam Mele, a legitimate big-league player (and later manager), was regarded almost with contempt because, for some reason, his card was too common. I don't know why; maybe the machine got stuck. Every kid in our neighborhood had at least five or six Sam Meles, so they weren't even useful for trading purposes. The only thing you could do with them was decorate them with beards and mustaches (which the players seldom came equipped with in those days), so the surplus cards came to be called "mustaches." To this day, in our family, a useless duplicate of any commodity is referred to as a mustache.

I expressed mild dismay over the current state of the art, but since I assumed Steve was no longer a serious collector, I suggested that his anxiety must be purely academic.

"I am thinking of the youth of today," he said. "It's a real hardship, and I am worried about how it may affect their interest in our national game. Those cards are a disgrace.

"And," he went on, "I am also very disturbed about Montreal."

"Why?" I asked.

"Because they are winning," he said.

"So?"

"Do you want a Canadian team winning the World Series?"

The last thing I would have thought Steve guilty of was xenophobia. But he obviously drew the line at foreign subversion of baseball, even by our friendly neighbors to the north, and even though none of Montreal's agents is a real Canadian. (On the basis of national origin, there is actually a much greater threat from the Caribbean element among the Expos. Three of them come from the Dominican Republic, and two of these are coaches, which could indicate that they are subtly easing their way into influential management positions. The only fallacy in this otherwise ominous hypothesis is that coaches are the least influential members of any baseball organization. Once in a while, they can get a man to stop at third base. But that's about it.)

I chided Steve for this narrow-minded attitude, but gently, since I felt sure it was adopted for purposes of stirring up controversy rather than out of any deep-seated feeling. But I am not one to take any threat to baseball's tradition lightly. Quietly, on my own, and without consulting the commissioner, I have come to Montreal to see for myself.

Thursday
May 31st

SEND IN THE CLOWNS

MONTREAL—The French they are a funny race. So ran the opening line of a bawdy poem I remember from somewhere. The second line is unprintable, at least by my prim standards, but fortunately it has nothing to do with the subject at hand, anyway. The subject is baseball in French—or more prop-

erly, baseball in a French atmosphere. My first reaction was
that it is revolting. But first reactions, conditioned to shock,
are likely to be extreme. It is not revolting. There is no way
you can make baseball revolting, especially when played by
two good teams like the Expos and the Phillies.

Irritating is what it is. Irritating as hell.

I do not, be it understood, have any objection to the
announcements in French and English that issue from the
public-address system every few moments. I am, in fact,
pleased that baseball has added a beautiful language to its
repertoire. French is a worthy new partner for the tongues
in which the game has traditionally been played, which are
English, Spanish and Japanese.

What I do object to violently is the notion which apparently prevails here that a baseball game is merely the central
attraction in a giant carnival. Music blares, clowns cavort
and the game announcer sounds like a circus ringmaster,
introducing each batter as if he had come directly from a
command performance before the crowned heads of six
countries. "Le quatrième frappeur, batting fourth," he says
in a voice fraught with tension, then with a rising inflection,
drawing out every syllable, "To-neee Peeer-EZZZ!" I rather
expected Tony to be shot out of a cannon, or at least to
cartwheel up to the plate, but he just walked up there
swinging a bat, like any other sixteen-year veteran who
knows his business. (I could not see the announcer, of
course, but I assume he was wearing a top hat and a swallow-
tail coat.)

Perhaps, before I paint myself as a totally sour observer,
I had better break this whole thing down into good and bad
—what I like about baseball in Montreal, and what I hate.
There is a lot of both, as you may not have guessed up to
now.

I like, first of all, getting to the ball park. You take the
subway, which is clean and fast. I asked a man where I
should get off for the Olympic Stadium. He did not speak

English, so there ensued one of those comic conversations so beloved of humorous essayists in an earlier day. I thought he told me to get off at the Pont Neuf, which I was pretty sure was in Paris unless they'd moved it. (It's possible; London Bridge is in Arizona.) He solved the problem by pointing to the Métro diagram on the wall behind him. The station he indicated was Pie IX, which I guess is named in honor of the ninth Pope Pius. So my confusion was, I stoutly maintain, excusable. What can you do with a language in which "nine" and "new" are the same word?

Anyway, the man gave me to understand that he himself was getting off at Pie IX. How nice, I thought, that this old man who doesn't even speak English is a fan of the great American game. He wasn't, though. When the train stopped at Pie IX, almost everyone got off, and my new friend (soon to be lost forever), looking around in wonder, asked me what was going on at the stadium. A track meet? A football game? "No, no, baseball," I said.

"Ah, baseball," he said, looking mystified, and hurried off in the other direction.

I had, foolishly, wondered if there would be any difficulty in finding the park when I got off the subway. There would be great difficulty, actually, in *not* finding the park (presumably my recent friend knew the only escape route). You proceed from the station through caverns measureless to man, all magnificently tiled and decorated, until you finally emerge into a large chamber which might look like the entrance area of any ball park except that it, too, is completely tiled and enclosed. Before you have even entered the stadium, you begin to get some idea of how Montreal went $9 billion (or some other totally unreal sum) into debt when it built this place for the '76 Olympics.

I bought a program, which cost a dollar and a half and contained articles in French on Pete Rose, English on Ross Grimsley, and both languages on Bill Lee. Inside I discovered a detachable scoreboard (*carte de pointage*) on thin stiff cardboard, the very best kind.

(All this was last evening. This afternoon, now a wise old Montreal veteran, I went again. Unwilling to pay another buck-fifty for the same program, I looked for and found a stand that sold the scorecards separately for 25 cents. These are exactly the same sort of cards we used to get at Navin Field—now Tiger Stadium—for a dime in the '30s. They have increased in price only 150 percent, and are thus a bargain when compared with hot dogs, for example, which also used to cost a dime and are now almost a dollar.

(I also discovered, on my way home last night, that the subway stops directly beneath my hotel. So it is possible to travel from the ball park to the hotel without ever going out-of-doors. If the planned stadium roof is installed, you will be able to go from your hotel to the stadium, see a ball game, return to your hotel and go quietly to bed without ever knowing that a violent storm is going on outside. That is, you will if you stay at that hotel, which I will publicly name upon receipt of what is known, I believe, as "a mutually agreeable sum.")

The Olympic Stadium is awesome. Gigantic and futuristic, it seems to contain enough seats for *tout le monde* (French for "everybody" but literally "all the world," which in this case is more accurate). If, in some distant century, it becomes necessary to transport thousands of earth colonists to Alpha Centauri, I picture them making the trip in something that looks rather like the *Stade Olympique*. People say it's cold and impersonal, and that there's not a bad seat in the house. I don't know exactly how you make a stadium warm and personal (I think it takes time and a lot of weathering), but it's true that there are no bad seats, although some of them are rather far from the action. They are comfortable seats, too, which is nice to know if you've been in a few ball parks.

I had nearly perfect seats, thanks to my son who lives in Toronto but has connections in high places all over Canada. This is the same son who once so admired Roadblock Jones, and used to carry one of those little athletic-equipment bags with ROADBLOCK printed on it in small, neat white letters. The years fly past, and I miss them. Some of them.

The playing field in the stadium is, of course, symmetrical and hard as a rock. But I'm not going on about that again.

The scoreboard is a veritable Niagara of information, pouring forth all the data about every batter who comes up except his mother's maiden name. It also flashes frequent advertisements, sometimes simultaneously with the game information. I was momentarily confused, while reading some player's batting *moyenne* and total of *coups de circuit*, to discover *"y'a rien comme un Coke"* nestled in among the numbers. Did this represent the player's personal view, I wondered, or was it just a general statement of fact? If the latter, it was inaccurate. There *is* something like a Coke. It's a Pepsi. Other soft drinks are even better, of course.

So there are a lot of good things about baseball in Montreal, including for the first time a very good team. But they don't quite atone for the come-to-the-fair, greatest-show-on-earth, tell-ya-what-I'm-gonna-do hype and hoopla that you have to endure in order to enjoy them.

What in God's name makes people think there is something disagreeable about hearing the normal sounds that ought to go with a baseball game? The murmur of the crowd, for one thing, that goes on long after the cheers have died down, or starts up when a favorite pinch hitter emerges unannounced from the dugout. Somebody (I think it was Harry Heilmann) used to call it "the voice of baseball."

The voice of baseball is inaudible in Montreal, drowned out by organ music played, at a decibel level that would wake The Grateful Dead, whenever there is a moment's interruption in play (which in baseball, as its detractors are fond of pointing out, is most of the time).

And through it all gambols Youppi (or Jouppi), the lovable little clown who symbolizes Montreal's total alienation from the spirit of baseball past. He leads cheers, which is hardly necessary because Montreal fans cheer too much anyway. (They are like Southerners when they saw their first hockey games, applauding every time the goalie stopped a dying shot fired from the far end of the ice.) He interferes with players warming up. He struts around aping the umpires. Like a dead animal in a formal garden, or an ink stain on a damask tablecloth, he befouls the dignity and beauty of the game.

At last night's game, the dugout roof was wet from a late-afternoon rain. Youppi, between innings, would race along it and slide—presumably splashing the box-seat holders, but certainly obscuring their vision. This is typical of a management which apparently thinks the spectators have no right to a view of the field when the ball is not actually in play. I can't believe that none of those spectators was tempted to poke the clown in one of his movable eyes with a sharp stick. If I ever sit in one of those seats, I will bring a sharp stick with me.

The man inside Youppi (a sort of dog or small bear) is actually a rather talented pantomime comedian. On the stage, or especially in a circus, he would probably be a smash. At a ball game, he's a pain in the ass.

There *was* a ball game, incidentally. Two of them, in fact. The Expos won them both, completing a three-game sweep of the Phillies without giving up a single run. In both the games I saw, the Phils outhit them, but that doesn't show in the standings. Montreal now leads Philadelphia by three open lengths.

Bill Lee, wearing the longest beard seen on a baseball field since the days of the House of David, pitched a superb game last night. He gave up a leadoff double to Luzinski in the fourth, plus two other doubles, but none of the Phils who got them ever moved past second base. It is foolish for a

Bill Lee, before the beard.

spectator to assume he knows what a pitcher is thinking, but Lee *seemed* to be in absolute control and totally confident. He mixed his pitches beautifully, and several times threw first-pitch change-ups. You're supposed to show them the heat first and then throw the change. Lee showed them the fastball while they were waiting to bat, then let them see the slow one as soon as they got into the box. It worked. Everything worked. In the second inning, Gary Carter, the Montreal catcher, followed a Perez single with a line drive into the left-field stands, straight as a string and barely fair. Since the fence is only 99 meters from the plate at the foul line, it hardly seemed as if it ought to count, but it did and that was the ball game, 2–0. (The distance translates to 324.7992 feet, long enough to make a home run respectable, if not quite "prodigious.")

This afternoon, I went out to the ball park a full hour before the game. I hadn't done that in years, but I looked forward to it, remembering from my boyhood the shouts of the players during infield practice in the almost empty stadium. I got the almost empty stadium, but no shouts. Or no audible ones. From the moment I entered, the atonal notes of the monster organ attacked my ears and my sense of decency. For one solid hour it went on. What *is* it with these people that they think an organ indifferently played at racehorse speed and amplified to seismic volume is preferable to silence? If this is entertainment, I am ready at last to concede that civilization is crumbling.

Despite the awful racket, though, the stands filled gradually until there were about 22,000 present. I settled back in my marvelous seat, the whole field spread out before me, and watched the managers conferring at the plate, the pitchers warming up, all the hallowed procedures that signal the imminent start of a ball game.

Then out came Youppi, and I wished I were back at Tiger Stadium behind a post.

It was an interesting game, though. André Dawson led off the Montreal first with a double. The next batter moved him to third with a sacrifice bunt. Highly questionable strategy. In the first inning, you may sacrifice the man from first to second with none out, but if he's already on second you go for the big inning. You don't sacrifice the man from second to third unless he's the tying or winning run.

What did I know? Dawson *was* the winning run, but I didn't realize it until two hours later when the game ended, 1–0.

You have to be smart to be a big-league manager. Or lucky. Dick Williams is obviously both. He has won pennants on various North American coasts and is now shooting for one on the banks of the St. Lawrence. There is one school of thought which holds that a manager has little to do with a team's success. You get the right players, according to this theory, and all you need is a manager who won't louse things up. Precisely. That's what a good manager is: one who won't louse things up. Williams is that sort. He won a pennant at Boston with a cast of clean-shaven types, and he won two more of them at Oakland with a team that annually led the league in fur. The only possible inference is that he rolls with the punches and guesses right more often than not.

There is no way Williams could have known that Dawson was the winning run. Scott Sanderson, his pitcher, was 3–3, and not an especially good bet to pitch a shutout. He did, though, and that's what the papers will talk about tomorrow. Probably none of them will single out Rodney Scott's sacrifice bunt as the key to victory, but it was. When Warren Cromartie followed with a fly to center field, Dawson came home with the ball game.

If Williams had let Scott hit away, he might have gotten more runs or he might have gotten none. But he sensed somehow that this was a game in which one run in the first inning would be useful. Luck, maybe, but flawless managing unquestionably.

Conclusion: The Expos can win it all. (Chin up, Steve!) What they lack is that peculiar thing, pennant-race experience. Once you have been in a close struggle down to the wire, you are better fitted to win the next one. I don't know why, but it proves out. Still, I suspect that at the finish, the Expos will be, as they say at the track, "there or thereabouts." If the latter, wait till next year.

❖   ❖   ❖

In the eighth inning of today's game, Garry Maddox was sent in to run for the Phils' Tim McCarver, who had gotten a pinch-hit single with one out. Maddox tried to steal second. He is a good base runner, but this time he got a terrible jump on the ball (I was surprised he went through with it), Gary Carter made a perfect throw to second and Maddox was an easy out.

The fans gave Carter a two-minute standing ovation. I couldn't figure out what was going on. I thought the word must have passed through the stands that he had changed his name to Cartier, but no, it was just misplaced Gallic exuberance. Although it isn't limited to the Gauls. Tim Burke, writing in the Montreal *Gazette*, says that "you don't get much of an argument these days when you declare flat out that Carter is the best baseball player alive right now." I think if he declared that anywhere but in Montreal he might get an argument.

❖   ❖   ❖

A big black headline in today's *Journal de Montréal* reads: BILL LEE SE COUPE LA BARBE. After last night's win, Bill Lee shaved off his beard, astonishing his teammates, according to the story. Lee, who has a reputation as an oddball, and is an articulate and intelligent man (do you suppose he reads books?), had earlier explained why he grew the beard in the first place. He wanted to remind Don Zimmer, his manager at Boston last year, "every time he sees my picture," that the Red Sox had been eleven games in front when Lee was dropped from the starting rotation. They blew it on the last day of the season plus one, as you may remember.

I still recall with pleasure a TV interview I saw last September in which Lee explained to a reporter why the Yankees were catching the Red Sox in the stretch. "They have positive momentum," he said, "while we have negative momentum."

❋   ❋   ❋

Thirty years or so ago, I read a fine little story in *The New Yorker* (by Joel Sayre, I believe) describing the author's consternation when he had thought he might be required to explain baseball to André Gide. (Why is too complicated to go into.) Quickly, he tried to formulate a glossary of baseball terms in French. He had a lot of trouble with "pop fly" but finally came up with *crac-mouche*. I don't know what they call a pop fly in Montreal, but I'm pretty sure it's not that.

❋   ❋   ❋

The popular name here for the Olympic Stadium is "The Big O." Until they stop the music (and Youppi is humanely destroyed), you can read that as "the big zero."

❋   ❋   ❋

It occurs to me that the hideous way they present baseball in Montreal may after all have very little to do with French-Canadian manners and mores. It may have more to do with expansionism. New teams come into the major leagues without any feeling for baseball and the way it has been played for a hundred years. They don't realize that change should be gradual, not forced but growing out of the exigencies of a world in motion. They think, because baseball is entertainment, it is synonymous with show business. Above all, they do not understand the simple principle that less is more.

(But then, why *should* Montreal lack a baseball tradition?

The game has been played professionally here since the '90s. Were those different people—baseball fans instead of circus addicts—watching the Montreal Royals all those years? Or is it that having attained "major" status at last, they thought just baseball wasn't enough, that it had to be hoked up with ancillary tinsel? If so, how sad.)

The Youppi Syndrome, I believe, actually began in San Diego with a goddam chicken. I understand it's spreading. If Southern California does slide into the Pacific one dark night, it will be ample retribution for that. Nothing less would be.

To my friends in Detroit: We didn't know how lucky we were. Sure, it's been a long time since we've had a winner, but we can go to a baseball game and see (perhaps from behind a post) and *hear*—what else?—a baseball game.

To my friends in Toronto: If anyone there is thinking about dressing some guy up as a bird and calling him Bloojie, find him and stop him. Whatever it takes, do it!

Friday
June 1st

THE APPLE

NEW YORK—The last time I visited New York, my oldest son was carrying his ROADBLOCK bag and my youngest had to have his steak cut for him by a kindly waiter. Both of *them* have been back to the Big Apple many times. But for me it's been well over twenty years. Some quick impressions:

Place looks about the same. Can no longer afford steak for youngest son, which he could now cut unaided if here, although *his* son might need help.

Staying at famous old hotel. Publisher got me room at discount. Still costs seventy bucks a day. Hotel name and location beyond reproach, but room a bit timeworn. Opened door of medicine cabinet, entire cabinet swung out, affording view of ancient hotel innards; seems to be crumbling, but going to be here only three days.

Called hotel laundry, was told no service until Monday. Washed underwear, draped it around room. Maid must wonder how I can afford $70 room. Me too.

Figured would eat one meal in posh restaurant. Hotel boasts same. Checked menu outside door:

> Your first course. Russian beluga caviar on an ice socle.
> *For Two persons.* $85

Italics theirs. If can find another person with $42.50, may give it a try. Otherwise never know what socle is. (Looked up "socle" in dictionary. Says "plain rectangular block plinth." No help.)

Ate in deli. More my speed. Walls of every New York deli, no matter how decrepit, covered with signed pictures of famous inscribed: *To my pal Louie who makes the greatest chopped liver in New York.* Had egg-salad sandwich, coffee. Hot day, no air conditioning, table grimy, but had second cup of coffee, hoping Candice Bergen would drop in. No luck.

Passed tiny *boîte* on 39th Street jammed between two large crumbling buildings. Called "Sandwiched Inn." Liked it. Easily amused by New York humor. Provincial?

No tickets available for Yankee game tonight. Didn't care. Very tired, and game was on TV. Yankees beat White Sox, 4–0. In fourth inning, Rivers tripled. Randolph hit grounder to short. Rivers ducked back toward third, short-stop threw to first, Rivers broke for plate, scored. Scorer said no RBI, he scored on throw! Strange ruling. New school of punitive scoring?

End of cute, staccato narrative style, No Pepys I. And so to bed, hoping can remember how to write complete sentences.

Saturday
June 2nd

PEACE IN THE BRONX

NEW YORK—Last year, during the World Series, I wrote some mildly critical things about the New York fans. "Simple observation," I said, "discloses that a high percentage of them are unregenerate jerks. They throw things, make obscene gestures and utter vile epithets at the players. As an annual fall ritual, they demolish the ball park and tear up the field, with the apparent approval of the Yankee management, which seems to feel that if they were forced to adopt a veneer of civilization they might not want to come to the games. No one has dared appeal to their better nature for fear this *is* their better nature. Are they part of the Yankees' home-field advantage? Probably. I have a feeling the New York players are as terrified of them as their visitors, but they've had all year to get used to them. Seeing them at close range for the first time must be rather like waking up in a Brazilian jail. Throwing them poisoned meat would be only marginally effective because, like many subhuman species, they have a certain low cunning, and they breed faster than you can get at them."

(Before I go on, I wish to retreat slightly. Not because I over-stated the case—not by much, anyway—but because the conduct I deplored is becoming more and more typical of fans of every sport, everywhere. Have you ever seen an angry British soccer crowd? Nor is it limited to sport. It is no longer just baseball's problem. It is the world's.)

One of the things I hated most about New York crowds was their intimidating effect on umpires. Last year, during a Sunday game at Yankee Stadium, Mickey Stanley, the Tiger right fielder, had a fly ball taken right out of his hands by a clown wearing a glove who leaned over the wall just as Mickey was about to make the catch. The umpire, mindful of the 50,000 shrieking fans in the stands, didn't call it. Two runs scored, Rozema was robbed of a deserved victory, Guidry won his thirteenth straight and three months later the Yankees tied for first and won the pennant in a play-off.

The play was clearly visible. The endless TV replays confirmed what had happened, but it *was* clearly visible the first time, on a smallish screen, at natural speed. I will never believe the umpire didn't see it, but I am willing to concede that he probably was instantly able to convince himself that he hadn't seen it because, considering the location, it was the prudent course.

I went on about this for days, calling down the wrath of the gods on umpires with no pride in their profession, bemoaning the deterioration of standards of decency in American life and making other near-hysterical charges, all the while wondering (in saner moments) what I was getting so abnormally upset about. It is, as you know, only a game.

It was the crowd, of course, that made me so mad. I thought it outrageous that a volatile mob could, in effect, take charge of the game, that a Yankee fan could enter the field of play and alter the result in the Yankees' favor and that the menacing presence of 50,000 other Yankee fans could enable him to get away with it. Although I've calmed down now, I still do.

Tonight I braved this howling rabble. Quite fearlessly. Before I left on this trip, my son Tony said to me—in jest, I believe—"Do you think you'll be safe in Yankee Stadium?" Reading what I had written, it almost did seem as if going to a game at Yankee Stadium were tantamount to challenging a family of grizzlies with a whip and a chair. But it's really fairly safe. In the mass, Yankee crowds are a frightening sight (especially when we watch them on television tearing down the fences). Individually, they are baseball fans, and so am I.

I suppose I was, subconsciously at least, hoping to witness one or two instances of mildly hideous behavior to confirm

my thesis. If so, I picked the wrong game. It was Jacket
Day (or night). I was surrounded by families of five, parents
with young children, many of them obviously attending their
only game of the year, buying pennants, souvenir baseballs,
Yankee yearbooks, hot dogs, soft drinks, absolutely everything that anyone could be persuaded to sell them. This
cozy, family-picnic atmosphere was so far from the Hell's
Angels picture I had painted that I am afraid I experienced
a slight letdown.

Yankee Stadium has been completely rebuilt since the last
time I saw it, but the playing area is not symmetrical, and
the surface is real grass, so it doesn't look like a game board,
as so many of the new fields do. The outfield, especially in
left, is huge, as the Dodgers found out last year during the
Series, when the home runs they had hit in Chavez Ravine
became easy outs in the Bronx.

Very few of the hateful embellishments of Circus World
have been added, although from time to time the p.a.
system does boom out the "Charge!" which sounds silly in
a park where baseball fans have known when to yell and
when to boo since long before any of the present players was
born. It sounded merely forlorn when someone with a bad
sense of timing activated it in the eighth inning with the
Yankees trailing, 7–0, and meekly going down in order. But
a few fans dutifully echoed it anyway. There were, as I said,
a lot of children there who probably didn't realize that response to mechanized stimuli at ball games is not compulsory.

Ken Kravec, the Chicago pitcher, held the Yankees to
three harmless singles, and made his sixth victory look easy.

I loved it.

❖   ❖   ❖

In the first inning, Alan Bannister, the Sox' banjo-hitting
second baseman, hit one into the left-field seats. It was close
to the line but clearly a fair ball. Sitting in the second row
in left, I almost yelled, "I got it!" Rising lightly to my feet,

I had it all the way, except that the presence of people behind me made it difficult for me to circle under it. It actually landed about three rows in back of me, but it was still the closest I have ever come to catching a home-run ball at a big-league game. (In fifty years of going to ball games, I have never caught or even touched a ball, fair or foul, nor have I ever sat with anyone who did.)

This was Bannister's fifth lifetime home run in roughly a thousand times at bat. It was, in fact, the winning run, too, so he'll probably remember it as long as I do. Longer, now I think about it.

✿   ✿   ✿

Jim Kaat, recently acquired by the Yankees from the Phillies, has been pitching in the major leagues for over twenty years. But he's never pitched for New York before, so the Yankee publicity people have never bothered to learn how to spell his name. In the program he's listed as: Katt 36. (The number was wrong, too.)

✿   ✿   ✿

Before the game, a group of musicians marched onto the field and the scoreboard informed us, YOU ARE BEING ENTERTAINED BY THE N.Y. CITY MISSION SOCIETY DRUM AND BUGLE CORPS. In the row behind mine, a wise-ass kid about ten years old said, "*This* is entertainment?" Yes, kid, it is, and count your blessings. You've never heard the organ at The Big O.

✿   ✿   ✿

The Stadium scoreboard spent a good part of the evening welcoming organized groups of fans to the game, to wit:

THE ST. LOUIS COSMIC CANDY DISCO CHAMPS
CENTRAL SUBPALPI CLUB OF ANSONIA, CONN.
JIMMY RYAN'S TAP ROOM   BOUND BROOK, N.J.

I hope they enjoyed themselves as much as I did.

✿   ✿   ✿

How the rich get richer. Tomorrow is Jacket Day II at Yankee Stadium, and they will have another full house (attendance tonight was 53,589). The gimmick is that the jackets are provided by a famous automobile company (which, if all we hear is true, should be saving its money). Thus, for an outlay of nothing at all, the Yankees fill up the stadium twice—for games with a non-contender—with adults and children, many of whom normally don't come to ball games and all of whom pay the full price for their seats. Now you know where George Steinbrenner gets the millions he pays ballplayers to come and work for the Yankees. (Think how many games the Minnesota Twins have to play to take in the money the Yankees will make this weekend.)

       ✿   ✿   ✿

I didn't get a jacket. I would have liked one, but I was forty-five years over the age limit.

Sunday
June 3rd

BROTHER ACT

NEW YORK—I spoke to my wife on the telephone today. Mary Ellen is not what you would call a true baseball fan. On most days, she would rather take a walk than watch, say, the Pirates playing the Phillies. But she *is* a thoroughly devoted Tiger fan, and today she rhapsodized over the dramatic game she had seen on television Thursday evening. Pat Underwood, a Tiger pitcher just up from Evansville, made his major-league debut in Toronto. The Blue Jays' pitcher was Tom Underwood, Pat's brother. The Tigers won the game, 1–0, on an eighth-inning home run by Jerry Morales. Pat Underwood's record is now 1–0. Tom, who has been a pretty good big-league pitcher for five years, is 0–7. Do not look, anytime soon, for an article by Tom Underwood entitled "It's Great to Be a Blue Jay!"

Monday
June 4th

GOOFY

NEW YORK—Lefty Gomez, one of the great Yankee pitchers of the '30s, was known in his playing days as "Goofy," but he wasn't, and he certainly isn't today. He's now seventy years old, or sixty-eight (depending on whether you believe the record book or his publicity handout), and he hasn't thrown a pitch in anger since 1943, but he's still making an honest living out of baseball. He is an appealing and amusing man with all his wit intact, and he claims he got the nickname because he invented a revolving fishbowl guaranteed to prolong the life of your goldfish by making it unnecessary for the little creature to waste his energy in swimming. I would have thought the fish could do with the exercise, but the idea is a striking one, even if no prototype was ever built.

Lefty was also known as The Gay Castilian, but I suppose he'd just as soon forget that. It's true that he was a light-hearted sort who loved a joke (which is what "gay" used to mean), but except for his name, he was about as Castilian as apple pie. He doesn't speak Spanish, as some Venezuelans discovered too late when they hired him to manage their team in a winter league. (He did okay, anyway. He has the gift of communication.) Besides, who ever heard of a Castilian named Vernon, which was Gomez' first name before it became forever Lefty?

When I was offered the opportunity to have lunch with Lefty Gomez at Christ Cella's restaurant, I hesitated at first.

Lefty Gomez, circa 1935, and today.

I thought it might compromise my amateur standing. I have made a point of not talking to ballplayers while compiling these chronicles, for a number of reasons. I was afraid I might like them too much, which would color my judgment. Or not like them at all, which would dampen my zest for the whole project. The main reason, though, is that I am a lousy interviewer. The routine questions are boring, and I am diffident about asking the right ones—the ones I don't already know the answers to. If I do manage to ask them, people refuse to answer. Sometimes they get mad, which makes me nervous.

(In all modern novels, men start talking to strange women and, within half a page or less, they are discussing shockingly intimate subjects, and you know what's coming next. This never happened to me, but it happens so often in books that I get the idea it's fairly common. I feel I have been cheated of something most people take for granted. Well, it's

probably too late to learn now. And just as I could never
maneuver women into making outrageous suggestions on a
few moments' acquaintance, neither could I induce men to
reveal startling secrets with a few probing questions. I think
I must blush when I ask them.)

So I hesitated before grabbing the chance to meet Lefty
Gomez. But only briefly. Lefty, I reasoned, is not a ballplayer
anymore. He spends his time traveling around the country
promoting the products of a famous sports-equipment firm.
In a sense, his profession is having lunch, and it would be
mighty small of me to deny this baseball giant a chance to
practice his trade.

The lunch was given by the Gillette people to promote
their sponsorship of the All-Star Game ballots, and I had
been told to ask for a man named Artie Solomon, who had
arranged it. I was immediately on my guard. I am a stranger
in New York, but not a complete rube, and I know the big-
city rules for self-protection, the oldest of which is "Never
trust anybody named Whitey, Doc or Artie." I was prepared
for a flabby, middle-aged man waving a soggy cigar, his
undershirt slightly exposed at the beltline, a man perhaps
formed in the mold they forgot to break when they made the
late Joe Jacobs, the fight manager known as Yussel the Mussel
and best remembered for saying, "I should of stood in bed."

Well, of course, times have changed, and great razor-blade
cartels do not hire replicas of old fight managers to put on
their publicity luncheons. Artie Solomon turned out to be
a pleasant, soft-spoken young man and a gracious host with
iron control of his emotions. He managed to grit his teeth
and remain silent every time Lefty mentioned the sporting-
goods company for which he works, which was about four
times for every one mention of Gillette, the company that
was paying the tab for lunch, as well as Artie's stipend. (I
trust that if he reads this, Artie will note that I have done the
right thing, and am available for further lunches.) The food

was excellent, the talk entertaining, and I should have been the poorer had I stood in bed. (The use of "stood" as the past tense of "stay" is a New York tradition that seems to be dying out, although New Yorkers still stand on line, bunk into each other and graduate high school.)

Besides Lefty, Artie and me, there were only three others present: a man from *The New York Times*, a man from the Associated Press and a man whose connection I never did learn, although I had the impression he was some kind of trainee. He kept asking high-school-journalism questions like "Did any funny incidents ever happen to you at an All-Star Game?" This was even more unapt than it seems, since Lefty had just told two or three funny stories about the midsummer classic they call it (such as the time he went to the plate against the great Carl Hubbell, and Gabby Hartnett, the National League catcher, said to him, "Are you trying to insult Hubbell—coming up here with a bat?").

When I was introduced to Gomez, I told him we'd met once before. He looked blank, as well he might have, since my last meeting with him had been in 1934 at the governor general's mansion in the Philippines, when Lefty had passed through with a group of traveling major-league players. (That must have been one of the greatest teams ever assembled; it included Babe Ruth, Lou Gehrig, Jimmy Foxx, Charlie Gehringer and Earl Averill, all now in the Hall of Fame, as is Gomez.) I was glad I brought it up because it gave Lefty the chance to tell a few stories about that trip, including one which defies belief. He said that Babe Ruth and his family were kept sitting in the lobby of the Manila Hotel for an hour while the royal suite was prepared for them. It turned out, says Lefty, that they were waiting for General MacArthur to vacate the suite so the Ruths could move in. Now, it's true that Ruth was known as the savior of baseball, but if you believe Douglas MacArthur would be forced out of his quarters for anyone short of the original

Saviour, then you'll believe Menachem Begin is really Glenn
Miller. (During the war, the Australians used to ask us if
we'd read the new best seller *MacArthur Is My Co-pilot*
by God.)

I didn't mention, incidentally, that I was only fourteen
when I first met Gomez, while he was already a big-league
star, but he must have suspected I was younger than he,
because most people are. Still, he looks great, nothing like
seventy, or even sixty-eight. In spite of triple-bypass heart
surgery just a year ago ("first triple I ever had"), he looks
as if he could work an inning or two tomorrow if the Yankees
need him (and I think they do). That's the standard thing
to say about an old ballplayer, and in this case it's obviously
an exaggeration, but I'll be happy if I can feel as good as he
seems to at his age, whatever it is.

(Although I am younger than Lefty, I was clearly older
than anyone else present, and I took a sort of childish pride
in the fact that after the first few minutes, Lefty began
directing all his anecdotes at me because I was obviously the
only one there who remembered half the players he mentioned. Surely, I must have been the only one who remembered Myril Hoag. I even remembered that Hoag wore a
size-four shoe, although I didn't think it necessary to bring
it up. That would have been pushing total recall of trivia
almost to the breaking point.)

No Castilian, Vernon Louis Gomez was a farm boy who
left Rodeo, California, to come to the greatest city on earth
and was above all astonished to discover it had two railroad
stations, whereas one had seemed like plenty back in Rodeo.
But he learned fast, and was soon keeping company with a
beautiful musical-comedy star named June O'Dea. They've
been married for forty-seven years now. These celebrity
marriages seldom last, but this one seems to have a good
chance of making it.

Lefty relates that on one of his first dates with June, she

arrived at the ball park a bit late, to find him angry and upset because he'd been knocked out of the box in the first game of a doubleheader. "Don't worry," she consoled him, "maybe you'll win the second game." A couple of months later, he says, he gave up a game-winning home run to Charlie Gehringer of the Tigers, and when he met June after the game she said, "Gomez, how long do you have to play in the big leagues before you realize you can't pitch Gehringer high?"

A charming story, I think. Like most of Lefty's, it has a slightly familiar ring, probably because he's been having lunch professionally with sportswriters for many a year. No storyteller can come up with new ones every day, but Lefty's are his own—he employs no writers. He is a genuinely funny man and, on brief acquaintance, seems like a genuinely nice one.

He is also one of the great pitchers of baseball history, as witness: 189–102 lifetime won–lost record; 6–0 in World Series play; five All-Star starts, three All-Star wins (both records).

Obviously, he is an ideal man to carry the look-sharp banner in the razor-blade company's endless quest for public approval of its Mickey Mouse balloting system. As the luncheon was breaking up, he made a gesture to that end. "I'm glad you all agree that the present voting system is the best possible," he said. No one contradicted him (who would argue with such a decent fellow?), but I, for one, think the present balloting arrangement is a bad joke perpetrated on the players and fans by a cabal of blade and baseball executives for the usual reason: money. I'll get back to that.

For now, I will simply say that I have waited all my life to have lunch at a famous New York restaurant with a "former immortal" (in Mark Harris' classic phrase), and it turned out to be worth it when I found out I'd been waiting for Lefty.

UP AGAINST THE WALL

Boston—Fenway Park is a cozy little· cage in which to watch a baseball game, and I enjoyed being there last night, but I didn't think of it as a religious experience, and so many people seem to. (Typical remark: "I envy you, going to Boston. I've always wanted to see a game in Fenway Park.") It's the aura of The Wall, I guess—the looming left-field fence which on television looks as if it's right behind the infield, and in person looks pretty much that way too.

For those who haven't been there, I can report that Boston fans are constantly on the move. I don't know where they're going, but between innings the aisles are always jammed with thousands of them going somewhere. Certainly not to the toilets, unless the Fenway has a MEN to match its monster. And a WOMEN too.

Boston fans also ooh and aah every time a Red Sox player hits a high fly to left field, no matter how shallow. They too are under the spell of The Wall, confident that anything hit out that way is likely to find it. They aren't far wrong, at that.

But baseball is baseball in Boston. There is no organ music, no little man dressed like a small animal (or a sock), and the park announcer could give lessons to the carnival barker who fills that post in Montreal. As Jim Rice, one of the great players of the game, advances to the plate, the announcer says, in an absolute monotone, "Rice, left field." Information. All we need.

The game itself was not much, especially after the fifth inning, when the Red Sox got three home runs and a triple off Texas pitching and scored eight runs to take a 13–3 lead. But I was intrigued by a lot of little things, such as Johnny Pesky's ability to hit pop flies. Pesky, a former Boston star now in his sixtieth year, closed out infield practice by hitting a high fly ball to the catcher, right up the elevator shaft. It came down within three feet of where it started. I couldn't *throw* a ball that straight up. A rare talent.

Far from offending us with organ recitals, the Boston management seems indifferent to music of any kind. They did play the National Anthem before the game, but it was apparently recorded on one of those cylinders that very old Boston families still keep in cedar chests in their attics. When the music stopped, I half expected to hear Thomas Edison reciting "Mary Had a Little Lamb."

There was also a moment of silence for Bill Liston, a popular local baseball writer who died Sunday. As we stood quietly, a bell tolled tinnily over that same sound system. Well, it was the authentic voice of Fenway Park, so I guess Bill would have liked it.

Jim Rice had a double, triple and home run in his first three times at bat. When he came up for the last time, in the eighth, he was obviously trying to hit a single to complete the cycle. But Rice doesn't know how to hit a single; not deliberately, anyway. He flied out weakly to right field.

When you talk about baseball in Boston, though, inevitably you get back to The Wall. I have avoided calling it by its popular nickname (I made a little bet with myself), but it is green and it is monstrous, which my dictionary defines as "shocking, absurd, hideous, malformed." The key word here is "absurd," for that describes the effect it has perennially had on the Red Sox bosses, who in trying to build a winner find themselves constantly with their backs to The Wall.

What the Red Sox do, year after year, is stock their team with right-handed hitters who can occasionally hit a ball against the fence when at home, but are liabilities anywhere else. This year, they are also trying to win a pennant without a left-handed pitcher, while Bill Lee, whom they let go, throws shutouts in Montreal.

I wish I could take sole credit for all this insight, but I can't. It was brought home to me by a perceptive piece of

writing I read in *Esquire* in April, written by a man named
Bill James. I was (most fans are) vaguely aware of the situation, but James pins it down. He points especially to Dwight
Evans, George Scott and Butch Hobson, all of whom hit like
Chuck Scrivener once they get out of town. Evans and Scott
are at least good fielders. Hobson makes third base a disaster
area.

At the end of last season, I was mesmerized by Butch
Hobson's fielding average. I had not thought it possible,
before, that a big-league infielder, playing a full season, could
finish with a fielding average below .900. Last year Hobson
fielded .899 and made forty-three errors! The next-highest
error total in the league at any position was Fred Patek's
thirty-two. Patek plays shortstop, a harder position, and had
almost two hundred more chances. Aurelio Rodríguez, who
led all third basemen, fielded .987 (and incidentally out-hit
Hobson by fifteen points).

Still, I thought Hobson might be the victim of a bum rap.
It's well known that he played last year with an injured arm,
so his fielding average was presumably misleading. Last
night I paid particular attention to what he did in the field.
He did nothing. He did not touch the ball once during the
game. He could have touched the ball had he been Rodríguez
or Nettles or almost any other third baseman, because two
ground balls went right past him for hits. Neither was an
easy chance, but almost any other third baseman would have
made a try for them, and a superior one would have handled
one or both of them. Hobson just looked at them. Pro-rate
those over a full season (surely not two a game, but a goodly
number, none the less), and it becomes clear that any fielding average Hobson compiles will be misleading, but not
to his disadvantage. Add to this his .211 batting average on
the road, and you begin to see how that wicked left-field
fence keeps tricking the Red Sox into building teams that
always finish high, but hardly ever win it all.

❊   ❊   ❊

Aurelio Rodríguez. Third baseman *extraordinaire*.

Back at my hotel, after the game, I saw several of the Texas players walking through the lobby. I couldn't identify any of them, but you can always recognize ballplayers. "How'd the game come out?" someone asked. "The Bosox prevailed," one of them answered.

✿   ✿   ✿

The Red Sox' win last night followed a disastrous road trip. In today's *Boston Globe*, Don Zimmer, their manager, is quoted as saying he can't imagine why the team does so well here and so badly on the road, but he's glad to be home anyway. Come, now, Don.

Thursday
June 7th

WITHOUT FEAR OR FAVOR

Home again. I had a call today from a friend who had been watching television and couldn't believe his eyes. He wanted to know about the scoring on a couple of plays in a game that I attended in Toronto, a ground ball that got past Aurelio Rodríguez and a fly ball dropped by Al Woods, the Toronto left fielder. Both of them were called hits, and my friend took strong issue with that. He's quite right. Both of them should have been errors. The Toronto scorer apparently has a batter bias. Most scorers, unfortunately, seem to favor either batters or fielders. Those who favor batters are, obviously, tough on pitchers. When almost everything that gets through the infield is called a hit, it plays hell with the old earned-run average.

Of course, neither of these is as bad as a hometown scorer, such as the one who apparently works (or worked) in Boston. Last year, in a game on TV, he scored three flagrant Detroit errors as hits. Think about *that* when you examine the averages Boston batters compile at Fenway Park.

The whole question of official scoring is one that baseball should do something about but, as with so many other simple problems, prefers to ignore. All official scorers at major-league games are part-time employees on piecework. They are, in almost every case, sportswriters doing the job as a sideline to their full-time work.

The difficulty is that there is almost always unconscious bias involved. I'm sure most official scorers try to carry out the assignment as conscientiously as possible. But they also have regular jobs to do, and they are to some extent dependent on the goodwill of the players for their cakes and ale. In Detroit, both major daily newspapers have taken official notice of this, and have forbidden their writers to work as official scorers. So the job has fallen by default to Ed Browalski of the *Polish Daily News*.

Most fans are only marginally conscious of the official scorer most of the time. They question a call occasionally, but seldom get very upset about it. The spotlight falls with an unpleasant glare on the scorer, however, when a pitcher is working on a no-hit game. As the potential masterpiece moves into the late innings, the scorer finds himself praying that no one will reach base on a batted ball, or that if he does it's a clean hit.

Last year, in a game against Oakland, Dave Rozema of the Tigers took a no-hitter through seven innings. In the eighth, the Oakland leadoff man hit what looked like a routine grounder to Phil Mankowski at third, but at the last moment it took a horrible hop and bounced off Phil's shoulder. Without a moment's hesitation, Browalski called it a hit, and the no-hit game was gone. He made the right call, beyond question, but it was a *fluke* hit, and he could have been strongly tempted to call it an error. Instead, he did what every scorer ought to do all the time. He did not consider the circumstances; he did not think about what inning it was, who was pitching or how many hits he had allowed. It would have been a hit in the first inning (or in a 10–8 game), so it was a hit this time, no matter who got hurt. Not all scorers are so capable of divorcing their judgment from their emotions.

(In the locker room after the game, Rozema said, "I knew it was a hit, but I was hoping the scorer would give me a break." Would he take a tainted no-hitter? someone asked.

Rozema, who has a sense of humor, smiled. "Sure," he said.

A few days ago, Bruce Kison of Pittsburgh lost a no-hitter on a grounder that got past his third baseman with two out in the eighth. Dan Donovan of the *Pittsburgh Press*, the official scorer, called it a hit, and it was the only one San Diego got. Kison was furious. I didn't see the play, but it doesn't take a genius to figure out, reading between the lines, that Donovan called it right. Listen to Kison. "It could have been a hit, it could have been an error," he said, "but since we were in our own ball park . . ."

The most revealing quote, though, came from Phil Garner, the third baseman. He said he would have been "willing to take an error" to save Kison's no-hitter, but at no time has he said that it *was* an error. I have never heard of a player who made a real error in such a situation who wouldn't freely admit that it was one.

Even if Donovan was wrong, which seems unlikely, Kison's whole premise is false. He wanted him to suspend the judgment he was being paid to exercise in favor of a hometown player. Clearly, this is a case in which the scorer did his job under pressure, and he's getting blasted for it.

It happens every year. Someone loses a no-hitter because the scorer called a close one against him, or gets a fake one because of a friendly call. In either case, many people get mad.

What baseball needs, in every ball park, is a full-time official scorer, a man (or woman) who knows the game, does not fraternize with the players and will consider every case strictly on its merits, as if he didn't know who the players were, or which side was batting. That's what the man in Pittsburgh did, and he's in trouble. One of the players he depends on for news is mad at him, and some of the fans who read his newspaper are, too.

The official scorer, under my system, would consider it

his duty to make the players and fans mad occasionally. And he wouldn't mind doing it because, when the game was over, he wouldn't have to turn around and ask them to help pay his salary.

There is unquestionably someone in every big-league city who is qualified to do this job—a former sportswriter, an ex-ballplayer, any veteran observer of the game with reasonably good judgment. It wouldn't cost much, just the difference between a modest living wage and what they are paying the part-time people who do it now. But it *would* cost a little, which is the reason it probably won't happen. Baseball people hate to spend ten dollars on something they can get for five that's almost as good. Like most people, I guess.

❃   ❃   ❃

My friend on the telephone recalled the rule of thumb from our boyhood that "if you touch it, it's an error" and wanted to know what had become of it. Well, obviously, it was never strictly enforced. You cannot give an infielder an error if he dives for a hard shot and barely gets his glove on it. And in the old days you didn't always *have* to touch it. I once saw Rudy York charged with an error on a ball he didn't come within 20 feet of. And quite properly, too. Rudy was the worst judge of a fly ball I have ever seen (although in later years Gates Brown made a brisk challenge for the title). When the Tigers persuaded Hank Greenberg (perhaps with a little money) to move to the outfield so Rudy could play first base, they knew what they were about. There was simply no other position Rudy could play. He was the world's finest designated hitter, unfortunately born forty years too soon. Even after he moved to first, he never took pop flies if he could get out of it. On high ones, he just got out of the way (not always easy in itself for Rudy) and let the catcher or second baseman take them.

Rudy York. He hated those fly balls.

Strangely enough, York was a good first baseman in all other respects. He used to lead the league in double plays started by first basemen. Quite an achievement for a big, slow *right-handed* fielder. He would have been a pretty good catcher, too, had it not been for the insidious pop foul.

✿　　✿　　✿

Unlike the fans, the ballplayers, especially the hitters, are always keenly aware of the official scorer. For the most part, they consider him the enemy. How could it be otherwise? No matter how many close ones he calls in their favor ("only fair"), sooner or later he will call one against them ("taking the bread out of my children's mouths").

I was official scorer at a Michigan–Northwestern game back in the spring of 1941. No tough calls (no pay, either). But after the game a Michigan player came up to me and said, "What'd you call that ball I hit to the third baseman?" The play was a little dribbler that I could have fielded bare-handed. I thought he was joking and I laughed apprecia-tively, but he insisted, so I said, "An error, of course."

"What?" he screamed. "That ball handcuffed him!" I laughed harder. I still couldn't believe he was serious. But he was. He was also a football player in season, and I de-cided to go elsewhere until he cooled down.

It shows how hitters love their hits, even when they aren't playing for money. That young man went on to become a famous football coach. But he never got that hit.

Saturday
June 9th

A ROSE IS A ROSE

Earlier this week, the papers were full of Pete Rose (not an unusual condition for the papers in any given week the last couple of years). Pete had just returned to Cincinnati for the first time since defecting to the Phillies, and they made a big deal out of his "homecoming." To make it more interesting, they even cooked up a feud (which, predictably, was boring). The Reds' general manager objected to Pete's being honored on the field, since he was now in the enemy camp. But it was all settled quietly, Rose got his local-MVP award, most of the fans cheered, a few booed, Pete went 0 for 4 at the plate (as is traditional in such cases) and the whole thing ended rather languidly.

Last year, Pete Rose was just another good ballplayer to me. He played in the wrong league. (It may be the best league, as he maintains, but to me it's still the wrong one.) I knew him by reputation, but my actual experience of him was limited to a few widely spaced TV games and what seemed like several hundred TV commercials in which he proclaimed that a man wants to smell like a man. These were, I confess, educational. All the TV commercials I had seen before had led me to believe that a man wanted to smell like a rose.

As it turned out, 1978 became The Year of the Rose, and I found myself writing about him more than any other player. In early May he got his three-thousandth hit. As with all such milestones, the press coverage was ample to the point of tedium. Not that Pete didn't deserve it. He is a great ballplayer, and I don't begrudge him his honors. But I do get just a wee bit fed up with hearing about how he did it all on sheer enthusiasm, despite a complete lack of baseball skills. The torrent of inanity crested in a statement by Sparky Anderson, then the Reds' manager, who seemed to be gunning for the funny-talking title which has been up for grabs since the death of Casey Stengel. As quoted by Jerry Green in the *Detroit News*, Sparky said of Rose: "God didn't gift him to run well. He does not have a good arm. He doesn't field well. He's below average in those things."

Then, in a truly majestic (possibly world-class) *non sequitur*, Sparky went on: "But baseball is the only game they don't check your IQ, your color, your religion. He was cheated when they handed out the abilities, but it shows you don't have to be big, you don't have to be good looking."

I don't really know what that means, but it seems to imply that Pete is small (not true) and ugly (eye of beholder), and it supports the myth that he is a punk ballplayer who somehow compensated by trying harder. If all it took were "desire," I know at least half a dozen people, one of whom is in this room, who would have been shoo-ins for the Hall of Fame.

"Desire" used to be a euphemism for lust, but now that the weighty writers have abandoned euphemism in favor of "honesty" (a euphemism), it has been adopted by sportswriters to describe what was once called guts or drive or the old college try. Whatever you call it, Pete Rose has it in abundance. Part of it, of course, is sheer confidence, a quality that he makes palatable by his aptitude for easygoing self-deprecation. (I recall with some satisfaction his answer to a question about his base-running ability: "I'm not bad. I'm no Joe Morgan, but I'm pretty good for a white guy.")

But the plain fact is that nobody had to teach him how to hit. He could always do that. If he couldn't, he wouldn't have been around long enough to demonstrate his ability to block ground balls with his chest and throw batters out at first—the universal touchstone for a third baseman who makes do with "desire" when he doesn't have "the good hands."

In many ways, Pete's career parallels that of my old hero, Hank Greenberg. Hank wasn't hired for his grace in the field, but he made himself a competent fielder through determination and endless hours of practice. The point is, though, that Pete Rose and Hank Greenberg both had something to trade. Their hitting bought them the time to learn how to play the game. It is to their credit that they both became good defensive players. A lot of good hitters never bother, which tends to shorten the career.

God didn't gift me to run well, either. There were those, in fact, who thought that God had played a rather mean trick on me in that department. I wasn't fat or especially clumsy; I was just *slow*. As a kid, I worked constantly on my fielding, and became pretty good at it. Since there were a number of

Pete Rose. He could always hit.

big, slow first basemen (Zeke Bonura, Dale Alexander, Hal Trosky) playing regularly in the big leagues during my youth, I figured this was my destiny, too. All of these strapping chaps were good hitters, but I didn't see that as a problem. Every kid thinks he can hit. That's the object of the game.

Then I got a bit older and had to bat against people who knew something about pitching. Not much, but enough to write the first faint words on the wall. The evidence began to mount that while Hank Greenberg's may have been a God of Wrath, mine was more of a practical joker. Far from making amends for my ponderous gait, He hadn't gifted me to follow the path of a ball in parabolic flight, either. In short, I couldn't hit a curveball with a snow shovel. And the first time I faced a pitcher with genuine skill I found I was no longer thinking of a baseball career, but simply of retiring from the scene without looking any more foolish than absolutely necessary. It wasn't till some time afterward that it suddenly came to me that I'd have to look for another line of work. It's a crushing moment, but sooner or later it comes to all of us who have plenty of "desire" but lack the equipment to utilize it.

(We won that game, incidentally, and I got a hit. God's parting gift?)

I salute Pete Rose. I question not his intelligence, his color, his religion, his size or his beauty. I ask not what he can do for me, but what I can do for him. I venerate his reckless resolve. And oh, how I envy him!

But please, tell me not again that he did it all without any talent—that "he was cheated when they handed out the abilities." There are too many of us out here who know better.

❊   ❊   ❊

A few weeks later, Rose began his consecutive-game hitting streak. By the first of August, it had reached 44 games, and I was becoming concerned about the threat to Joe DiMaggio's record of 56. This was odd, because I agreed with all that stuff about records' being made to be broken. I felt no pain when Maury Wills erased Ty Cobb's stolen-base record for a single season, or when Lou Brock wiped out his lifetime mark. Neither did I wince when Hank Aaron passed Babe Ruth's lifetime home-run total. Life goes on.

So why did I experience an obscure feeling of discomfort at the thought of Rose's breaking DiMaggio's record? It has been called "the record that will never be broken," but of course it will be. Like those monkeys pounding out all the world's great literature on an infinite number of typewriters, baseball players will break all the great records again and again as the history of the game stretches on into infinity (which is the way I like to think of the future of baseball).

But my uneasiness was well founded. To me, DiMaggio's 56 was sancrosanct, and it's not hard to guess the reason. Cobb's record was already ancient history and Ruth was nearing the end of his career when I first became a student of the game. My terminology is imprecise. A true "student" is impartial. He wants facts, without bias or preference for any individual. I was never that sort. But then, neither was I a DiMaggio fan. I always leaned toward the player who triumphed over innate handicaps or, if naturally talented, had the decency to glory in his skills (Willie Mays comes to mind). DiMaggio was one of those cold, colorless perfectionists who make the average pro look like an amateur. Indeed, he demonstrates more personal appeal in his coffee-maker commercials than he ever did on a baseball field. Anyway, Joe was a Yankee, and everybody (except Yankee fans) hated the Yankees.

So why, then, did I feel as I did? Simple. It's all in the timing. When Joe ran off that famous string, I was twenty-one and the world was green—although no more so than I. When the streak ended, I was at the Philadelphia Navy Yard being prepared for a war that everybody knew (but no one quite believed) was coming. We sat in the PX and talked about Ken Keltner's two sensational plays at third base, which finally convinced even DiMaggio that nothing lasts forever, a truism which he had seemed to be on the edge of forgetting.

Twenty-one! In all the years before and since, they have never come up with another age quite like it. Today's "adults," who achieve their legal majority at eighteen, must secretly know they are still children. But at twenty-one we honestly believed we were men, fully prepared to take on the game which we had yet to learn was rigged for the house. All the hope was real, all the horseshit still in the future and carefully hidden from view. (If you want a reason for believing in a merciful God, the fact that man cannot guess what lies ahead is the most convincing one I know.)

DiMaggio and his contemporaries were the heroes of my young manhood. They even went to war with us. Ted Williams actually *fought* in the war. But we feel a kinship even for those who just played baseball for service teams, recognizing that they also serve who only hit and run.

So I wished Pete Rose luck, but still hoped he wouldn't break Joe's record. There would be, after all, great honor in being better than everyone *but* DiMaggio.

Hardly had I written this when the streak ended. I was startled and a bit chagrined. Like many ballplayers and fans, I am terribly superstitious about baseball, while scorning superstition in other areas as childish nonsense. I always feel that my relationship to a game somehow has an effect on the outcome. If I turn on a game broadcast in the seventh inning to discover the Tigers leading by four runs, and the other team promptly scores five, I find myself wondering if it was my fault. *Post hoc ergo propter hoc.* Cause and effect. Silly, but there you are.

So, foolishly, I couldn't help wondering about the coincidence that my essay on the sanctity of DiMaggio's record was immediately followed by the downfall of the scrappy little legend in his own time. Ridiculous? Certainly. I was thousands of miles away (although that, too, is beside the point) and no one involved in that game even knew I existed. Still, I felt somehow at fault in the matter. Even so, I was glad he hadn't broken the record. It goes with my majority, and it's almost the only thing I retain intact from that year of promise. The dreams of fame, riches and Paulette Goddard all came to naught. But DiMaggio's *56!* goes on forever—or at least until some distant time when I won't give a damn.

        ❊   ❊   ❊

You may have noted that I fell into the familar error of referring to Pete Rose as "little," although I am fully aware that he is not. There is a tradition in baseball of the tough little man who triumphs through sheer determination. The prototype of this genre is probably Eddie Stanky, of whom it was said, "He can't run, he can't hit, he can't throw; all he can do is beat you." This was such a good line that it soon became a cliché and was said about countless other players, some of whom couldn't run, throw or hit and couldn't beat you either.

They also say about players of the Stanky type that they came to play, that they always give you 110 percent and that, for them, desire is the name of the game.

Stanky actually was fairly small at five-eight, 170, and Nellie Fox, another eminent member of this clan, was not much bigger. Rose, though hardly a giant, is a full-size man, and no one has ever accused him of not being able to hit. But he fits the pattern, if not the uniform, of the good little man who beats you. And I will always wish him well, if for no other reason than that he obviously loves to play baseball. Which is the name of the game.

Tuesday
June 12th

STAR-STRUCK

Jim Campbell is hooked on celebrities. That's the only reasonable explanation for his behavior. Campbell, the Detroit general manager, has just fired Les Moss and hired Sparky Anderson to manage the Tigers.

Sparky Anderson is a famous manager, even if he does talk funny. Les Moss was a virtually unknown manager. (He was named minor-league Manager of the Year in 1978, which is just one step from anonymity, given the general level of interest in minor-league baseball.) Moss was given fifty-three games in which to prove his capacity to build a winner. Anderson will be given five and a half years. He will also be given a salary larger than that of many of his players. There are few, if any, players on the team making less money than Moss was getting.

But isn't all this more or less routine? After all, big-league baseball teams are notorious for hiring and firing managers at a furious rate, often on rather flimsy grounds. Well, sure, but in this case it is worth remembering that Campbell stuck with Ralph Houk for five losing years, in which the team repeatedly looked better than it played.

Ralph Houk was a famous manager, although not a very good one. Last year, in his final season with Detroit, he seemed to have lost interest in the game. Yet he might still be the manager if he hadn't chosen to retire voluntarily.

Houk's fame proceeded from two sources. He won three pennants with the Yankees (1961–63) after taking over a ready-made championship team from Casey Stengel. And every ballplayer who ever played for him (as far as I know) says he was a wonderful manager. Together, these make a flimsy framework on which to hang a managerial reputation. There is another side to the coin, and it's the side that comes up every time I mentally flip it.

After Houk's three pennant winners, he retired to the front office and turned the team over to Yogi Berra. Yogi's team won the pennant, too, apparently proving that the Yankees didn't even need a manager, because Berra's reward was a pink slip, handed to him by Ralph Houk. Let's think about that. Houk fired the man for winning a pennant with the same team that he himself had been extravagantly praised for leading to victory. The obvious inference is that it didn't take much skill to manage that particular bunch of Yankees.

In 1966, with the Yankees fallen from glory, Ralph Houk returned to the field. (Do not let the word "triumphantly" slip into that sentence.) That year, he began a string of thirteen straight losers, alleviated only slightly by one second-place finish (in 1970, fifteen games back of Baltimore). The last five of those years were spent with the Tigers, where a fourth-place finish in 1977 was the closest he came to a championship.

Last year, Houk's boredom with baseball became so intense that he didn't bother to devise a set of signals that couldn't be read by anyone within hailing distance. The story went that a visiting reporter was calling all of Ralph's plays in advance from the press box, so transparent was his semaphore system. This was widely reported, but it apparently did not move Ralph to introduce an element of mystery into his wigwags. In the final week of the season, the Tigers were playing an important series with Boston. It was important because the Red Sox were in a down-to-the-wire race with the Yankees for first place, and the loss of a single game would have cost them their chance for the title. During this series, Carl Yastrzemski revealed that he had been picking up Houk's signs from left field and relaying them to his catcher. Ralph might as well have been using colored lights.

Another thing that happened in that series was indicative of Houk's attitude toward his players and his job. With a runner on first and none out, Phil Mankowski hit a little pop fly to the pitcher. The runner, Whitaker, naturally hurried back to the bag. Mankowski stood at the plate and watched. The pitcher, Mike Torrez, had him in full view, so he just let the ball fall to the ground, picked it up and threw to second, from where it was quickly converted into a double play. Rusty Staub then singled to right, which *would* have put runners on first and third with one out had it not been for Mankowski's laziness. As it was, nothing came of it, and the Tigers lost, 1–0. And, I repeat, this was a key game in the American League pennant race. Houk did not fine Mankowski, or make him sit down, or reprimand him publicly. If he said anything to him at all, his words were lost to history. You can't really blame him. Who wants to get tough when he's three days away from retirement? But the incident stands out as representative of the entire season. The Tigers played sloppy, slipshod ball all summer long. Their base running was an off-color joke much of the year, and their inattention on defense could have been made into a training film called *Coma*. These are things a manager can do something about. He cannot make a slow runner fast, or turn a weak arm into a strong one. But he can teach the elements of base running and how to be in the right place at the right time. Most of all, a manager can insist that his players master every baseball skill *of which they are capable,* and put them to use on the field in every game they play. Houk consistently failed to do this. And that was too bad because the Tigers' shocking base running and defensive indifference must have cost them half a dozen ball games. Although they finished fifth, they were twelve games over .500 and only thirteen games behind the winners in the best division in baseball. Obviously, if they'd won that extra half-dozen games, they'd have been in the race right into September. And when you're in the race—really in it—there's always a chance you'll get hot and win it. Because of Houk's indifference to the most basic fundamentals, the Tigers never had that chance.

I really can't speak with confidence about the earlier

years (although the record seems to speak for itself), but last year I was watching, and last year Houk was a bad manager. Yet so taken is Jim Campbell with name brands that Ralph could have stayed on as Tiger manager, presumably forever, had he chosen to.

As for the other factor in Houk's reputation, the players who said he was a wonderful manager, they didn't really mean it. Oh, they probably thought they did, but what they meant was that he was a wonderful *guy*. They liked him. Houk was always said to be a great handler of young players. In my innocence, I used to think that meant he was a good teacher. Actually, it meant precisely the opposite. He didn't teach them at all; he just kept telling them how good they were. If you were a young player and your manager never corrected you, never made you work overtime and constantly told you everything was going great, you'd probably go around telling people he really knew how to handle young players, too.

How come no manager is ever reputed to be a great handler of *old* players? Since pennant-winning teams, in most cases, are largely made up of experienced players, this would seem to be an even more useful skill. But nobody seems to have it. At any meet-the-manager press conference, you can pretty well list the attributes that will be claimed for the new man even before they are revealed. He will be "a solid baseball man . . . who demands that his players give him 100 percent . . . a no-nonsense leader who is, none the less, respected by his players . . ." and inevitably, "an outstanding handler of young players." It would be refreshing, for once, to hear: "Joe has little patience with overpaid, overrated kids, but he gets the most out of players who have been around long enough to know what the game is all about."

Houk and Moss, we were told, were good handlers of young players. They're both gone now, and Sparky Anderson is the manager, supposedly selected because he is, above all, a great handler of . . . but I hardly need tell you.

The fact is—and there is no way around it—Campbell's treatment of Les Moss was grossly unfair. It bordered on the indecent. What makes it worse is that one gets the impression Campbell was planning it when he signed Moss in the first place. Why else would he hire a manager and pay him a salary suitable for a utility infielder? How could Moss ever have won the respect of his players when they knew (and they always *do* know) how little the Tigers' management thought of him? Don't get me wrong. I could live very nicely on $35,000 a year. But for the manager of a major-league team, it's insulting. It virtually proclaimed Campbell's intention of dumping him if someone he liked better came along. They can pay off his one-year contract with the hot-dog money from one sellout crowd.

Anderson, on the other hand, has a five-year contract at a reported $110,000 per. If they fired him tomorrow, it would cost them more than half a million dollars. That kind of money ensures that Sparky will be around for a while, come hell, high water or twenty-game losing streak.

Baseball fans have strong opinions. As a Tiger fan, I am shocked, almost embarrassed, by the cruel firing of Les Moss, who had done nothing to deserve it (and in fact, no reason was given except that "Sparky was available"). But baseball fans are also fickle. If Anderson leads the Tigers to victory this year, or even next, I'll be calling him a great manager, and possibly even conceding that Campbell made a brilliant move. Rotten, but brilliant.

At least, though, I demand some evidence. Jim Campbell thought Ralph Houk was a great manager without any evidence at all.

As for Sparky himself, he's not making any big promises. Secure in his long-term contract, he can afford to be cautious. He did let down his guard slightly, however, when he assured

Sparky Anderson. He can afford to be cautious.

Tiger fans a championship by 1984. I figure the 1984 World Series to start in the home of the National League champion on Tuesday, October 9th. I will mark that date on my 1984 calendar as soon as I get it. If neither the world nor I has come to an end by then, I'll be there.

But October of 1984 is a long way off. If you want to know how long, consider the possibility that someone you haven't yet heard of (right now, she may be the attorney general of Nebraska) will be running for president when we all gather for that Series.

Frankly, Sparky, I was hoping for something a bit sooner.

✻　　✻　　✻

Realistically, about the only thing we can say with any certainty about 1984 is that October 9th will be a Tuesday. That my whimsical prediction about the presidential race of that year might come true is not quite beyond the frontiers of chance. Almost equally bold is my assumption that the '84 World Series will begin on or about the second Tuesday in October. If the junk merchants take over baseball, as they have basketball and hockey (and to a lesser degree football), who can guess when the Series will start? It may be held in the Orange Bowl during Christmas Week, and to qualify, the Tigers may first have to win a seven-game series with a wild-card team from the Three-Eye League.

This is the age of the gimmick in professional sport, as you surely know unless you are living on Sofu Gan and getting your news of the world from itinerant pearl divers. The gimmicks are all designed to make money, which would be okay except that most of them cheapen their games and ultimately debase the value of their championships.

This year, the two best teams in hockey were the New York Islanders and the Montreal Canadiens (in that order, some would say). The Islanders didn't make the Stanley Cup finals, and only a fluke last-minute penalty to Boston permitted the Canadiens to get there. A Stanley Cup series between the New York Rangers and the Boston Bruins would have been comparable to a World Series last year involving the Texas Rangers and the San Francisco Giants. If Texas had played San Francisco in the Series in 1978—even conceding that they were both good teams—would anyone really have believed that they were playing for the championship of the world?

Last year, among the twelve teams in the NHL play-offs (from an eighteen-team league) were the Colorado Rockies, with a record of 19 wins and 40 losses! In basketball, more than half the teams in the league made the play-offs, including four members of one five-team division.

Is it coincidence that nobody but a hard core of fanatics watches pro basketball during the regular season anymore? Even more pointed is the fact that when the almost endless basketball play-offs finally do end, hardly anyone but the fans in the two cities involved is aware of it.

Baseball is, uniquely, a game in which class is established only over the long season. In '78, the Toronto Blue Jays beat the New York Yankees and the Boston Red Sox four times each during the season. But when it was over, there were New York and Boston tied for first, and there were the Jays dead last. And all three teams were right where they belonged, as every baseball fan knew.

Baseball will survive, I have no doubt. But if its greedy leaders succumb to the temptation to create a trashy play-off system, it will soon be reduced to the level of celebrity bowling and the demolition derby—something which people who can't read can watch while digesting their dinner and waiting for *Laverne and Shirley*.

Wednesday
June 13th

THE GREAT (OR SEMI-GREAT) DEPILATION

Champ Summers has shaved off his mustache. The Tiger outfielder played for Sparky Anderson in Cincinnati, and he knows how the new manager feels about facial hair. The word is that he's against it.

Several other Tigers have followed Summers' example, but there are a number of holdouts. Aurelio Rodríguez, a Mexican citizen, is exempt from the ban. (With his mustache, Aurelio looks a little like Pancho Villa. Without it, he looks like a high-school kid. But that was a long time ago. Hard to say how he'd look without it now. Strange, probably.)

Jason Thompson, although presumably traveling on a U.S. passport (unless Californians have their own), has also declined to shave. When asked why, he replied, "No comment." Fair enough, because Jason's mustache is barely worthy of comment. If he keeps quiet about it, Sparky may never notice it.

Thursday
June 14th

WOULD YOU BUY A USED CAR FROM THIS MAN?

In yesterday's *Detroit Free Press*, an article about Sparky Anderson (there were several) described him as the kind of man you wish your father had been. That is not to be read as a criticism of fathers. I'm one myself. But few of us are (or had) fathers as downright wonderful as Sparky. He is decent, warm, generous, kind, fiercely loyal. Just about everything you'd want in a father. Or a son. But this reporter went too far in grading Sparky's honesty. Too far for the paper's advertising department, anyway.

It seems that some years ago, during a spell of unemployment, Sparky took a job selling Nash Ramblers—the automotive equivalent of being a utility infielder for the Oakland A's (or, as Les Moss found out, manager of the Detroit Tigers with an airtight one-year contract). "Trouble was," said the unthinking author, "Sparky Anderson is an honest sort of fellow, not at all the kind of man to sell cars." This is the kind of remark the average car buyer can identify with. But some car salesman must have felt that the writer should have found another way to measure Sparky's integrity.

In today's *Free Press*, there is a brief note on the sports page, which I shall quote: "The profile of Sparky Anderson

in Wednesday's *Free Press* contained a gratuitous reference
to automobile salespeople. The reference was unfair, and the
Free Press regrets this remark."

To suggest that a car salesman does not always tell you
everything you'd like to know about a car is no more than
to suggest that life is not always beautiful. But life, which
most of us will be reluctant to trade in even when it begins
to rust out, is not for sale in the advertising section of your
daily paper. Automobiles are.

In Journalism I, the lesson for today is: Avoid offensive
examples, specifically those offensive to people who sell
costly products in large volume. Especially cars. In Detroit.

Friday
June 15th

A LITTLE OLD STANDING O

When Sparky Anderson made his first appearance on the
field last night, he got a standing ovation, apparently a tribute
to this dedicated man for making it to the ball park on time.

The standing ovation in American sport has become a joke,
and I don't know how it happened. Or when it happened.
But I think I know what it means. It means Americans
have lost the capacity to distinguish between something
rather nice and something awe-inspiring.

On the second day of May in 1939, I skipped an afternoon
class and, together with a friend who also held baseball in
higher esteem than Geology 12, hitchhiked from Ann Arbor
in to Detroit to see the Tigers play the Yankees. I don't
know how many people were in the stands, but there couldn't
have been much of a crowd because we had no trouble
getting good seats. (This was still the Depression, and the

ticket sellers were so artless as to sell you the best tickets they
had left when you arrived half an hour before the game. This
is one reason you will sometimes hear an old guy refer to
those bad days as "the good old days.")

I stared at my scorecard mechanically as the park announcer ran down the Yankee lineup, but I was counting, and
when he got to the seventh man I turned to my friend and
said, "Jesus, they've got Gehrig batting eighth!" (My
friend's name was Jim. The name I used was an expletive.
In those days, hardly anybody I knew was actually named
Jesus.) No sooner had I spoken than the announcer intoned
the fateful words: "Dahlgren, first base."

And then we knew. After 2,130 consecutive games, Lou
Gehrig's streak was ending. Having already wasted my pro-
fanity on the far less shocking event I had thought I was
about to see, I said nothing. Jim and I just looked at each
other in wonder.

A few moments later, Lou Gehrig emerged from the dugout to carry the lineup card up to home plate. The disease
that would kill him two years later (but about which we
then knew nothing) had already begun to cripple him, because I clearly remember that he walked slowly and rather
stiffly toward the waiting group of umpires.

I also remember that the fans stood up and applauded for
what seemed like a long time but was probably about two
minutes. There was no shouting, just sustained vigorous
applause. But they were *on their feet*, which meant something in those days. A standing ovation was a ritual act,
meant to honor a man's whole career, or some deed of
superhuman courage or skill. It was important because it
was unplanned; people knew when to do it—and when not
to do it, which was most of the time.

Lou Gehrig got another standing ovation when he made
his famous farewell speech at Yankee Stadium, of course.
Babe Ruth got one in Pittsburgh when, a week or so before

retiring forever, forty years old and worn out, he miraculously summoned the strength to hit three home runs in a single game—the last of them one of the longest ever seen in that park.

On April 8th, 1974, Hank Aaron broke Babe Ruth's lifetime home-run record by hitting his 715th off Al Downing of the Dodgers. If you were living in the United States at that time, you remember what happened. They stopped the game, interviewed Aaron on national TV, made speeches and presented him with a plaque. It was unseemly, because it interrupted the rhythm of the game and made Aaron's feat seem like part of a planned entertainment. This was one of the great *individual* accomplishments of athletic history. Hank Aaron did it all by himself, over a period of twenty years. And once it was done, he seemed to diminish, rather than grow, in stature as the show-biz types took over. He became the star of the show instead of the whole show, which he deserved to be for a few minutes, until the people sat down and the next batter stepped up to the plate. (Actually, most of the huge crowd, instead of sitting down, left the park after Aaron's home run. They were not baseball fans but celebrity chasers. I cannot speak for Hank, but had I been in his shoes, I would have preferred an unchoreographed standing ovation from the few thousand genuine fans who stayed for the whole game.)

In an earlier day, before the invention of the media hype, the people would have stood up and cheered for several minutes, Hank would have waved his cap at them and that would have been enough. But the standing ovation has become meaningless in an era when people do not know the difference between a good thing and a great thing. When we see a manager getting a standing ovation for showing up (or a catcher for throwing a runner out at second), it becomes easier to understand how a stupid and pointless book about a sea gull can sell eight million copies, and a rather pretty girl from Nicaragua who has never in her life done anything worth knowing about can become world famous.

A week or so ago, when the Tigers were in California, Mark Fidrych joined George Kell at the TV microphone. (Did a nice job, too, for a pure amateur.) At one point, a fat man in one of the field boxes fell over the rail while reaching for a foul ball and hit the ground rather hard. As he was being helped back to his seat, the people around him stood up and cheered. "He got," said The Bird, "a little old standing O." The terminology seemed to me significant. The term "little old" indicates good-natured approval. The reduction of the key word to a single initial denotes a tired familiarity; the thing is so commonplace that the speaker can't be bothered pronouncing the entire phrase.

When John Wayne, shortly before his death, made a farewell appearance at the Academy Awards, he got a standing ovation. John Wayne was an American institution, whatever you thought of him, so he certainly deserved it, but in this instance it had no more impact than an Entertainer-of-the-Year award from the Davenport Elks, because they would have done the same thing for Lawrence Welk or Henry Kissinger or any other Famous Name.

For an athlete or an entertainer, the standing ovation used to be the equivalent of the Nobel Prize—a reward for a lifetime of excellence. During all those years that John O'Hara, the novelist, yearned in vain for a Nobel Prize, I'll bet he never once referred to it as "a little old Nobel P."

❋   ❋   ❋

I find I cannot leave the subject of Lou Gehrig's last day without commenting on the movie made of his life. It was called *Pride of the Yankees*, and it was extravagantly praised, which is not surprising. How could a critic do anything but extol a movie about an American hero who went bravely to

an early death, starring another American hero, Gary
Cooper? Released shortly after the country went to war
against Japan, when we were desperately looking for heroes,
the picture couldn't miss. None of which alters the fact that
it wasn't very good.

Gary Cooper never had any trouble convincing anyone
that he was an honest, brave, wonderful guy—or any success in convincing me that he was Lou Gehrig, or any other
ballplayer. But the most damaging, ultimately ruinous, defect
of this film was that the writer didn't know much about
baseball. Or if he knew, he didn't care, which is worse.

You would think that a sense of drama would be the one
almost indispensable tool for a screenwriter. But the most
dramatic moment in the Lou Gehrig story (which I happened
to witness) was eliminated from the movie. In real life, the
words "Dahlgren, first base" coming over the public-address
system stunned the crowd into a moment of unplanned
silence, which was followed by the unprecedented sound
of several thousand people sighing in unison. Then Gehrig
trudged painfully up to the plate, carrying the lineup card
without his name on it. It was one of the most moving
moments in sports history, high drama of the sort you cannot make up. So they made up something *else*!

In the movie, the Tigers and Yankees are involved in a
close game when we hear the park announcer say, "Your
attention please: Dahlgren batting for Gehrig." Cut to the
radio announcer exclaiming that Gehrig's consecutive-game
streak is ending. It was disgusting: bogus theatrics hatched
out of Hollywood's inability to understand that truth is often
better than anything the hacks can dream up.

The movie version was ridiculous, as well as crudely
insensitive. Not only did it not happen that way but, as you
will have realized if you know anything about baseball, it
couldn't have happened that way. Putting in a pinch hitter
for Gehrig would not have ended his streak. The tragedy
had to be acted out before the game began.

As for the game itself, the real one wasn't very close. After Lou had sat down on the bench for the first time in fourteen years, the Yankees went out and won it, 22 to 2. The movie people couldn't see the significance of that either.

Saturday
June 16th

FROM HERE TO INFINITY

Sheldon Burnside, a pitcher whose name intrigued me last year before I even knew who he was, has now become a "player to be named later." Or so he thinks, and you can't blame him. He's been sent down to the minors, but instead of going to Evansville, the Tigers' farm club, he finds himself in Indianapolis, a Cincinnati outpost. Examining the evidence, Sheldon has a sneaking suspicion that he may be headed for the Reds as part of the Champ Summers deal. His reasoning appears sound.

Last season, in his first appearance with the Tigers, Sheldon gave up four Yankee runs in one-third of an inning, making his earned-run average 108.00. He lowered it later, but it occurred to me that if he had never pitched again, he would have shared an unenviable distinction with three other pitchers. Harry Heitman (Brooklyn, 1918), Frank Wurm (Brooklyn, 1944) and Fritz Fisher (Detroit, 1964) all have lifetime ERA's of 108.00. That's not the highest, however. That mark is held by Joe (Fire) Cleary of the 1945 Washington Senators with a lifetime ERA of 189.00. That works out to seven earned runs in one-third of an inning, and will be hard to top.

There are, of course, several pitchers in the book with ERA's of "infinity," designated thus: ∞. They are the ones who pitched in a big-league game but never got anyone out.

Since they are officially recorded as having pitched 0 innings, there is no way to compute their earned-run average. Obviously, Cleary's biggest mistake (he seems to have made several) was retiring one man. I don't know who that batter was, but come to think of it, he holds a unique distinction himself. He's the only man who ever failed to reach base against the pitcher with the worst ERA in history. Struck out, in fact.

Monday
June 18th

A DEAR JOHN LETTER

In the advertising business, or the aluminum-siding business, or most any normal business, they know what to do with an old guy who can no longer carry his full share of the load. Especially an old guy who was once a brilliant contributor, one of the people who made the business go. They appoint him Director of Contingency Planning, the president issues a memo announcing his "promotion" to a position in which he will be "dealing with issues of vital importance to the continuing expansion of our essential modal parameters" and they give him an office where he can sit and wonder what that means. Some of the ambitious young bloods in the firm may gripe a bit over the fact that he's still drawing a substantial salary they'd like to cut up among themselves. But no one calls him a jerk. At least, not to his face.

Well, not all companies are that compassionate. Some of them, it's true, will fire the old guy. He may not even get a gold watch out of it, but he'll be given a warm handshake and told what a fine man he is and he'll be missed, and if it weren't for the stockholders' stubborn insistence on a youth movement . . . but what can you do? A few people will re-

John Hiller, back from the brink.

member what a fireball he once was. And for the most part, those who don't will keep quiet. Nobody will tell him to drop dead.

John Hiller is an extreme example of a man who was once a brilliant contributor, one of the people who made the business go. The business being the Detroit Baseball Club, as you surely know. He is not old. At thirty-six, he is less than a year older than Rusty Staub, who, you will recall, still figures he has five $200,000 years left. Or is it two $200,000 years and three $300,000 years? (Rusty, like the Geritol lady, obviously figures he's going to get better instead of older.) But Hiller has lost his fastball, which is comparable to a bookie's losing his telephone. He has lost none of his skill. He can still throw the curve and his justly celebrated change-up. But the fastball is not so much a skill as a talent bestowed at birth, and what the Lord giveth at birth He taketh away at thirty-six. Without the fastball to set it up, the change looks like batting practice with a softball. *You* could hit it. A major-league hitter destroys it.

So Hiller has been having a tough year. He's given up some clutch home runs that have cost the Tigers ball games. The good days, once the norm, have become rarities. Obviously, he is not what he used to be, and he says he's had it. At the end of the season, says John, he'll call it a career.

What has prompted Hiller's decision even more than his unhappy performance is the detestable behavior of the fans. "I've had guys not more than six feet from me holler, 'Why don't you go have another heart attack?'" he says. The kind of mentality which this sort of thing bespeaks is beyond description, so I won't try, but I remember the days when we thought the Nazi movement couldn't possibly have happened here, and I weep for my lost innocence. Who are these people? They shouldn't be at baseball games, they should be home nailing their children's hands to the wall.

It's well enough to say these are just a few monsters, not typical of Detroit fans at all. (Good Lord, if they were typical, who would dare go to a ball game?) But that's not just five guys up there booing when Hiller leaves the mound after getting pounded. Baseball fans, who honor the memory of men who played twenty or fifty years ago, seem peculiarly insensitive to the problems of last year's heroes.

They don't do that in any other park, Hiller says; only in Detroit do they boo their own players when the gift begins to rust. I think he's wrong there; I know I've seen it in other cities. But it is a shame wherever it happens. Sure, we are all apt to express our misgivings privately when the ex-hero with depleted talents strides to the mound or the plate. But we ought to have enough respect for the achievements of the past to keep them to ourselves. As they do in the aluminum-siding business. Usually.

If this is the last year for John Hiller, he'll have little to regret. He's an admirable young man. Note how easily I slip into the habit of calling him young, once I start to think of him as a "civilian." As a ballplayer he's skirting senility, but on the long course he's still a youth (still eligible for the Yale Younger Poets award if he's interested). Hardly a callow one, though. He shucked off his callowness while sitting out the 1971 season after a heart attack at the age of twenty-seven. Against all odds, he came back from the seeming tragedy to become one of the best relief pitchers in baseball —*the* best for a couple of years. He loves the game, works hard at it, examines and criticizes his own performance, helps the younger players and counts himself lucky to be here. Or did until recently.

Many people, having gone to the brink of disaster and back, attain maturity for a while. But they tend to forget where they've been. Hiller remembers. It took courage and determination to do what he did. It took intelligence and character to make it permanent. Whether he retires this year or not, John Hiller's baseball career will be over soon, but he'll still have a ways to go in life. I have no doubt that he'll handle it well.

Tuesday
June 19th

HERE TODAY

Billy's back. Just as I did not predict, Billy Martin has returned to manage the Yankees after an absence of less than a year. They needed something, but I thought it was a relief pitcher.

Last year, when George Steinbrenner announced, five days after firing Billy Martin, that he would bring him back to manage the team in 1980, I was skeptical. "It is a bizarre development," I said, "but I'll be surprised if the pledge is ever redeemed." I may be right, at that. He's back, true, but George Steinbrenner's credo is "Miracles Now," and if Billy can't deliver them, who's to say what may happen between now and next opening day? In the capricious atmosphere of Yankee Stadium, 1980 may be two interim managers away.

When Billy Martin lost his job (technically he "resigned") last July, I was far away. I heard the news on my little radio through a wailing wall of static at two thirty in the morning. It wasn't until I got back home, and was given a copy of *The New York Times* for July 30, 1978, that I began to understand the implications of what had happened. It turned out that there was more to Billy Martin's problem than simple Mediterranean choler. The legend on his personal coat of arms, it seems, might well have been *In vino bilis.*

It had never been any secret that Billy took a drink on occasion. People had even been known to comment that the occasions were not always adequately spaced. As an alcoholic, I fully understand the temptation. I have known the thirst. The unmitigated fact, though, is that a large capacity for booze produces a reduced capacity for efficient performance in any recognized field of endeavor.

The *Times* piece, compiled by two reporters named Gerald Eskenazi and Murray Chass, contains an almost hour-by-

hour account of Billy's activities during the days preceding
his resignation. There are repeated references to statements
made in bars or over drinks. Indeed, one might have been
forgiven for inferring that Billy seldom spoke at all, off the
field anyway, except when in a bar or over a drink.

On Sunday, July 23rd, the day before his resignation,
Martin made his celebrated statement about Reggie Jackson
and George Steinbrenner: "The two of them deserve each
other. One's a born liar; the other's convicted." (Steinbrenner
was convicted of making illegal campaign contributions to
Nixon.) The remark was made to Chass of *The Times* and
another reporter shortly after Martin "had had a few drinks
at the bar" at O'Hare Airport in Chicago. The reporters flew
with the team to Kansas City, from where they telephoned
Steinbrenner for his comment. "Steinbrenner sounded
stunned. He asked Chass to repeat what Martin had said.
He asked whether Martin had been drinking." When reached
by Al Rosen, the Yankees' president, at his hotel in Kansas
City, "Martin was in a room drinking with some of the
Yankee staff." He denied making the statement, "but Rosen
wondered how two reporters would have identical quotes"
if he hadn't. At one o'clock in the morning, Billy phoned one
of the reporters. "Martin's words were slurred," the reporter
said. He accused the sportswriter of being "out to get me
fired."

The next day, wearing dark glasses, Martin announced his
resignation to a hurriedly assembled news conference.

One of the things that had originally triggered Martin's
anger was learning, while in Chicago, that Steinbrenner had
once discussed with Bill Veeck, the White Sox owner, the
possibility of exchanging managers, Martin for Bob Lemon
(who was then the Chicago manager). Billy found this out
while "drinking with Veeck" after a game at Comiskey Park.

For the skilled observer, a pattern is beginning to emerge.
Reading the entire piece with a trained eye, one notes that
at no time does the writer accuse Martin of abstinence.

Drinking impairs one's ability to do one's job. There are no exceptions to this, notwithstanding the romantic protestations of writers and other artistic types. It is true that there are people who are so good at their jobs that they can do them fairly well despite being more or less drunk. For a person in authority, however, being known as a drinker can be ruinous. And nowhere is this more likely to be true than in the case of a baseball manager. His players must *believe* he is qualified to make decisions, quite apart from whether he is or not. In matters of game strategy, if they question his judgment, their execution will be halfhearted. It hardly seems necessary to point out that a manager whose players suspect he is befogged by drink is not in a position to be a dynamic leader.

Almost anyone who understands baseball could run a team "by the book," always following the established rules of strategy, making the high-percentage choice. And in fact, there have been many managers who operated that way, some of them rather successful. (If you have the best players, you will usually win, whatever your method.) Walter Alston of the Dodgers was that sort, and he kept his job for twenty years. The great managers, though, have been those who were prepared to throw away the book when the situation called for it, *and were able to recognize that situation.* Leo Durocher was a prime example. Many of his players have attested to how exciting it was to play for Durocher, because he was always willing to try the unexpected, and ingenious at devising ways to do it.

Obviously, if a manager's mind is not clear—or even if his players merely suspect that it isn't—every unorthodox maneuver is going to raise doubts as to whether he knows what he's doing. If it doesn't work, this will be taken as proof that he made a stupid move, although the truth may be that it didn't work because the players involved didn't carry it out with conviction. Whatever the reason, the manager is plainly operating under a severe handicap.

This is equally true of every other phase of a manager's job. Instruction and discipline, for example. How can a manager either correct flaws in performance or enforce rules of conduct if the players have no confidence in his judgment?

Finally, there is the ancient but still valid precept that a leader ought to set an example for his men. In the same *New York Times* story from which I have been quoting, Billy Martin says (in a bar): "The rules are made by me, but I don't have to follow them." Rank hath its privileges, granted, but the prudent man doesn't abuse them and then brag about it.

It is an odd fact that I never suspect alcohol as the source of a difficult situation until the mud hits me in the eye. I am not normally so generous. I am suspicious of the honest politician, the munificent philanthropist, the public-spirited businessman. I do not for a minute believe that Miss Universe's consuming ambition is to heal sick children. I even imagine the utopian visionary is a secret cynic. I am a skeptic (although not yet quite a cynic myself, I hope), but I seem to have a block about alcohol.

You might think that having been down the road myself, I would be inclined to blame every instance of erratic behavior in others on drink. But quite the opposite is true. For years I have heard stories about Billy Martin's violent outbursts of temper (which have led to fistfights with his own players), of his wildly changing moods, of his damaging public statements. One undeniable fact about Martin is that he has been a winner everywhere he has managed. And he has always lost his job after angry confrontations with the people who hired him. What makes him behave that way? I used to wonder. The simple answer never occurred to me.

Now that I know, I have a great deal more sympathy for him. But I wouldn't hire him to manage my ball club unless I were convinced that he had given up drinking forever.

❀   ❀   ❀

Billy Martin. Angry man.

It is ironic that Billy Martin lost his job once because he said that George Steinbrenner and Reggie Jackson "deserve each other." For it strikes me that if ever two people deserved each other, they are Steinbrenner and Martin. What they have in common is arrogance and insensitivity. Billy seems to think he is above criticism, and he bristles whenever a reporter asks him a question which he interprets as reflecting on his intelligence, manhood, honor, courage, truthfulness, religious convictions or the way he wears his hat. And almost every question, except the straight tell-me-how-good-

you-are used by the TV man with thirty seconds to fill, *does* reflect on one of those things. Or so Billy seems to think.

Steinbrenner doesn't bristle. On television, he often comes across as a rather pleasant, easygoing man who's just trying to get fair value for his money. In reality, he is overbearing and, off his record, odious. He is also very, very rich, which permits him to be these things with impunity.

In June of last year, Steinbrenner, accompanied by his puppet president, Al Rosen, followed the Yankees from town to town, issuing daily bulletins on Billy Martin's tenure. It was appalling. In Boston it was made clear that if the Yankees lost three straight, Martin was out. Then they came to Detroit, and we heard that three losses in four games would signal the end for Martin. He was literally holding his job from day to day. Billy Martin is a difficult man, but he didn't deserve that.

Later, when Reggie Jackson went hitless in a double-header loss to Milwaukee, Steinbrenner publicly excoriated him. Jackson retaliated by saying he would play out his contract and retire, it was all just too painful to tolerate.

George Kell, the Tigers' TV announcer, was critical of Jackson. "I never found it painful to come to the ball park," he said, "and I can't understand these players today who say it is." Kell never played for a man who called him a bum every time he grounded out, either, but he seemed to think Steinbrenner was justified. When a man pours millions of dollars into a ball club, he said, he has a right to demand a winner. But does he have a right to act like a jerk? I guess maybe he does, at that. The ability to pour millions of dollars into anything carries with it certain inalienable rights, one of which is to be forgiven for behavior that would get most of us thrown out of a Sicilian bordello.

If George Steinbrenner disapproves of the way his manager runs his team, he can tell him so privately, or he can get rid of him. But to ask a man to manage a baseball team (or anything else) while his employer is criticizing his every move to millions of listeners and readers daily is beyond reason and decency.

And look at the performance of the people the Yankee owner was attacking. Billy Martin, whatever you may think of him, had won two consecutive pennants and a World Series. Reggie Jackson took Steinbrenner's money and delivered the package he had ordered. He hit .286 with 32 home runs and 110 RBI's, one of the best years of his career. He also helped the team win a pennant, and hit .450, with 5 home runs, in the World Series. This is the man Steinbrenner felt it proper to sneer at in public after one bad night.

I am sick of the notion that seems to prevail these days that great wealth automatically makes you a wonderful guy, even though the evidence indicates that you are an offensive buffoon. You can't stop Steinbrenner from acting that way. Ownership of a famous baseball team gives him instant access to the press and TV, which promptly report everything he says. But at least you can label him for what he is: an obnoxious clod. In a $600 suit. (I wonder if I would act like that if I had money. I wish I could find out.)

          *   *   *

Is $600 for a suit enough to indicate great wealth? I have no idea what a rich man pays for his suits these days. Never having paid any considerable fraction of that amount for a suit, I find the thought of a $600 one most impressive. If it's too low, substitute an appropriate figure.

Wednesday
June 20th

OF TELEGRAPHIC RECONSTRUCTIONS AND OTHER FOND MEMORIES

There's been a lot of griping lately about potato chips' desecrating the sacred image of baseball. That's because every time a Tiger hits a home run, a local potato-chip company sends a case of chips to some worthy charity. They do this not out of altruism, but with the clear understanding that Ernie Harwell will mention it on the air. ("That home runs sends a case of potato chips to the Stigmata Sancti Home for the Bloody but Unbowed.") Ernie—or, to be precise, the Detroit Baseball Company—doesn't do this out of an excess of public spirit, either, but rather for a fee paid by the chip chaps.

Quite a few people think this is chintzy, and I agree. But it is hardly new. The gratuitous commercial tie-in of this sort has been a part of baseball broadcasting for as long as I can remember. Harwell displays a certain reticence in delivering his potato-chip message, persumably reflecting a belief that it's undignified for an outfit as prosperous as the Tigers to scratch for the last dollar that can be squeezed out of a meager gift to orphans or codgers. But Harry Heilmann, whom many grizzled fans remember as the most popular announcer the Tigers ever had, used to revel in this sort of thing, especially in the pre-war (i.e., Depression) days when every sponsorial nickel was eagerly coveted.

The first Tiger announcer I remember was Ty Tyson, a soft-spoken man with a dry sense of humor, many of whose sardonic remarks I did not appreciate at the age of nine, when I began listening to baseball on the radio. I heard Ty get ruffled only once, and that was not during a baseball game. Long after his Tiger days, he was doing a Michigan–Cornell football game from Ithaca. It was halftime, and the Michigan band was spelling out the word BUICK on the field, in consideration of the fact that the car company had paid for the musicians' trip. You could hear the Buick theme music in the background as Ty went into a routine commercial announcement. "This game, like all the Michigan games this season," he said, "is brought to you by the Buick dealers of Greater . . . my God, what am I saying? I mean the *Chrysler* dealers of Greater Detroit!"

In the middle '30s, Harry Heilmann began doing the Tiger games on another station in competition with Tyson. Heilmann was a rare, maybe unique phenomenon in the sports-broadcasting business. He had, on the surface, almost no qualifications for the job, beyond the obvious one that he had been one of baseball's greatest hitters (four times A.L. batting champion with .394, .403, .393 and .398). He was unpolished, ungrammatical . . . and marvelous. His sheer exuberance and obvious love of the game were so contagious

that he soon became Detroit's favorite announcer, driving
Tyson right off the air. (They remained close friends. I still
recall Tyson's tearful announcement of Heilmann's death
from cancer in 1951.)

Heilmann worked hard at improving both his delivery and
his English and eventually became almost glib—but he never
quite outgrew his enthusiasm for slipping in an extra plug
for the people who paid the bills. He did it with such good
humor, though, that no one ever seemed to resent it. I remember a Red Sox outfielder rather oddly named Colonel
Buster Mills. He was known around the league as Buster
Mills, but Harry always managed to refer to him as Colonel
Mills at least once during every game. It was the perfect
lead-in for a mention of General Mills, makers of Wheaties,
the Breakfast of Champions.

Another sponsor during the Heilmann years was the
Socony-Vacuum Company, one of whose products was an
insect spray called Bugaboo. "There's a fly to right field,
fairly deep," Heilmann would say. "Pete Fox drifts under it
and . . . Bugaboo! another fly is dead."

Socony's principal products, though, were oil and gasoline,
and Heilmann worked their brand names into the com-
mentary with fair frequency. During the annual Detroit visit
of Al Schacht, the famous baseball clown, Heilmann would
always invite him to come to the booth and chat about the
game. Since Schacht spent most of his time on the road, he
wasn't familiar with many of the players. Once, as Rudy
York advanced to the plate, Schacht said, "Who's this
fellow?" York was a power hitter, famed for his home runs
but not noted for asceticism in matters of food and drink.
His weight was officially given as 220, but that probably
represented more an ideal than a reality.

"That's Rudy York, Al," Heilmann said. "He's got plenty of
that old Mobilgas power."

"He looks like he's inflated with it," said Schacht.

(Rudy was undisciplined in all things. I had the strong

Harry Heilmann. A great hitter, a unique broadcaster.
"Trouble! Trouble!"

feeling that as a hitter, he never speculated on what the next pitch would be. He just stood up there and if he could reach it he hit it. He was the antithesis of his more famous teammate Hank Greenberg, one of the most cerebral sluggers ever to play the game. It has been said that every great hitter is a guess hitter. If Rudy was, as I suspect, an exception to this rule, he could always have resorted to the standard cliché of the unorthodox: "It works for me." It did indeed, as 277 home runs and 1152 RBI's over a twelve-year career will attest.)

Heilmann was a master of an art form that no longer exists: the telegraphic reconstruction. When a baseball team went on the road in those days, it was cheaper to keep the announcer at home and let him "reconstruct" the game (fake it) from a studio. A telegraph operator sat nearby taking terse dispatches from the scene of action (Ball . . . Strike . . . Foul Ball . . . Greenberg doubles to left), which he handed to the announcer, who would then call the play in great detail, relying heavily on his imagination ("That was a fast ball, low and away." "It's off the wall, and Hank races for second!").

Most baseball announcers have pet phrases to describe a batted ball that looks as if it's going out of the park. "It may be . . . it may be!" Or, "It's going . . . going . . .!" These code words alert the listener to what's coming and build suspense, yet leave the broadcaster an out if the ball doesn't quite clear the fence. Heilmann's home-run signal was "Trouble! Trouble!" Trouble for the other side, naturally, since the buzzwords were generally used only to portend a quad-rangular by the home team. A home run by the visitors did not evoke the same kind of excitement.

No one was fooled by the telegraphic reconstruction. Every regular listener knew the announcer wasn't really at the game, but we didn't think much about it unless it was obvious that the announcer himself was not sure what had taken place on the field. This sometimes happened when the telegraphed message was too succinct in describing a compli-cated play. (I stress that the play-by-play was sent not by teletype, but by Morse code—one man banging out dots and dashes on an old-fashioned telegraph key. The staccato sound of the telegraph was often clearly audible in the background, and there were stories of people who regularly picked up a few bucks in barroom bets by their remarkable ability to predict what the next hitter was going to do. To an expert telegrapher, of course, the dit-dah-dit was as clear as the spoken word.)

Heilmann sometimes read mail from his listeners on the air. He began one broadcast with a gleeful rendition of a complaint from a loyal fan named Otto Schwarzhauser, who objected to Harry's prolonging the suspense when a Tiger hit a home run in a reconstructed game. "I'm a butcher," he wrote, "and the last time you did it I got so excited I almost cut my thumb off. You already know it's a home run, so why don't you say so?" Came the sixth inning of that day's game, with the score tied, and a Tiger hitter got hold of one. "There's a long drive to right field," Heilmann exclaimed. "It's well hit. Trouble! Trouble! Look out, Mr. Schwarzhauser."

Harry Heilmann collapsed while covering the Tigers during spring training in 1951, and died about three months later. Just before he died, he was told he had been elected to the Baseball Hall of Fame. It was a lie, but I hope he believed it. The following year he did make it. He had been out of baseball for twenty years, and the honor was long overdue. To many of us, he was equally deserving of a spot in the Radio Hall of Fame. Tiger games on radio were never quite as much fun after he was gone.

Heilmann was followed in the Tiger booth by Van Patrick, a noted football announcer whose principal qualification was self-esteem. His fame as a football broadcaster emanated solely from the number of games he had called. He used to fly around the country doing three or four games in a single weekend. By the time he died he must have broadcast several hundred games, and knew less about football than half the people in the stands at any one of them. I know it's bad form to speak ill of the dead, but honesty compels me to state that he was a terrible announcer. His style was reminiscent of people like Bill Stern and Harry Wismer, two famous and terrible announcers of the days before television, when accuracy was not at a premium because the listeners couldn't see a thing.

Patrick's monumental ego, offensive enough in small doses, became unbearable when he was on every day. He seemed to have no interest in baseball and saw the game mainly as a vehicle for promoting himself. If it's possible to be simultaneously boring and maddening, Patrick did it. His broadcasts were redeemed only by the occasional comments of his colorful "color man," Dizzy Trout. Diz, who had been a star pitcher for the Tigers throughout the '40s, was a funny man, sometimes even intentionally. He was nearly illiterate, but thoroughly devoted—not so much to broadcasting as to the team. On more than one occasion, when an altercation developed on the field, he threatened to go down and take on the opposing player himself. And when a bad call went against the Tigers, he didn't shrink from expressing his opinion of the umpire.

Trout's namesake, Dizzy Dean, who was a broadcaster in St. Louis, made capital of his own highly original grammar for years ("slud" as the past tense of "slide," etc.), but one got the clear impression that he was working at it. Diz Trout's malapropisms and mispronunciations were artless and innocent. He had lived in Detroit for at least twenty years and played for the Tigers for fourteen, but he could pronounce neither the name of the city nor that of the team. He called them the "DEE-troit Taggers." He delighted me every time he referred to the player list as the "rooster." My wife's favorite Troutism, though, was the word he used (and she uses to this day) for the cover that is put over the field when it rains. He called it the "tarpoleon," which rhymes with Napoleon.

During breaks in the game, Trout used to entertain us with little anecdotes from baseball's past: odd incidents, unusual records and the like. We were supposed to believe he was ad-libbing these from his vast store of baseball lore. In fact, they were written for him, and he was usually reading them for the first time. This was evident because they contained modestly erudite words, not in Diz's normal vocabulary, which he often mispronounced and occasionally couldn't say at all. Sometimes, after taking two or three shots at a word, he would just skip it and go on. More than once, however, faced with a tough multi-syllable, he would simply abandon the whole project and, after a suitable pause, start talking about something else. So after an intriguing buildup we were left with no punch line because Diz had run into a word like "unpremeditated." ("One of the most unusual double plays ever made," he might say, "happened in a 1927 game between Beaumont and San Antonio in the Texas League. No fewer than six players, including all three outfielders, handled the ball on the play, which was completely unpred . . . unperdimate . . . unpredeminate . . ." Pause. "Well, the Tigers are coming to bat in the bottom of the fifth . . .")

Sometimes Diz was amusing on purpose. A common baseball expression in those days, referring to any player of great size, was "He looks big enough to work for a living." Diz's version was "He looks big enough to carry a sign."

Van Patrick used to get openly irritated at Diz Trout's outbursts, especially his unblushingly partisan comments about the opposing team or the umpiring. Patrick would huffily remind him that his conduct was unprofessional. It surely was, but it was also unpretentious and sincere and the perfect antidote to Patrick's consummate pomposity.

Van Patrick and Diz Trout are both dead now, possibly gone to a place where everyone has what he wants. I picture Patrick in a sumptuous office, its walls covered with autographed pictures of the great (*To my old pal Van, with best wishes for all eternity—God*), while Diz doubtless pitches a two-hit shutout every fourth day and spends the intervening days lecturing on baseball in the local language, which he speaks flawlessly.

Nowadays there are four principal announcers doing Tiger games: Harwell and his backup man, Paul Carey, on radio, and George Kell and Al Kaline on television. Ernie Harwell has been the Tigers' radioman for about seventeen years. He is a pro. He roots with restraint, and he never knocks the team, but he lets you know, when the occasion calls for it,

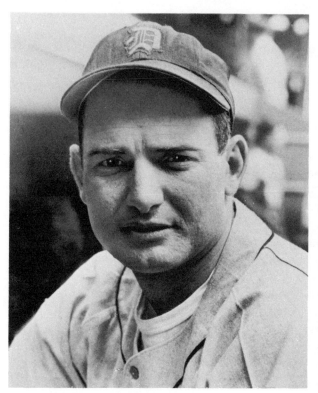

George Kell, left, and Al Kaline in their playing days.

that an outfielder "didn't play that very well" (he botched
it) or that a gift hit from the official scorer was "a fairly easy
chance" for an infielder (the scorer botched it). Ernie tells
you what happened and, if possible, why. That's what a baseball announcer is supposed to do, but few in the profession
do it as well.

Al Kaline has been a refreshing surprise. The inarticulate
kid who became an outfield superstar is now a TV com-
mentator whose remarks add to your appreciation of the
game, instead of just filling dead air time. Honesty is what
Al is selling, and considering that it's the Tigers who are
buying, he should be commended for always giving full
value. The system under which the radio and TV announcers
are employees of the baseball club has been justly criticized.
Often, it makes them shills for the team. But it hasn't
bothered Kaline. Thoroughly unassuming, he never says he's
going to tell it like it is. But in contrast to many of the self-
styled fearless commentators who do commit that solecism,
he really does say what he thinks. When the Tigers are playing bad baseball, Kaline will tell you about it. He is the
ideal partner for Kell, who is a good reporter but seldom
editorializes.

Al Kaline was the kind of ballplayer of whom it is said
that "he comes to play and always gives you a hundred and
ten percent." We use these exhausted phrases now only in
jest, and that's too bad because they would have a certain
impact when applied to a Kaline if they hadn't been used up
in describing players who rise to a great occasion. For Al, the
occasion was a whole career. He was with the Tigers for
twenty-two years, and he played on a lot of bad teams, but
he did not lower his standards to fit the company. He gave
not 110 percent, which is a meaningless hype phrase, but as
close to 100 percent of himself as any player the game has
known. He was a gifted ballplayer but, in my opinion, not
quite gifted enough to become one of the game's all-time
greats on talent alone. That he did become one is a tribute

to such tired old virtues as determination and hard work. He was born a star; he made himself a superstar.

The qualities that make Kaline a good baseball announcer are the same ones that made him a great player. He *knows the game* as well as anyone I've ever heard talk about it. And he'll let you know when someone is doing it wrong. With anyone less sincere, this could quickly become offensive. But one of Kaline's prime assets as an announcer is an air of quiet concern. Let an outfielder fail to back up second on a key play, or carelessly throw to the wrong base, and he'll tell you about it, not in anger but in sorrow. It's as if it hurts his feelings to see a young player dishonoring the uniform he wore with such distinction. I suppose that sounds as maudlin, in a cynical age, as a homily on maidenly virtue, but that's the way Kaline strikes me—as a simple man who believes the laborer should be worthy of his hire (especially at today's hourly rates, I should think, although he never mentions that).

Al is equally outspoken on the delinquencies of opposing players, and this I find funny because we are not used to hearing such frank appraisals of professional athletes. Last year, during a series with Minnesota, whose third baseman was a young man named Mike Cubbage, Kaline commented, "I don't see why the Tigers don't bunt more against Cubbage. He has the worst arm I have ever seen." This probably didn't make Cubbage feel too good, but there was no malice in it. A man can't help it if he has a bad arm, and Kaline's disdain is reserved for players who do have the tools and don't make proper use of them. The criticism implicit in the remark was directed at the Tigers. Against this third baseman with a terrible arm, the Tigers did not bunt, either because they didn't know how or, worse yet, because no one had the intelligence to think of capitalizing on this weakness. Criminal negligence, in either case.

George Kell, who does the play-by-play on TV, is a former Tiger third baseman (1946–52) of great skill, as well as a

pretty good game announcer. Neither he nor Kaline is a
master of English grammar and diction, but I guess you can't
have everything.

Kell and Kaline are often accompanied in the booth by a
third man, Channel 4's chief sports announcer. I do not
name him because, as these things go, he will probably be
somebody else by next month. Whoever he is, he is involved
in an obvious conflict of interest. He works for the TV
station but appears "with the approval of the Detroit Baseball Club." It is patently impossible for a man to be an impartial reporter of the Tigers' activities while he is dependent
on their "approval" for his position as a game broadcaster.
Suppose, for example, he discovers that one of the players
is secretly fomenting a revolt against management. Does he
put on his reporter's hat and break the story on the eleven-
o'clock news? Or does he quietly go to the club's general
manager and warn him of the problem? And that would be a
minor dilemma compared with his discovery, say, of some
highly unethical act by the baseball club itself. He has, in
effect (if not technically), two employers whose interests
are not always the same.

Ideally, the game broadcasters would be employees of the
radio or TV station, responsible only to the people who hired
them, and rated solely on the accuracy and expertness of their
reports. Ideally, too, the course of true love would never run
rough, and Hitler would have been accepted at art school.

Saturday
June 23rd

YOU'VE GOT TO BE THERE

What ever happened to speed and control? Once considered the two most important assets a pitcher could have,
they seem to have disappeared from baseball, or at least from

its language, to be replaced by two new things called "velocity and location." No player or manager can talk about pitching in public nowadays without stressing the vital importance of "velocity and location."

In every profession there is an apparently irresistible impulse to change the language as soon as the common people start to catch on to it. (In medicine, for example, there is a permanent committee of learned physicians who work around the clock revising the jargon, to keep the practitioners one jump ahead of the patients. After countless hours of doctor shows on TV, once esoteric terms like "subdural hematoma" and "myocardial infarction" no longer fool anyone, so these word healers can never rest.) Baseball is no exception, and so we got "wheels" for legs, "Chinese liner" for "Texas Leaguer" for pop-fly single, "frozen rope" (rescued from its original obscene function) for line drive, and a thousand other colorful terms. But at the other end of the scale, we also get pretentious inanities like "velocity and location," which is not only stilted but inaccurate.

"Velocity," it's true, is just a high-flown synonym for speed —offensive only in its pomposity. But "location," in any normal usage, doesn't even mean what these speakers intend it to mean.

To talk about a pitcher's location is not to discuss where he throws the ball but where he *is*. Still, it's a fact that, even in it's normal sense, location is indeed a vital factor in a pitcher's effectiveness. If he's going to be of any help, he ought to be at the ball park. He ought *not* to be anywhere else, especially any place where liquor is exchanged for money.

Baseball history is full of stories of players who suffered from a shaky sense of location on game days, including some very good ones. Four who come immediately to mind are Rube Waddell, Grover Cleveland Alexander, Flint Rhem and Boots Poffenberger. Alexander was much the best of them, but the others all had their moments. Waddell was a dull-witted clown, famous for chasing fire engines and often stopping for a drink (or a dozen) on the way back from the fire. According to oral history, Waddell once considered an offer of $2000 to jump from the Athletics to another team, but Connie Mack dissuaded him with a counter-offer of 400 one-dollar bills. Rube was the prototype of the crazy southpaw. Because of him, the mental processes of left-handed pitchers have been suspect ever since. He was also a superb pitcher, who won 196 games and would doubtless have won a lot more if, as Branch Rickey once implied, he had gotten a little more sleep.

Flint Rhem has contributed a number of stories to base-ball lore, including one that has become a legend of the game. He disappeared for several days, finally returning to announce that he had been kidnapped by four men who tied him up and forced strong drink down his throat through-out his ordeal.

During Grover Alexander's last years with the Cardinals, he and Rhem were teammates. Once Alex took a few days' unauthorized leave when he wasn't scheduled to pitch, and Rhem (who *was* supposed to pitch) vanished at the same time. When they returned, Rhem said he had gone along because, knowing Alexander's drinking habits, he had thought someone ought to look after him. There is no record of what Alexander said. Maybe nothing. They were usually satisfied just to have him back.

Cletus Elwood (Boots) Poffenberger, who pitched for the Tigers in the late '30s, also had a tendency to turn up missing from time to time. He had spent some time on the Tigers' farm team at Beaumont in the Texas League, and he liked the town. When, at one point, the Tigers proposed to send him to the minors for a period but wanted him to go to Montreal, which was in a faster league than Beaumont, Boots rebelled. It was Beaumont or nowhere for him. The incident secured Poffenberger's little niche in the baseball eccentrics' hall of fame. He liked the bright lights, the music and the wine when it was red or any other color. It was generally held, among baseball men and the world at large, that for anyone with these proclivities to demand Beaumont, Texas, when Montreal beckoned was comparable to an art lover's selecting an original drawing of Orphan Annie and Sandy in preference to the *Mona Lisa*.

Monday
June 25th

TIME IS NOT OF THE ESSENCE

One of the things which happily differentiate baseball from other team sports is the absence of the clock. No matter how desperate the situation late in the game may be, there is always plenty of time. When the home team is four runs behind with two out and the bases empty in the ninth, the spectators start heading for the exits. But most of them don't actually leave until they have seen the final out. And if the batter beats out an infield hit, and the next gets a walk, there is a flurry of excitement. The people who were leaving start looking around for a place to sit, or jam up the exit ramps, refusing to move, and they root for a miracle finish. Sometimes they even get it.

In football, if the score is 31–7 and there are only four minutes to play, especially if the home team is losing, the fans get up and leave. They know there is no hope. They may miss some exciting plays, maybe even a couple of touchdowns patched together out of strange passes and the carelessness of the visiting team (its victory assured), but they know that the winner has already been determined.

When the score is close, the contrast is even greater. In baseball, with the tying run on second and a good batter coming up, everything seems to slow down. The batter takes his time getting into the box and setting himself for the pitch. The pitcher studies the position of the outfielders, checks the runner at second, stares interminably at his catcher. And the tension builds while nothing is happening.

In football, conversely, with the final seconds ticking away and the trailing team trying desperately to score, everything is speeded up. The ball is snapped the instant the teams are lined up, the blocking assignments are not carried out, the quarterback heaves the ball frantically even when there's no one there to catch it. It becomes *a different game*, totally unlike the one they have been playing all afternoon. And this new game is one for which the officials don't seem to be prepared, one which they appear unable to handle. That's why, in the last couple of years, there have been so many questionable decisions which, because they came in the closing seconds of a close game, directly affected the outcome.

I thought of this contrast yesterday as I watched a Baltimore pitcher named Don Stanhouse, who holds the ball so long he appears to be hoping the batter will fall victim to some crippling disease if he is patient enough. Stanhouse, I think, overdoes it. But we have, after all, nothing but time. No harm is done, except to my composure. And I remembered a football game I saw on television which produced the worst call I have ever seen by an official in a professional sports event. All because of the clock. Oakland was trailing San Diego, 20–14, with a few seconds left to play. Ken Stabler, the Oakland quarterback, was attempting to pass from about the San Diego twenty-yard line when he was grabbed by an opposing lineman. With his arms partially pinned to his sides, Stabler threw the ball forward underhand. It hit the ground, and the play should have been over. It was an incomplete forward pass, no question about it. But the officials chose to regard it as a fumble. Along came Pete Banaszak of Oakland, who made no attempt to pick up the ball but instead shoveled it forward another five yards or so. Wantonly illegal, as every schoolboy knows. Finally, Dave

Casper, also of Oakland, entered the picture. He pushed the ball along for the final five yards until it crossed the goal line, then fell on it for a touchdown. In a movie, it would have been funny. It was funny, because it didn't even occur to me that the officials would allow it until I saw Oakland lining up for the extra point.

San Diego won the game, and it was taken away from them and given to Oakland. There is no other way to say it.

I emphasize again that none of this would have happened if the clock hadn't been running out. If there had been time for even one more play, Stabler wouldn't have thrown the ball, nor would either of the other Oakland players have reacted the way he did to a loose ball. The clock changes the game, and in effect changes the rules. A play that could not have happened during the first fifty-nine and a half minutes of the game *did* happen during the final few seconds, and the officials were incapable of dealing with it.

I offer no suggestions. I am no more thrilled by the idea of bringing TV sets onto the field to decide such questions than Pete Rozelle is. But it's a fact that football's credibility has been badly damaged by such incidents—of which this was the worst, but hardly the first. I'm just glad baseball doesn't have anything comparable to football's last-minute panic.

Has Stanhouse thrown that ball yet?

Tuesday
June 26th

CAN THE LEOPARD CHANGE HIS SPOTS?

Sparky Anderson has taken charge. Okay, we wanted strong leadership and he's apparently loaded with it. But in today's chapter of Seeing Who's Boss, Sparky has trifled with what I thought was a tradition of almost sacrosanct dimensions. He has eliminated the orange stripes from the Tigers' socks.

He had a good reason. The players looked sloppy, he said. And I would agree that from the knees down at least, their appearance was a denial of the meaning implicit in the word "uniform."

Professional sport has always been a branch of the entertainment business, although until recently it was the custom to deny this. With today's soaring salaries, the players have become sharply aware of the importance of what is known in the public-relations dodge as their "image." A player's salary is based in part on his popularity, and his popularity is not always based entirely on how well, or even how hard, he plays the game, but on an intangible quality which I guess could be summed up in the overworked term "personality." Unlike most other entertainers, though, ballplayers do not sing, play guitars or tell jokes. They must somehow win the fans' approval by purely visual means, and few of them are content to let their bats or their gloves do all the talking.

The most flamboyant example of charisma far in excess of ability is that of Mark Fidrych. And this is not to minimize his considerable ability. Mark's antics were the more pleasing because they seemed to be totally ingenuous, but whether by art or by innocence, he put on a great show (and will again, if there is any justice). Other players, not so naturally charismatic, have to resort to whatever tricks of manner or dress they can contrive. One of the favorite ways of expressing individuality is by the distance above sea level at which the pants are worn.

Like J. Alfred Prufrock, ballplayers generally wear the bottoms of their trousers rolled. The subtle distinction lies in the location of the point at which the trousers encounter the socks. Lately, some players have taken to pulling the pants almost to the ankles, so the socks are barely visible. Others wear them somewhat higher, but buy (or perhaps have made to order) the "stirrup" socks which are unique to baseball with stirrups which come to the knee, or perhaps beyond, so they appear to be wearing fragments of stocking on each side of the leg. They look like socks specially designed for a hilarious movie about a ragtag traveling baseball team. They look, in short, silly.

The Tigers have traditionally worn black socks with several thin horizontal orange stripes. But as Sparky Anderson was quick to notice, the varying sock designs combined with the whimsical trouser lengths to conceal some of the stripes. Thus, there was conservative Rusty Staub, who rolls his pants just below the knee in the old-fashioned manner, displaying all of his orange stripes, while others showed only two or one, or in some cases none.

Sparky examined the disarray that prevailed below the Tigers knees and called a halt. All players, he decreed, would henceforth wear their pants at a reasonable length, and to eliminate the variation in number of stripes showing, the stripes would simply be eliminated. Plain black socks would be in.

I can't disagree with Sparky's attempt to bring some order out of the chaos that dominated Tiger legs, but I wonder if he consulted the club's history book before he did it. If I remember my Tiger lore and legend (*legend*: an unverifiable story handed down from earlier times and popularly accepted), the stripes were not originally adopted to reflect the team's nickname; quite the reverse. The original Detroit ball club, the story goes, took the field with orange-on-black socks for some reason unknown. No doubt some aggressive sock merchant was stuck with a pile of them and gave the team an offer it couldn't refuse. Say ten cents a pair. If that is the case, then the name "Tigers" sprang indirectly from the exercise of stinginess or thrift or prudent financial practice, a Tiger tradition which is still generally observed. In any event, Sparky has tampered with not only the decor but the very lineage of the club and its honored name. As

with everything else he does, though, we'll forgive him if
he gives us a winner.

❋   ❋   ❋

One player who took issue with Sparky's legwear edict
was Ron LeFlore, who always likes to test the water before
going in. He said, well, he'd have to think it over. Sparky
said, well, he'd better hurry because the game was going
to start shortly. So Ronnie thought it over quickly and decided to acquiesce. This little incident (remembering the
noise over whether Ron would play left field or not) illustrates the difference between the degree of authority exer-
cised by a manager with a five-year contract carrying large
numbers and that of a man who is asked to lead but is given
a meager salary and is instantly expendable. Ron could defy
Les Moss because the Tigers, having nothing invested in
him, would not back him up. (Or maybe they would have,
but Moss couldn't be sure of it.) Money is power, and the
Detroit management, with over half a million dollars tied
up in Sparky Anderson, is not about to let him be overruled
by one of his players, no matter how good.

The moral of all this? Don't take the job unless you get
the money, I guess. But so anxious are most ex-ballplayers
to manage a big-league club that many of them would take
a job on any terms. Only a few managers can dictate demands. Sparky is obviously one of them. That should make
him a more effective manager. We'll see.

Sunday
July 1st

NEVER ON SUNDAY

Toronto—Unless you are a religious fanatic, it seems a
safe guess that when you look back upon the great events
of your life you will find that few of them happened on a

Sunday morning. I do not, perish the thought, mean to include the part of Sunday morning which is really an extension of Saturday night. That, indeed, is when a great number of memorable events are apt to occur, especially when you are young and in love. Or in something.

I'm talking about the typical American Sunday morning when you don't have to *do* anything. You get up when you feel like it, read the paper indolently, drink many cups of coffee, eat when you get good and ready, and in general devote yourself single-mindedly to sloth. It's a *long* morning, often not ending until what, on any other day, would be considered midafternoon.

Nothing noteworthy has ever happened to me on one of those Sunday mornings. But hardly anything awful ever happens then, either. And it always seems unlikely that it will, especially if you avoid section one of the Sunday paper. Inflation, energy crisis, the threat of nuclear meltdown are all suspended until three P.M. Through the windows you see nothing but sunshine and blue sky (or black clouds and driving rain, which may be even better; you're not out there). If you have the blessed faculty of being able to forget the existence of Monday, you are at peace.

Leafing, with all due indolence, through the Sunday *New York Times* this morning, I came upon the box score of yesterday's Detroit game, which Cleveland won 4 to 2. The Indians had been in a long losing streak, for which the Tigers came up with the cure. I was sitting in the living room of my son's fabulously expensive home in Toronto. (My son is not rich. All homes in Toronto are fabulously expensive.)

"Kip gave up three runs in six and a third innings," I said to Terry, a confirmed Torontoan but, like me, a lifelong Tiger fan. He nodded gravely, as if I had imparted some rare pearl of inside wisdom.

After a moment, he said, "What's the matter with Whitaker?"

"Broken finger or something," I said.

"When's he coming back?"

I glanced at the paper. "He played a little yesterday," I said, "but Wagner played most of the game."

He nodded again and returned to his reading, but I shortly interrupted him once more. "Wagner got two hits," I said, "and they only got six altogether."

Who the hell cares? I thought some time later. What possible significance could be attached to two hits by a second-string infielder on a fifth-place team in a game lost to a sixth-place team? Well, none at all, except in the sense that a profound remark by an eight-year-old may foreshadow an adult mind that will startle the world. Wagner will never be a great hitter, but his much-improved hitting this year could portend something for the future. "You can't win the pennant without a strong bench," and next year we're going for it all. In baseball, there is always next year. There is no year after next.

Grasping at straws? Certainly. It's the sort of thing you wouldn't have time to mention on Wednesday. But on a lazy Sunday morning it seemed important.

*   *   *

A NOTE ON CIVIC TERMINOLOGY: In the foregoing, I referred to my son as a Torontoan. Torontoans themselves, for some puzzling reason, seem to prefer the wretched designation "Torontonian." Anyone with ears will surely recognize that this is not only awkward and pretentious but virtually without useful function. Supposing you were unfamiliar with the term; what would you say to someone who told you he was a Torontonian? Let's say you meet him in Laramie or Arles, and you inquire politely about his background.

"I am a Torontonian," he says proudly.

"Ah, yes, one of the great Armenian families. But where do you live?"

Or possibly, suspecting him to be a refugee: "What's the political situation in Torontonia these days?"

You might even think he was an expert on poisonous spiders. Granted, that may be reaching a bit, but no more so than to think you would guess he was a resident of Toronto. Toronto is a marvelous place, and most of its citizens are properly proud of it, so it is the more mysterious that they should choose to conceal their provenance behind such an unfortunate term.

"Torontoan" may not be especially pretty, but it's quicker and, more important, it retains the accent in its original position. "Torontonian" shifts the stress to the third "o" and adds one more syllable, creating a word of unwieldy length whose meaning is open to the most extravagant conjecture.

Torontonians of the world, arise. Become Torontoans. Please.

Tuesday
July 10th

THE LEGAL MIND AT PLAY

Last night, for the first time this season, I lost track of the Tigers completely. They played a game against Minnesota, but I didn't hear one minute of it, or learn the result until I saw this morning's paper (they lost). Even in the worst of seasons, this happens to me only once or twice. But the first time it does happen I realize that I have conceded the pennant. Not consciously. I still *think* they have a chance to turn it all around; but in my heart I have given up. I know that because last night I forgot them.

But the evening could hardly be called a negative one in the baseball department. My wife and I were being entertained by my sister, Mary, and her husband, Phil, who is both

a baseball fan and a federal judge. So in addition to disposing
of slightly more than my share of food (I don't drink, so I
try my best to compensate for it at the buffet), I came into
possession of an extraordinary document, which the judge
had secured for me. This was a copy of the opinion of the
United States Supreme court in *Flood v. Kuhn et al.*, 1972,
the landmark case that started the ball rolling toward the
jackpot for professional ballplayers, although it gave no aid
or comfort to the petitioner. He was Curt Flood, late of the
St. Louis Cardinals. He lost the decision, but he lost it in
language which made it abundantly clear that he was going
to be the last loser. All of today's free-agent millionaires owe
a debt to Curt Flood, who cleared the way for them. There
is no record that any of them has ever offered a payment on
the debt, but I'm sure Flood expects none. This is the way
of the world. The pioneer gets the credit, someone else
gets the cash.

Incredibly, although the court ruled against Flood, it conceded that baseball's favored position in the eyes of the
judiciary was probably "unrealistic, inconsistent . . . illogical."
In effect, the court said to Curt Flood: Look, we know you're
getting shafted, but this court has a long and honorable
history of shafting baseball players (see *Federal Baseball
Club v. National League*, 1922, and *Toolson v. New York
Yankees*, 1953), and we're not about to break with tradition.
Of course, if you were a football player or a hockey player
you would get simple justice, but since you are a baseball
player you are out of luck.

That's a paraphrase, obviously, but I now return to direct
quotes. "If there is any inconsistency or illogic in all this, it
is an inconsistency and illogic of long standing that is to be
remedied by the Congress and not by this Court," said the
court to Curt. (You will note that pursuant to the rules of
English punctuation, I write "court" exclusively with small
letters, whereas the court bestows upon itself a capital C—
another instance of inconsistency and illogic sanctified by

long standing.) It is shattering to my composure when the U.S. Supreme Court *seems* to say, like a Victorian father in 1972 beating his daughter for displaying too much ankle in public, "This is the way it's always been and, by cracky, right or wrong, this is the way it's going to be." With that kind of reasoning, it's a wonder the justices didn't invoke the Dred Scott decision and send Flood back into slavery.

After dinner, Phil, as we call the judge (we revel in informality when dining *en famille*), discoursed at length and with some vigor on what is wrong with American education. He handed down several *ex cathedra* pronouncements, most of which had to do with the failure of American teachers to understand the nature of their responsibilities. Since knocking American teachers is a favorite American pastime these days, this might have provoked only favorable comment in other company. But my wife is an American teacher, and not one to suffer obloquy with serenity. Voices were raised. Strong phrases, possible even the dread "ivory tower," were used.

I took no part in this unseemly exchange, which gave me an opportunity to devour the text of *Flood v. Kuhn et al.*, along with a second piece of pie. I found it a truly remarkable literary work for reasons quite apart from those I have already mentioned. It was, in fact, for these other reasons that Phil thought the syllabus worthy of the attention of someone writing a book about baseball.

(I did not ask him what he thought of the decision itself. I'm not sure he could have told me, since I believe him to be thoroughly devoted to both justice and the law, which, as we know, are often in painful conflict. Anyway, if he had told me, I assume it would be imprudent to quote him. I'd prefer not to know things that are off the record.)

By the time a truce, or at least a cease-fire, had been declared in the great education debate—with neither side conceding a single point, moot or otherwise—I had thoroughly digested Part I of the Flood–Kuhn opinion, the section which

Phil had found so amusing. I found it equally so; astonishing, even. The court's opinion is delivered by Mr. Justice Blackmun, who finds it worthwhile to devote Part I to a history of baseball. Starting off, like one of those terrifying anniversary-banquet speakers, with, "It is a century and a quarter since the New York Nine defeated the Knickerbockers 23 to 1 on Hoboken's Elysian Fields," Blackmun takes us through the founding of the Cincinnati Red Stockings, the introduction of Sunday baseball, "the appearance of the American League, or 'junior circuit,'" the "discouraging episode of the 1919 Series," which is putting it rather sweetly, and various other events of more or less importance in what the better historians like to call the annals of the game.

In the most surprising passage in Part I (possibly one of the most surprising passages in the history of jurisprudence), the justice reels off the names of eighty-nine former ballplayers, ranging from Ty Cobb and Babe Ruth to some comparative unknowns. In a footnote, so help me, he apologizes to "others equally celebrated" whom he might have forgotten. Presumably, these would include Joe DiMaggio and Ted Williams. Most students of the game would consider them at least equally celebrated with Al Bridwell and Tommy Leach, who made the list. For my part, I regret the omission of Flint Rhem and Hippo Vaughn.

He quotes a Ring Lardner joke, cites "Casey at the Bat," includes three stanzas of an obscure poem by Grantland Rice and gives us the full text of Franklin P. Adams' "Tinker to Evers to Chance" poem. It is silly and pointless, irrelevant and immaterial, and in a way rather touching. It tells us clearly that here is a man of distinction, a jurist who has risen to the top of his profession, who still wants it known that he is a knowledgeable baseball fan with a proper reverence for the traditions of the national pastime. I can't really quarrel with that.

But there is more. The final topper comes from the former swivel-hipped scatback, Byron (Don't Call Me Whizzer)

White. I quote his contribution in its entirety: "MR. JUSTICE WHITE joins in the judgment of the Court, and in *all but Part I* of the Court's opinion." (Italics mine.)

Justice White does not explain which segment of Part I offends him. Perhaps, like me, he objects to the very mention of General Abner Doubleday, although it should be noted that Justice Blackmun does *not* credit the general with anything more than being known. Very wise. The slightest suggestion that Doubleday might have invented baseball would have cast grave doubt on the validity of the opinion and the sagacity of the highest court in the land.

Curt Flood probably has his doubts, anyway.

Thursday
July 12th

TAKING THE GLOVES OFF

I don't know just how far down memory lane I have to go to reminisce about the days when ballplayers always left their gloves on the field at the end of an inning. I can't remember when they changed the rules and made them take the gloves back to the dugout with them while their team was at bat.

Many young fans won't know what I'm talking about, and maybe they won't believe me. But it is a fact that until some years ago (fifteen, twenty, I'm vague about it) all the players except the pitcher and catcher, at every level from the backyard up to the majors, left their gloves right out on the field near their positions while they were batting.

Now that I have convinced you this is true, there is nothing to reminisce about. Which is a story in itself. In all the years I watched (and played a little) baseball, I never once saw a batted ball hit a glove on the field, or a player trip over one, or anything. It was as if the square foot of territory that each glove occupied were consecrated ground. It was, in fact, as if they weren't there. So the game did not change one iota when they took them away.

Well, there is one story. I read somewhere recently that Charlie Gehringer, the great (the adjective is inadequate) Tiger second baseman, once had an embarrassing experience as a result of that old custom. Charlie hit a ground ball to the infield, and was thrown out at first for what he *thought* was the final out of the inning. He rounded first; circled behind Oscar Melillo, the St. Louis Browns' second baseman; picked up his glove from the grass and prepared to take his position in the field. Melillo, as Gehringer tells it, turned to him and said, "This is awfully nice of you, Charlie, but I think I can handle it by myself."

Friday
July 13th

A LITTLE NIGHT MUSIC

Last night, we watched an amazing sight on television. For two hours, we looked at rotten people walking around on the field at Comiskey Park. This was not billed as a special, which was probably just as well because, after the first few minutes, it was more wearying than *The Best of Donnie and Marie*. It was, actually, billed as a baseball game, and I guess that's what it was, because today we have learned that the Tigers have been awarded a forfeit victory over the White Sox.

I have described these people as "rotten" although I am not in a position to assess their character, either individually or en masse. Some of them may be, if the truth were known, deeply involved in the campaign to save the whale, and believers in truth in advertising. They were, it is true, mostly young and almost all devotees of rock-and-

roll music, which in itself is a turnoff to anyone my age.
People of my generation are made uncomfortable by the sight
of young people enjoying themselves in ways we find mysterious. And to us the greatest mystery of the age is the
appeal of rock music. But that's all quite beside the point.
If they had all been wearing three-piece suits, carrying
American flags and singing "Stardust," they would still have
been rotten because they were walking around on a baseball
field when I (and presumably even a few thousand at the
park) wanted to see a ball game.

I have always suspected that someday one of Bill Veeck's
promotions would strike back at him, and it finally happened.
Veeck's enthusiasm knows no bounds, but occasionally his
judgment is a little off, and this was one of those times. In
spades. It all began, apparently, when some local rock disk
jockey got the idea that a strong public statement against
disco music would be a major contribution to human better-
ment. (What he really wanted to do, needless to say, was
promote himself. And he succeeded. You cannot, they say,
argue with success.) He arranged with Veeck to admit for
98 cents anyone who arrived carrying a disco record. The
idea was to destroy all these records in public as a tribute to
Iggy Pop, Mott the Hoople, Rod Stewart, Death Warmed
Over and all the other great stylists of the genre—past,
present and future. Veeck saw a chance to fill up the ball
park—at rock-bottom rates, true, but a buck is a buck, and
98 cents is almost a buck. He filled the park, and today
probably wishes he had been content with something less
than capacity.

There were several things wrong with this idea. The rock
culture is a drug culture, and its devotees like nothing better
than to stand around and smile at each other and speak
their strange tongue. (In this respect, they resemble Latvian
immigrants, although there are fewer of these and they do
not have their own radio stations.) When an organized
attempt is made to bring large numbers of rock people to-

gether for standing around, it is called an "event." The basic,
unbreakable rule for holding a rock event is, or should be,
that you do not try to carry on another unrelated activity on
the same turf at the same time. As you would not hold a tea
dance in the middle of a prayer meeting, you do not hold a
rock event in the middle of a baseball game. Bill Veeck broke
that rule. Probably he didn't know about it, but he does now.

One of the most intriguing features of the whole business,
for those of us who were watching it from a safe distance
(Channel 4 in Detroit carried it live and, to use the popular
TV phrase, "in its entirety"), was the absolutely horrified
reaction of George Kell and Al Kaline. Kell and Kaline are
both ex-ballplayers and good baseball announcers, as I have
already indicated. They can describe and interpret a ball
game, and do a ninety-minute fill during a rain delay if
necessary. But they are not trained to handle a rock event,
or a riot (as this was somewhat extravagantly called). I
thought they did just fine, although some of the newspapers
today have criticized them for their lack of objectivity. What
nonsense! To expect objectivity from Al Kaline when the
Beloved Game is under attack is tantamount to asking the
late John Wayne to smile understandingly at someone
spitting on the flag. Kaline is as straight an arrow as you
are likely to find in a month of walking up and down among
the people of this land, and Kell is not far behind. They both
love the game, as well they should, and I suspect that Kaline
prays nightly for the souls of Babe Ruth and Kenesaw
Mountain Landis.

"I've *never* seen anything like this in my *life*," Kaline
would say, "and I hope I never do again!" Kell would echo
those sentiments, and that's the way it went for two hours.
Occasionally, they would speculate on the possibility of
clearing the field so the second game could be played. (It was
to have been a doubleheader. One game had been played,
although hardly under ideal circumstances. Objects, including firecrackers, had been thrown on the field, delaying play,

at frequent intervals. The rock event, which was to have preceded the second game, instead became the second game.) But mainly they expressed their contempt for these awful people who were making it impossible for the proper business of the evening to proceed. "These are not real baseball fans, and we don't need them or want them at the ball park," they both said, time and again. I cannot believe that Kaline, especially, would have been any more indignant had he been one of the Disciples witnessing the Crucifixion.

My wife and I laughed at the intensity of his scorn for these sacrilegious intruders upon consecrated ground, all the while, I suppose, slightly embarrassed at the realization that we agreed with him, although we might not have expressed it in quite such flamboyant terms.

I do not have my wife's power of attorney, but speaking for myself, I was disgusted, principally because I wanted to see a baseball game, but also because I am always appalled at the selfishness and thoughtlessness of modern man, and I don't mean just modern *youth*. For the first thirty or forty minutes, I had little reaction, except that it was a startling sight. After that, though, I began to mutter, okay, you've had your fun, now clear the field so they can play baseball, as advertised. They never did, and I was mad about it.

But I have a special perspective on this incident. I have seen the best minds of my generation (including my own, which was the best on my block, if you don't count a couple of people) made useless not by drugs, but by booze. Bill Veeck should have known better than to open his park to the rock people, some of whom doubtless *were* baseball fans, but who adopted the behavior of the greater number who weren't. He might have remembered what had happened a few years earlier in Cleveland, when the ball park was turned over to Alcoholics Defiant—an informal group that assembles at baseball games when, incredibly, the feature of the evening is ten-cent beer. The drunks turned that game into a far uglier spectacle than the rock people created in Chicago, whatever they may have been smoking. As far as I know, no one was hurt last night. The game in Cleveland wound up with visiting players' defending themselves with baseball bats.

The lessons for today. One, do not open your ball park to large numbers of people whose compelling reason for being there is inimical to the playing of baseball. Two, drunks of any age have small license to look down on those addicted to any other uncontrollable substance, even if they're young.

And for the record, one more comment. I hope the Tigers keep Al Kaline around forever. He is a naive young man of forty-five, who has spent his adult life sheltered from reality behind the walls of baseball parks and good hotels. But he is an honest, decent gentleman who stands up for the game, the team and a lot of other presumably worthwhile things. I wish him well all the days of his life.

       ❊   ❊   ❊

I wish Bill Veeck well, too. Veeck has always occupied a paradoxical position in my mind. He is bright, amusing and clever. He is the prototype of the lovable con man who always has a hustle going, but you forgive him because he makes it fun. He is the originator of a lot of the things that I hate about modern baseball: the mixing of carnivals and baton twirlers and everything else his fertile mind can conceive of with the sacred game. But somehow he makes palatable what is offensive in other parks. I think there are two reasons for this. First of all, he genuinely likes baseball. He must; he has left it a couple of times for personal reasons (health mainly, I believe), but he has always come back to it, although the lords of baseball don't want him and make it tougher for him to return each time. Second, his promotions usually don't interfere with *the game* (last night's being a notable exception). He may have a thousand flamenco dancers on the field before the game, but once it starts there is no hateful little creature, like the despicable Jouppi (or Youppi) in Montreal or the dread San Diego chicken, running around harassing the players and umpires and making a travesty of the game. This last is an offense which used to be specifically prohibited by the official rules, and is now widely encouraged for what are deemed good and sufficient (and are purely commercial) reasons. I'd prefer to see his exploding scoreboard transferred to Disneyland, which would seem to me more in keeping with the puerile notion that it represents: that you have to *tell* baseball fans when to cheer. But aside from annoying the visiting players, it doesn't intrude too deeply on the game. (And I'm sure Bill Veeck has no compunction about annoying visiting players.)

I felt sorry for Bill Veeck last night. He was obviously dismayed by the monster he had built, and he spent two hours out on the firing line, first pleading with the revelers to put out their fires and get off the field, and then pleading with the umpires not to forfeit the game. He has always had health problems. He lost a leg in the war and, I believe, only recently came out of the hospital after an illness. His own people were trying to persuade him to leave the field, but he was there to the ignominious end.

I wouldn't presume to offer Veeck advice, but I note that his White Sox, who often appear to be a pretty good team, are far down in the standings and that some of his players have been frank enough to blame the never-ending distractions on their home field for their plight. (They often have to do without batting practice because of a cow-milking contest or a water ballet.) And they have a strong case, because the Sox have a much better won–lost record on the road than they do at home, which is an extreme rarity, and in this case perhaps a significant one.

Just once, I'd like to see Bill Veeck go for quality baseball, to the exclusion of circuses and sideshows. He had a contender in Chicago a couple of years ago, and attendance was excellent. I believe those people came to see the White Sox, not the unicycle races.

＊　　＊　　＊

It was an interesting doubleheader the Tigers won in Chicago last night. The winning pitcher in the first game was Pat Underwood, and the second has been credited to Frank Zappa (his first major-league win).

Monday
July 16th

AN ACT OF FAITH

What follows is a tribute to the squeeze play, and the story of a couple of specimens that went wrong with surprising results.

The shimmering beauty of the squeeze play is that when properly executed, it cannot be stopped. The ugly side of it is that when it is badly executed, the team at bat is not only foiled but embarrassed. And although it is almost always the batter who fails, it is the base runner who is made to look foolish. There are few sights more heartrending than that of a runner frantically putting on the brakes, twenty or thirty feet from home, while the watcher waits at the plate with the ball in his hand and a triumphant gleam in his eye.

Offhand, I can think of no other play in baseball in which success depends entirely on the element of surprise. And the surprise must be achieved even though the defensive team is fully aware of the squeeze-play possibility. In a close game, with a runner on third and no more than one out, the squeeze is always a threat. The catcher knows this, but he does not know on which pitch it is coming, if it is coming at all. Unless his team has picked up the sign (and tipping

the squeeze sign ought to be baseball's First Deadly Sin),
he has to guess. If he calls for two pitchouts in a row and
nothing happens, he's got his pitcher in a hole. He must come
over the plate with the next one, and he still doesn't know
whether the batter is going to swing away or bunt.

As for the base runner, who is running down the line
toward home even as the ball speeds there ahead of him, he
must have absolute faith in his teammate at the plate. The
latter's job is absurdly simple (but sometimes devilishly
hard): No matter where the pitch comes in, he must get his
bat on it and he must hit it on the ground. If he bunts it
foul, the play is dead but the runner is still alive. If he misses
it completely, the runner is not only out but mortified. But if
he bunts it fair and on the ground, there is no defense against
it, no way the other team can react fast enough to prevent
the run from scoring. This is the key fact about the squeeze
when it's done right. The bunt doesn't have to be a good
one, provided the runner is dashing toward the plate with
complete abandon, totally confident of the batter's ability
to deliver him from evil.

(In recent years, two distasteful terms have entered the
baseball lexicon. These are "suicide squeeze" and "safety
squeeze." The former is the new and presumably more colorful name for the squeeze play. "Safety squeeze" is a term which
seems to be applied to any bunt with a runner on third.
Ridiculous. If the runner isn't coming, it isn't a squeeze play.
The squeeze play entails a calculated risk in the hope of a
big reward, possibly the winning run. The very idea of
incorporating a safety factor into the squeeze is repugnant.
Oh, it's quite okay to bunt with a runner on third and let him
decide whether he can make it home or not. But don't call
it a squeeze play. No risk, no squeeze.)

I have said that failure to execute the squeeze properly is
disastrous to the team at bat. But there are exceptions. An
interesting one in yesterday's Detroit game involved Tom
Brookens, a Tiger rookie just up from the minors. He was on

third with Alan Trammell at bat. The squeeze was on. Brookens raced for the plate. Trammell failed to hit the ball, but it was hardly his fault. The Chicago pitcher—a left-hander named Wortham—delivered a monstrous wild pitch, and Brookens was able to walk the last few feet to the plate.

I suppose a wild pitch on an attempted squeeze is not terribly unusual, but *this* wild pitch deserves special recognition. I am no novice at watching wild pitches. I have seen a pitcher throw the ball three feet over the catcher's head. I have seen a pitcher throw behind the batter (although that, rumor hath it, is not always as wild as it looks). But this one was unique. It appeared to be part of some other game; it certainly came nowhere near anyone in this one. Milt May, the White Sox catcher, never got out of his crouch, so it wasn't meant to be a pitchout, but even if it had been it's doubtful that May could have caught it. At least four feet outside and six feet high, it was the King Kong of wild pitches. (Brookens, since he was running on the pitch, was credited with a steal of home in his sixth major-league game. Many fine base runners have gone through a whole career without one of those.)

Earlier this year, a truly unusual play occurred in a Detroit–Texas game, the result of a combination of circumstances that might not come up again in a dozen years. Bump Wills, a good base runner, was on third for the Rangers. The catcher, by coincidence, was Milt May, then with the Tigers. Noticing that Wills was running far down the line on every pitch, Milt called for a pickoff play at third. Probably a good call, too, except that on the same pitch Texas put on the squeeze. To make things more interesting, the batter missed the sign. As Wills raced toward the plate and the batter stood idly by, May grabbed the pitch and came up throwing. Rodríguez, the third baseman, fired the ball right back to him, but Wills slid home safely. (Of course, those of us who were unaware of all the grand strategy—including, presumably to his chagrin, the batter—were mystified by the whole business until explanations were made later.)

In the two cases described, the squeeze play went awry and the runner still scored. But these are mere curiosities of the game. In any normal instance, if the batter fails to meet the ball, the runner is out, and that usually means the rally is over. So the risk is great, but so is the prize. I'd venture to say the prize is far more than the single run that scores on the play. Requiring perfect timing and faultless execution by two players in full view of the cheering thousands, the squeeze is the ultimate in teamwork. The aesthetic satisfaction that comes from doing it just right (especially since the consequences of failure are so disagreeable) builds the whole team's confidence in its ability to play winning baseball. It's the most exciting offensive play in the book.

❖   ❖   ❖

The rarest squeeze play in the book (so rare, in fact, that it's probably *not* in the book) is the two-out, two-strike version. With two strikes, if the batter bunts foul he's out. With two out, he must beat the play at first base or the run won't count. I saw it done once by Roxie Lawson, a Tiger pitcher in the late '30s. He made it look like a piece of cake. Laid down a good bunt and beat it out easily. Roxie was a lifetime .173 hitter. Had he been a good hitter, he would never have been allowed to try this unusual stratagem. I don't suppose I'll ever see it again. Still, if the score is tied and you want to surprise—really surprise—the opposition, it's worth keeping in mind.

FASCINATION WITH NAMES AND NUMBERS

John Paciorek, as every serious collector of baseball curiosa knows, is major-league baseball's leading lifetime hitter. No one ever hit for a higher average over an entire career. His career, which was all over before he reached his nineteenth birthday, consisted of one game for Houston in 1963, and it was quite remarkable as far as it went. He had three hits in three times at bat, walked twice, scored four runs and batted in three.

There are many other hitters with lifetime averages of 1.000, but most of them had only one time at bat. Among batters who never made an out, Paciorek's three for three is tops.

I have, as you can guess, been browsing through the record book, an utterly fascinating accumulation of baseball facts, ranging from the awe-inspiring to the ineffably trivial. Listed here is every man who ever played in a major-league game. Here is Ty Cobb, with his 4192 hits and .367 lifetime batting average (both "unbreakable" records), right below Joe Cobb, who has no batting average at all. Consider Joe Cobb. The books tells us that he was born in Hudson, Pennsylvania, January 24, 1895, and died December 24, 1947; that he batted and threw right-handed; that he was 5 feet 9 inches tall and weighed 170 pounds, and that his last name was originally Serafin. All this for a man who appeared in one game for Detroit in 1918, apparently going to the plate once and getting a base on balls. In the matter of vital statistics, we know more about Joe Cobb than we do about Shakespeare. Shakespeare never played big-league baseball, so we know not whether he batted left or right (although some readers of the sonnets have pegged him as a switch hitter).

I marvel at the scope of these great baseball record books which have appeared in the past ten years or so, products of the computer age. They have conferred immortality of a sort on men whose names were lost to history for fifty years or more. And of each of them, however slender his record, it can be said, "He was a good ballplayer." If he hadn't been, he never would have been offered a big-league uniform, even for a day.

For me, the big books are also an exercise in nostalgia, recalling names I had forgotten countless years ago. But surely their most intriguing feature, to any genuine baseball zealot, is the small glimpses they offer of the lives of otherwise unknown performers, and the puzzling questions they often raise.

Take Bill Bergen, for example. There is a mystery surrounding him that may never be solved. He was no one-day player; quite the contrary. He came into the major leagues in 1901, when he was already twenty-eight years old, and managed to stick around for eleven years, although he hit over .200 just once. His lifetime batting average was a limp .170. The question is: why? Why was this incredibly bad hitter allowed to go to bat 3116 times in major-league ball games? He was a catcher, and the assumption is that he must have been an awfully good one. My own theory is that his father owned the Brooklyn ball club, with which he spent most of his career.

Bergen, incidentally, was a teammate of three interesting players at Cincinnati in 1902, all of whom achieved fame (or something) with other teams. Harry Steinfeldt became the forgotten third baseman in the Chicago Cubs' infield immortalized in Franklin P. Adams' "Tinker to Evers to Chance." Sam Crawford was a twenty-two-year-old outfielder who hit .333 and then went on to Detroit, where he stayed for fifteen years, made the Hall of Fame and collected the amazing lifetime total of 312 triples. No one but Cobb (Ty, not Joe), with 297, has ever come close to that

Bill Bergen. A lifetime .170 hitter, but a long career. Why?

figure, and he had almost two thousand more at-bats than Sam.

The most remarkable player on that 1902 Cincinnati team, however, was Dummy Hoy, then forty years old and winding up a career that had begun in 1888. William Ellsworth (Dummy) Hoy was a deaf-mute who stood only 5 feet 4, but he had a lifetime batting average of .291, plus 607 stolen bases. He also was responsible for a small revolution in baseball tactics. The visual signals which are used by all teams were originally devised by Hoy's manager so he could communicate his wishes to him. Dummy Hoy died in 1961, just five months short of his 100th birthday. My father, as a very small boy, saw him play, I think. At least, he used to talk about him as if he had. Apparently, in those days, no one thought the name by which he was always identified at all demeaning.

Think about this. In 1906 the Chicago White Sox, the famous Hitless Wonders, were last in the league in hits, total bases and team batting average. They produced a fraction over seven hits per game and had a grand total of six home runs! They also won the pennant and beat the Cubs in the World Series. The following year, they hit only five home runs, and in 1908 they achieved the seemingly impossible. In that year, playing 156 games, the White Sox hit three home runs (and still lost the pennant by just a game and a half). I feel reasonably sure this is the single-season record for futility in the power department.

Just as there are many batters with perfect batting averages, there are any number of pitchers in the book with won–lost records of 1.000—that is, they won at least one game and never lost one. The vast majority of them have 1–0 records, but there are more than a half dozen with 3–0 marks. The leader in this category is one Ben Shields, who must have been one of the luckiest pitchers ever to play the game. He won three games for the New York Yankees in 1925,

Copyright 1888.
Goodwin & Co. N.Y.

Hoy, C.F. Washington.

William Ellsworth (Dummy) Hoy. A small revolution.

kicked around the majors and minors for six years before re-surfacing with the Philadelphia Phillies in 1931, where he won one game, despite giving up nine hits and seven walks in five innings of pitching. Over his career, he pitched a total of forty-one innings, during which he allowed fifty-five hits and twenty-seven walks and had an earned-run average of 8.34. But he was never charged with a loss. He is the only 4–0 pitcher in baseball history. (There have doubtless been several rookie pitchers with temporary 4–0 records, but they didn't know when to quit. Neither, apparently, did Ben Shields until it was forced upon him. But he got away with it.)

There is no mystery about Ben Shields. Plainly, the base-ball gods favored him with one of their unpredictable smiles. And he hung around long enough to prove he wasn't good enough, perfect record notwithstanding. But what about the others, the dozens of 1.000 hitters and 1.000 pitchers (plus all the pitchers with 0.00 ERA's)? What happened to them? Their records are, I realize, deceptive, but still . . . when a man has fulfilled his obligation to perfection, why is he not then given another chance? Pure logic would dictate that there shouldn't be any 1.000 hitters or pitchers in the book. And yet there are too many to count. I wonder about them all.

There are, incidentally, only three pitchers in the book with "perfect perfect" records: won 1, lost 0, ERA 0.00. They are Nellie Rees (Washington, 1918), Paul Jaeckel (Cubs, '64) and Nestor Chavez (San Francisco, '67). The best of them was Jaeckel, who gave up only four hits in an eight-inning career. Where did he go? He is today only thirty-seven years old, and the Cubs might well consider giving him another chance.

But wait, here's a surprising development. There are, it's true, only three double-perfect pitchers *in the book*. But here's one who's not in the book. You'll remember him,

Rocky Colavito. W 1, L 0, ERA 0.00.

though, if you're a baseball fan. The book I am using explains in the introductory notes that "men who were primarily non-pitchers are included in the pitcher register only if they pitched in five or more games." Rocky Colavito, he of the powerful biceps, 374 home runs and 1159 RBI's, was beyond question a non-pitcher—primarily. But he pitched three innings of relief for Cleveland in 1958 and, ten years later, three more for the Yankees. In the latter game, he got the win over Detroit (and the Tigers went on to win the World Series that year). In all, Rocky pitched six innings, gave up only one hit, had an ERA of 0.00, won one and lost none. He was not only a "perfect perfect" pitcher, but the best of the lot. You might never have known that if I weren't an inveterate reader of small print.

One of the captivating features of the record book is the players' nicknames, especially those from the early part of the century. I am, first of all, stunned by the amount of research it must have taken to dig them up. No computer, it would seem, can be programmed to do that kind of work. But it is the names themselves, regardless of how they were uncovered, that stir the imagination. What do they mean?

No one would ask that question about such famous nicknames as those of Ty Cobb, who was called "the Georgia Peach," or Frank (Home Run) Baker. Cobb was from Georgia and was a peach of a player, and Baker earned his title by hitting two home runs in the 1911 World Series and banging out an average of seven per year over a career that spanned the great transition in baseball. (Baker broke in in 1908, the year the Chicago White Sox hit three home runs, and he was a teammate of Babe Ruth's in 1921 when the Babe hit fifty-nine.) But how, for example, did Dave Altizer of Pearl, Illinois, become known as "Filipino"? And why was little Arlie Latham, who played for six teams in three different leagues before the turn of the century, called "the Freshest Man on Earth"? (In 1909, evidently still fresh after a ten-year absence, Arlie Latham made a farewell appearance with the New York Giants at the age of forty-nine, and stayed long enough to steal his 791st base. It should be noted, however, that stolen bases before 1900 cannot be compared with twentieth-century steals since they were awarded on an entirely different basis.)

Names like Whitey, Hoss, Brickyard, Dapper Dan and Big Bill are easily enough understood, and we can imagine how Benny (Earache) Meyer earned his designation. We can guess why Dirty Jack Doyle played for twelve different teams in seventeen years, too. Since he won 203 games, Al Orth (1895–1909) probably didn't mind being called "the Curveless Wonder," but what did Bill Lattimore do in his four-game stay with the 1908 Cleveland club to earn the title "Slothful Bill"? And how, in God's name, did Hub Perdue of the Boston Braves and St. Louis Cardinals (1911–1915) come to be called "the Gallatin Squash"?

In the area of literary nicknames, there have been a number of "King" Lears and at least one "King" Lehr. More surprising, though, is Hal Janvrin, who played for several teams between 1911 and '22 and was called "Childe Harold." (Literary allusions are not common in baseball, but an interesting one comes along now and then. In recent years it has become fairly general to say of a poor infielder that he plays like the Ancient Mariner. That is, "he stoppeth one of three.")

Blue Sleeve Harper, Trolley Line Butler, Peaceful Valley Denzer, Dauntless Dave Danforth, Snooze Goulait, Buttermilk Tommy Dowd, Little All Right Ritchey, Sea Lion Hall. There's a story in every one of those names—undoubtedly in many cases a painfully dull one, but that's the chance you take. (Sea Lion Hall's baptismal name, incidentally, was Carlos Clolo. Figure that out.)

Finally, you may be interested to know that from 1908 to 1911, Albert Schweitzer (probably not the same one) played for the St. Louis Browns. His nickname was "Cheese."

Wednesday
July 18th

VOTE EARLY AND OFTEN

The American League, it can now safely be said, will always find a way to lose the All-Star Game. Last night, the winning run scored on four walks and a phony balk. That is, it was a National League balk called by a National League umpire against an American League pitcher, and the leagues do not have the same balk rule!

The winning run was walked in by the great Ron Guidry, who had just been brought into the game. The batter was Lee Mazzilli of the Mets, who, one inning earlier, had hit a pop-fly home run down the left-field line off the Texas Rangers' relief ace Jim Kern. It must have been one of the shortest home runs in All-Star history, but it counted, and if Steve Kemp had hit it I would have loved it.

The Mickey Mouse hits off the concrete infield of Seattle's Kingdome were evenly divided. Davey Lopes of the Dodgers got one in the second inning, and Bruce Bochte of Seattle matched it in the sixth. Both hits figured in the scoring, but they evened up, so there is no great lesson to be drawn from them—except the self-evident one that the All-Star Game should, by Congressional fiat, be declared illegal, immoral and dumb unless played on a real baseball field. (That'll be the day.)

As for the balk, it seems serious to me only as evidence of the fact that the two leagues are playing a slightly different game, which becomes slightly more different every year. Very few of us understand the balk rule. It often seems to depend on the angle at which the pitcher's toe is placed on the mound, or an imperceptible movement of the shoulder. I suspect that even in their own league, only pitchers and umpires understand the balk rule, and not all of them. So how can a pitcher be expected to conform for a single game to

a rule distinct from the one he has learned at great pain over
a period of several months, or several seasons? It doesn't
make sense, and it could make trouble. Okay, the All-Star
Game is just a glorified exhibition game, but what about the
World Series? A balk call could cost a team the world's
championship. And if it's called against a pitcher for a move
that he has been told all year is perfectly legal, chances are
he's going to get a bit huffy about it—possibly to the extent
of killing the umpire.

We hear constantly that the two leagues have different
strike zones. We hear also that this umpire will "give you
the high one" while that umpire won't. The strike zone is
clearly defined by the rule book, so it should be exactly the
same in both leagues, and no umpire in either league should
ever have to "give" you anything.

The strike zone, as I understand it, extends downward
from the armpits. This means that a ball thrown right across
the letters on a player's uniform (which are usually just
below armpit level) is a strike. Indeed, we used to speak
of a "letter-high fastball" as a perfect pitch to hit. But no
umpire will call it a strike anymore. In fact, from long
observation of American League baseball, I would say that
a pitcher is lucky to get a strike call on anything more than
two or three inches above the waist.

It is an abomination, certainly, that in one league pitchers
bat while in the other they don't. But that doesn't involve
umpires' decisions. Surely, the action of the game itself, the
movement of the players and the ball, on which an umpire's
pronouncements are based, should be governed by the same
laws throughout baseball. The rules are in the book. Would
it be too radical simply to enforce them?

I realize this is an outlandish suggestion, but the commissioner could do something about it. Here at last is a
problem that is clearly not "a league matter," since it involves all of baseball and has arisen precisely *because* the
leagues have been allowed to operate independently of each

other. And it would not require inter-league conferences to arrive at a system agreeable to all. The system is already established. The commissioner could simply order all hands to conform to it. He won't, though.

❀   ❀   ❀

The All-Star balloting produced its usual quota of nonsense. Last year Don Money was elected at second base, although he was not a second baseman. This year there was a huge outpouring of votes for Carlton Fisk as catcher, although he was not catching. Rod Carew, who was injured early in the season, was chosen at first base for the American League, and actually led all players in the voting. Not that Carew isn't a great ballplayer, but you just cannot be an "all-star" when you're not playing.

The fans also elected a complete outfield from the Boston Red Sox, including Carl Yastrzemski, who is primarily a first baseman now. They cast few votes for Don Baylor of California, who is leading the league in RBI's by a wide margin. That worked out all right at game time. They put Yaz at first base in place of Carew, who couldn't play, making room for Baylor in the outfield. But the voting system was revealed once again as preposterous.

Much of the blame, as always, falls on the razor-blade company's ballots, which are printed before the season begins, guaranteeing that you can vote only for *last* year's stars. A man who is hitting .400 this year cannot be chosen if he had a lousy year last year, because his name won't even be on the ballot. Sure, there's a provision for write-in voting, but how many write-in candidates can you name who ever won an election in which millions of votes were cast?

If the fans must choose the team, give them blank ballots and make them write out their choices. If they can't do that without a pre-selected list to choose from, they shouldn't be voting anyway.

But the only sensible way to choose an all-star team is to

let the players vote, not more than ten days before the game. (If that had been done this year, Don Baylor would have been elected to a starting position, and you may be sure that he's aware of it. Ask any player who is having by far the best year of his career, and who sees himself being outpolled by a half dozen better-known players who are having ordinary years, how he feels about the present system. It is nonsensical, totally without merit.) The commissioner, who knows which way the razor cuts, would doubtless protest that this would "take the game away from the fans." The truth is that it would give the game back to the real fans who would like to see the game played by the outstanding players of the current season at every position.

❄   ❄   ❄

This year we were subjected to the spectacle of the Cardinals' Garry Templeton chirping, "If I ain't startin', I ain't departin'." I heard it quoted so much I guess a lot of people thought it was cute. It was, in fact, an arrogant expression of contempt for the welfare of the game that pays his salary, especially unseemly in a shortstop who made forty errors last year.

Any player selected for the All-Star Game who fails to show up without a *legitimate* excuse should be suspended for two games immediately following.

I mean, let's do it right or call it off!

Saturday
July 21st

HAIL AND FAREWELL

And so it is with heavy heart that we say goodbye to Rusty Staub. The Staub story in Detroit came to a mournful end yesterday, when the Tigers sent Rusty off to Montreal to play in the wrong league.

At first blush, it would seem like a triumph for Rusty, and I suppose he will choose to interpret it that way. (At the moment of writing, I have seen no quotes from anyone.) After all, he asked to be traded, and he was traded. What's more, he's going back to Montreal, where he had the best three years of his career, batting .296 and averaging 90 RBI's and 26 home runs a season, and was an immensely popular local hero, affectionately known as *le grand orange.* Best of all, the Expos are in first place, so Rusty has a chance to play on a pennant winner.

All this is very misleading. The truth is that the deal seems more like the first step on the road to oblivion for Staub. When he played for the Expos, they were a brand-new expansion team, and he was the star of a last-place club. Things have changed in Montreal. They now have one of the best outfields in baseball (Cromartie, Dawson, Valentine), so there is not the slightest chance of Staub's breaking into the regular lineup. He will be a pinch hitter, nothing more, for as long as he stays with the club.

I would not be so bold as to examine Jim Campbell's motives, but with or without malice, he has had his revenge on Rusty, while also weakening his own club. By trading him to a National League team, where Staub's proper position —designated hitter—does not exist, he has dealt him right out of a job. Rusty will sit on the bench for the rest of the season, going to bat maybe thirty or forty times. He may help the Expos win a pennant (one timely pinch hit can do that), but there is no chance at all that he will compile the sort of figures that lead to multi-year big-money contracts.

It's plain enough why Montreal wants him. When you're a contender, you try to close every loophole. Picking up a good left-handed pinch hitter for the stretch drive is called "buying pennant insurance." It doesn't guarantee a pennant, but it means you've left no stone unturned.

Rusty Staub had a long career as an outfielder, but he was always painfully slow, and he's not getting any faster. The

American League, where he would never have to put on a
fielder's glove, is his natural milieu now. I wonder if he
thought about that when he asked to be traded. For as long
as he stays in the National League, Rusty will be a fringe
player—a sad and sudden comedown for one who was the
second-best RBI man in the game just a year ago.

Pinch hitting offers an opportunity to be a hero, it's true,
but it also dramatizes failure, since the pinch hitter seldom
appears unless the game is on the line. Let Rusty be found
wanting two or three times with the game in the balance, and
Montreal's *grand orange* will soon become *le grand limon*.

Last words. To Rusty Staub: May all your restaurants
prosper. To Jim Campbell: Don't eat at Rusty's.

Wednesday
August 1st

MAN WITH A MISSION

STOUGHTON, WIS.—This is a place whose previous claim
to literary fame was a fleeting mention in one of Ring
Lardner's little nonsense plays. All I plan to tell you about
Stoughton is that it's a charming little country town, heavily
populated by persons of Norwegian ancestry who often say,
"*Oofda*," which means, among other things, "wow" or
"ouch" or "damn, that's heavy." (One of the local fast-food
joints features an Oofdaburger.) The people here are, as
far as I can see, generally pleasant to newcomers, as long as
they know their place.

We came here because our son Tony has lived here for
years and likes it. He's a gregarious type and knows almost
everyone in town, including Ryne Duren, the former Yankee
relief ace. Today Tony and I had lunch with him, and he took
issue with something I had written about him last year. I had
suggested that he was a negligible threat with a bat in his

hands. I didn't actually say he was a bad hitter. I just quoted some figures: AB 114, H 7, BA .061. "What you failed to mention," he said, "is that I was expert at getting on base by other means." He was, he said, one of the best at getting hit by a pitch.

"In one game," Duren said, "I started for the plate, then stopped and spoke to Hank Bauer, who was waiting to bat after me. 'If I get on base,' I said, 'will you drive me in?' Bauer said, 'Sure, but how are you going to get on base?'" Hank, for some reason, was skeptical of Duren's ability to get a hit.

"'Don't worry about that; I'll figure out something,' I said—too loudly, as it turned out," Duren went on. "I stepped into the box and the first pitch came in high and close, perfect for my purposes. Unfortunately, the umpire had overheard my conversation with Bauer, and he may also have been influenced by the fact that I started to moan even before the ball hit me. Anyway, he wouldn't have any part of it. All I got out of it was a bruise."

Ryne Duren is a Man with a Mission. Last year he wrote a book called *The Comeback*, which deals with his career as a big-league pitcher, his descent into the abyss of alcoholism and his return to the world. He has been for several years director of the alcoholic rehabilitation program at Stoughton Community Hospital.

In case you're too young to remember, Ryne Duren pitched in the major leagues for ten years, during many of which he wasn't quite sure where he was. "I never really knew what it was like to pitch a sober inning," he says in the book.

At his best and fastest, Duren was a superb pitcher. Good hitters were afraid of him—afraid they couldn't hit him and equally afraid that he might hit *them*. In 1958, his best year with the Yankees, he was 6–4 with twenty saves (tops in the league), plus a win and a save in the World Series. Two years later, after a fight on a train, he was shuffled off to the Angels. There were three or four other clubs, and many drunken incidents, before he left baseball and drifted into less lucrative professions like washing dishes and pumping gas. In his ten-year major-league career, he had twenty-seven wins and fifty-seven saves, probably just a fraction of what he could have done if he'd had his mind on his work. But drunk or not, he averaged more than one strikeout per inning, a distinction he shares with Sandy Koufax, Nolan Ryan and very few others.

We talked some about baseball and a lot about booze, because, as I said, Ryne Duren is a driven man. "All my life," he said, "I was repelled by the very thought of drugs. I hated even to take medicine when a doctor prescribed it. And all those years I was an addict. I never understood what was wrong with me until I faced the fact that alcohol is a drug. That's the first thing we must make clear if we're ever going to take any serious steps toward reducing the problem."

In this area, Ryne Duren has already done something about the problem. Through his own treatment and a lot of subsequent hard work, he made himself an expert on the condition he had once known only from the inside. He has done an excellent job here, but he knows it would take thousands of programs like his to make any impact on the growing incidence of alcoholism across the country.

It has always seemed to me that baseball is one of the worst professions for the latent alcoholic. The combination of vigorous young men, lots of money and extravagant public adulation is potentially lethal. Baseball players are often on the road for ten or twelve days at a stretch, and they have a lot of free time. Most of them are under great pressure to do better, or just to keep their jobs. Alcohol relieves pressure. I know all about it.

Duren, who hasn't had a drink in ten years, charges that about a third of the players in the majors drink too much, and that the people who run baseball don't want to know about it. "Would you like to do something about it?" Tony asked him.

"Sure, I'd like to work with ballplayers on the problem, but to do that I'd need baseball's blessing, which I don't have a prayer of getting."

"Why?"

"Because alcohol, especially beer, is the source of millions of dollars in revenue for them—from ball-park sales and especially, from TV commercials. They're reluctant even to do anything about drunkenness in the stands, which is getting worse all the time. The last thing they want is me coming around saying alcohol is a drug. They don't like to think of themselves as drug peddlers."

But they are, he did *not* say, although the inference was hard to avoid.

We talked some more about players he had known. I asked him about Billy Martin.

"I always liked Billy," he said. After a pause, he added, "I saw him recently on TV, being interviewed by Barbara Walters. She asked him about his drinking. He said it wasn't a problem, he was only drinking beer now."

He shook his head, and we both smiled ruefully. We've both been there, and we both know that "I'm only drinking beer" is the entrance to the pit.

A friend of mine who had a serious drinking problem and knew it once asked me for help. Except that he didn't want *too much* help. "I'm not interested in joining AA," he said. "I just want something that'll keep me from drinking in the daytime." Sad, but so funny I couldn't help laughing.

"I'm sorry, Jack," I said, "they don't have a club for that."

They don't have one for people who are "only drinking beer now," either.

NAMING THE BABY

If you have ever written a book, you must have found, as I have, that one of the toughest problems you face is choosing a name. Along about the middle of it you think of a title that's not too bad, and you figure, Fine, I don't have to worry about that anymore, and you get on with your work. Then, as the moment nears when you actually have to type the name in the middle of a blank sheet of paper and put it on top of the pile, you begin to fret about it. What's bothering you is the certain knowledge that there is a perfect title, plus the positive realization that you aren't going to be able to think of it.

It seems so easy. After all, you're a writer, you write hundreds of words every day (and all your friends say you write such amusing letters), so why can't you think of four or five words to put on the cover? You recall some of the baseball books you have liked. The titles all seem just right, as they always do in retrospect because the contents were so good. *The Summer Game* and *Five Seasons*, Roger Angell's two fine collections of his *New Yorker* pieces. Or Donald Honig's *Baseball When the Grass Was Real*, one of several excellent books based on interviews with old ballplayers, following the format originated by Larry Ritter with his marvelous *The Glory of Their Times*. Honig's latest, *The October Heroes*, would be worth reading just for the remarks of Les Bell, 3B, Cardinals, 1926. Old Pete was *not* woozy with drink and knew exactly what he was doing, says Bell. You could read it.

One way to get a title is to borrow it from a poet, and two of my favorite baseball books used that device. Roger Kahn got his *Boys of Summer* title from Dylan Thomas, and Mark Harris took *Bang the Drum Slowly* from the anonymous author of "The Streets of Laredo." The latter, by the way, is the best baseball novel ever written. Of course, that's only my opinion. Among those who disagree with me, many favor *The Southpaw*, by the same author.

There was a book a few years ago called *Moe Berg*, a functional title, covering the subject in seven letters, and an intriguing one if you know who Moe Berg was—one of the most interesting men ever to play the game. The book was apparently written by a committee (three authors are named). About the only thing a committee can do better than a single person is elect a chairman, so the book is not as good as its subject warrants. But it is notable for one quote from Ted Lyons, the old White Sox pitcher who spent his life in the second division and still won 260 games. Lyons was not your average, inarticulate ballplayer, as this demonstrates: "A lot of people tried to tell him what to do with his life and brain and he retreated from this. Moe Berg had to be his own man. He tried to be a run-of-the-mill guy. He was different because he was different. He made up for all the bores of the world. And he did it softly, stepping on no one." I'd settle for that last part on my tombstone.

I went through a little poetry, some favorites of mine: Yeats, Dylan Thomas, Anne Lalas. Good lines to spare, of course, but not just what I needed for a title. Sylvia Plath has a reference to baseball in her *Letters Home*. "Spent Saturday in the Yankee Stadium," she writes, "with all the stinking people in the world watching the Yankees trounce the Tigers." (She must not have gone on Jacket Day.) I didn't see how I could use that. In the end, I went to a less exalted form of poetry, the pop music of the vaudeville era. Jack Norworth's lyric for *the* baseball song has already been heavily mined for book titles, but there were a few lines left. I thought of calling mine *Some Peanuts and Cracker Jack* (useful aids to the enjoyment of baseball, which I hoped the book would be, too) or *Out with the Crowd* (since that's where I learned to love the game). I finally chose the present title, though, because I liked the impression of total commitment it conveyed. Not that I want you to take it literally, of course. In reality, I *would* care if I never came back. I don't want to sit in an empty ball park all night. I want to go somewhere, have a good dinner, talk about the game . . . and maybe catch a night game on the telly.

※   ※   ※

My wife has pointed out that I may have overlooked an exciting possibility in the words of the baseball song. I could have called the book *Root, Root, Root* or, for brevity's sake, simply *Roots*.

Tuesday
August 14th

LOOSE ENDS

The All-Star Game seemed like a good place to stop this book, especially since the Tigers weren't going to win the pennant (but wait till next year!). But I keep thinking of things I hadn't gotten around to talking about, and perversely (for my present purpose) baseball doesn't stop making news after the All-Star Game. So with your permission—actually, you have no choice—I'll try to wrap up a few loose ends. Brevity is not my long suit, but I'll strive for it this time.

• I haven't mentioned, for one thing, the grotesque way in which the Yankees' Goose was cooked. In a clubhouse scuffle with Cliff Johnson, a huge utility player, Rich Gossage injured his thumb so badly that it required surgery, and the Yankees lost the pennant. They probably would have lost it anyway, but this foolishness ensured it.

The carelessness with which so many professional athletes treat their bodies has always puzzled me. A player will work all winter on his strength and coordination, then break his leg trying to jump a fence on the first day of the season. And I keep remembering Jim Lonborg's skiing accident. In 1967, Lonborg was close to being the best pitcher in the game. After pitching two great games in a losing cause in the World Series, he decided to go skiing. He did come back, but he was never as good again.

It seems to me that if I were a ballplayer who commanded vast sums of money for the things I could do with my arms and legs, I would try to take care of them. Maybe not, though. Maybe I'd be as negligent as they are with the invaluable tools of their trade. But a carpenter wouldn't.

• I was wrong, in a way, about Rusty Staub. He is playing some, at first base, and he's had some useful hits. But I still think he'll never be more than a part-time player in the National League, so there's no way he can compile the kind of record that produces money in the amounts he seems to think are his due.

• Lou Brock got his three-thousandth hit. It was a line drive that smashed the hand of Dennis Lamp, the Chicago pitcher. While we were watching Lou on television being swarmed over by his jubilant teammates, Lamp was presumably writhing in agony somewhere off camera. Brock, who is forty years old, is having a great year, but still says he will retire at season's end. On top. It's the only way to go.

• The Tigers drafted Rick Leach, the Michigan quarterback, in the first round and paid him $150,000 to sign a contract. Last year they got Kirk Gibson, a glue-fingered receiver from Michigan State. (Somebody said they now have a better passing combination than the Detroit Lions.) I'm happy they got Leach, since I am a Michigan fan, but a lot of people were surprised; they didn't think he was a good enough prospect to go in the first round. I told you, Jim Campbell is hooked on celebrities. One thing: if Leach and Gibson do make it into the Tiger outfield in a couple of years, they'll be a great draw. That is, if they're any good.

• Thurman Munson died. He was flying his own plane, and he cracked it up. It's always shocking when a famous athlete dies at the peak of his career, so the world mourns a bit too ostentatiously for a day or two. The day of his funeral, the Yankees came from behind with a dramatic five-run late-inning rally to beat the Orioles. Everyone was as ecstatic as if they'd clinched the pennant, because they "won it for Thurman." It was a fine tribute, I guess, but I wonder what it means. When the '39 Yankees crushed the Tigers on the day Lou Gehrig sat down, that was nice because Lou could watch them do it. As to whether or not Munson was watching, there are two schools of thought. Well, we'll all know someday, or we won't know anything. Anyway, I guess his wife and family were pleased, and they were the ones who needed a lift. It was too late to do anything for Thurman.

• Willie Horton is having a fine year at Seattle, and that's good news. Willie gave Detroiters a lot of thrills in the good years; he loved to hit, and he liked playing for the Tigers. They let him go two years ago because he couldn't get along with Ralph Houk. But now it turns out they might have done better to let Houk go and make Willie manager. Last winter, in Venezuela, Willie took over a team that was fifteen games under .500 in mid-season. Under his direction, the club ran off an incredible sixty wins against only eight losses. Nobody ever thought of Willie as managerial material before, but you simply can't argue with 60–8!

There was a funny incident involving Horton early this year. He angrily accused Dick Drago, a Red Sox pitcher, of throwing at him. Drago, as is the custom, denied it, but added apologetically, "Maybe I did throw a little too hard." Never before, to my knowledge, has a pitcher apologized for throwing too hard. Certainly not when he wasn't throwing at the batter!

• We come now to the Great Mooning—one of those

incidents that may make it Great to Be a Yankee, but cast some doubt on the validity of the Yankees' vaunted dignity and elegance. You have this female fan, see, young and presumably attractive—at least, from certain angles. She exposes her backside to the Yankee players assembled in their bus outside Comiskey Park in Chicago. Naturally, these high-spirited kids do not avert their eyes. The next night she's back, and the Yankees are signing autographs for her in a place where she won't even be able to see them. Gross, but boys will be boys, and only a few of the Yankees are over thirty-five. It's a shame no one took a picture of this great moment in Yankee history. It was reported that Billy Martin, the inspirational leader of the club, tried to do just that. He indignantly denies it, but no one denies that the young lady gave performances three nights running, and it's hard to believe Martin didn't know about it. Whatever his personal standards of conduct are, he should have known the incident would embarrass the club, and he should have ordered his players to knock it off (if that's the phrase).

Incredibly, Mickey Morabito, the Yankees' publicity director, reportedly told a writer, trying to check the story, that if you hung around with his club long enough you'd see just about everything. When something like this happens, the publicity director's job is to say it couldn't have happened, and anyway the whole thing had been greatly exaggerated. But the Yankees' publicity director seemed to take some pride in confirming it.

Doesn't anyone in a position of authority on that club have any common sense?

• Sparky Anderson has been running a tryout camp in Detroit during the second half of the season, shuffling players into and out of the lineup, and into and out of the league. The young pitchers look promising, Aurelio Lopez is the find of the year in relief, and we're expecting great things in '80. If the pitching comes around, and Champ

Summers continues to hit home runs at his present startling rate, it's hard to see how they can miss, now that they have a genius at the helm. Your serve, Sparky.

Wednesday
August 15th

COMING TO WATCH

"Not sixteen per cent of the human race is, or ever has been, engaged in any of the kinds of activity at which they excel." A man named Paul Mairet said that. I read it in *The Viking Book of Aphorisms*, one of those handy collections that enable you to quote famous people without actually having to read them. Consequently, I have no idea who Mairet is, or what he's famous for (certainly not for his literary style). But I am always bewitched by the sort of mentality which thus reduces something everyone knows in a vague, general way to a precise mathematical certainty. How did he arrive at that figure? Since he was so exact, are we to infer that 15 percent of the people *are* working contentedly away at things they do brilliantly? I would have thought the number was smaller.

Most of us have known dozens of people who had jobs they didn't understand very well (and consequently hated). I myself have had several such jobs. Right after the war, in mild desperation, I took a job as a bookkeeper and spent six months writing numbers in a big green ledger. When I left, I was told they were sorry to lose me because I had been "coming along fine." To this day, I do not have the slightest idea of what I was doing. The company, a large one, collapsed a year or two later, and I think I know why.

Since then I have had many jobs, some of which I did more or less well, but I rarely achieved a level of performance that could legitimately be described as excellence. And

I found myself constantly surrounded by people who didn't excel at all, some of them in positions of considerable responsibility.

(I will get to the point in a minute. What I am doing here is saying goodbye, because the book is about to end, and it's hard to say goodbye to anything that's been so much a part of your life for so many months. I worry about all the things I wanted to say but didn't, and all the really terrific things I never even thought of, but will after it's too late. For those omissions, as the Spanish say, *no hay remedio*—there is no remedy. But I wish there were.)

Considering this state of affairs, then, should we not be grateful for the existence of a large field of human activity in which almost all the participants do excel—especially since we can watch them while they do it? I am talking about big-league baseball, of course. I think few of us really recognize the degree of excellence it takes to play the game in the major leagues. But almost every fan of long standing can remember an outstanding high-school or college player he has seen, one whose skills so far exceeded those of the players around him that he seemed to be playing a different game, but who never came close to making it in the bigs. Once you have watched such a player fail, you begin to get some idea of just how good you have to be to play in the majors at all, let alone become a star.

I am, I see, once again in danger of launching a defense of baseball, which needs none. My intent, more precisely, is to put in a good word for those of us who like being spectators, despite the scoffing of the devotees of participation. Very simply, I would rather watch baseball played with skill and grace and style than go out myself to ski or play golf or tennis without any of those things. So as long as they come to play, I'll happily come to watch.

I don't believe in reincarnation or life after death, but not believing is a far cry from denying them absolutely. I am always willing to be proved wrong. I don't always take it gracefully, but in this case I think I would be pretty good about it. If I do come back, I hope it's as someone who can go to his right on a hard ground ball with a little more haste than I ever could in the present session—and, I hardly need add, hit a curveball. Failing that, I'd like to have season tickets.

But perhaps there will be a full schedule of games on The Other Side. If so, I'll just sit there watching, storing up memories and statistics in my mind with which to entertain all the people I love, who I am confident will be along sooner or later. And if the play is up to major-league standards, *then* I won't care if I never come back.

Index